Glam Italia!
101 Fabulous Things to Do in Naples

Adventures, Intrigue and Glorious Mayhem in Europe's Most Exciting City.

© 2024 Corinna Cooke
All Rights Reserved

No part of this publications may be reproduced, distributed or transmitted in any form or by any means, electronic or mechanical, including photocopying, recording, or by any information storage and retrieval system without prior written consent by Glam World Publishing, LLC.

ISBN: (paperback) 978-1-7323799-9-2
ISBN: (eBook) 979-8-9913790-0-7

DISCLAIMER
The author is not a travel agent.

All opinions and views expressed are those of the author based on personal travel experiences. Businesses and websites recommended by this author may change ownership, rebrand, or close through no fault of the author. The author has not received any compensation or sponsorship from any recommended business.

Cover art and all images by Marta Halama.
Photography by Tracy Battaglia
Photography by Karianne Munstedt.
Formatting: Polgarus Studio
Cover Design: eBook Launch

Contents

1. Introduction 1
2. How To Use This Book 11
3. A Very Brief History of Naples 15
4. Getting Around 23
5. The Naples Pass 31
6. A City of Staircases 35
7. The Fabulous Metro Art Stations 43
8. The Neighborhoods of Naples 53
9. Piazza Bellini 63
10. Street Art in Naples 67
11. Caravaggio in Naples 79
12. Amazing Underground Sites in Naples 93
13. Ten Unmissable Museums 117
14. *The Veiled Christ* (Cristo Velato) 135
15. Eight Incredible Churches in Naples 143
16. Remarkable Castles and Palaces in Naples 177
17. The Royal Palace of Caserta 191
18. The Teatro San Carlo 199
19. Interesting & Unusual Things to See in Naples ... 203
20. Pompeii 223
21. Other Stupendous Archaeological Sites 239

22. The Greek Temples at Paestum 263
23. What to Eat in Naples 275
24. Naples – The Home of Pizza 291
25. Which Wines to Drink in Naples 297
26. The Best Coffee in the World 305
27. Island Hopping: Procida, Ischia & Capri 315
28. The Reading List: Ten Wonderful Books Set in Naples 341
29. Arrivederci 347
30. What Next? 351
Acknowledgements 355

1.
Introduction

Naples sneaks inside your soul and changes you.

Hi, I'm Corinna – welcome to my book! This one is designed to guide you around one of the coolest cities in the world and make you fall in love with it along the way.

This is not intended to be the definitive guide to Naples. Honestly, there can be no such thing, because Naples has too many incredible, exciting, fantastic experiences to fit into a single book. Or perhaps into a hundred books. So instead, this is a collection of (more than) 101 things that have personally thrilled *me* to my core in this dynamic, vital city.

While writing this book I thought about the first time I stumbled upon each of these places and experiences in Naples, and how they made me feel – how my pulse started racing, how my jaw dropped, how overwhelmed, thrilled and excited I felt. And that's what I hope you'll find within these pages – a series of places that resonate with you, places that you don't just *want* to see, but *need to experience* for yourself.

A couple of decades ago in my former life as a makeup artist, I worked with a woman whose husband worked for some NATO-like outfit that involved the family moving to a new post every three years or so. For twenty years they had moved in and out of the most exciting countries in the world, experiencing an array of cultures, and her stories were equal parts astounding and marvelous. She told me stories all that day, and at the end I asked which had been her favorite place, or was it even possible to have favorite? She didn't hesitate for even a second. 'Naples!' she exclaimed. 'Once you've lived in Naples, nowhere in the world can compare.'

This was back in the days when the city of Naples had a pretty raunchy reputation, and I couldn't understand why someone would choose it over say, Paris. She took me by the shoulders, looked me in the eye, her perfect grey bob swinging right into place, and told me that Goethe had it right: 'See Naples and die'. This wasn't a warning of inherent danger, but a warning that after experiencing Napoli, *everywhere else is less*. All I could think of as I drove home that day, was how and when I could I get to Naples. I was a single parent of a young child at the time and couldn't buzz around Italy as frequently or as freely as I do now.

I didn't get it back then, but now that I've seen it for myself, I do. I get it in spades. Blood moves differently through your veins in Naples. The city has a raw, wild, high-octane energy. Maybe it's a power surge from Vesuvius mixed with underground rumbles from the *Campi Flegrei* that creates the dynamic voltage of this place. Whatever it is, come here and take a moment to stand still and feel it surge through you. You too will see that after Naples, everywhere else is less.

Shortly thereafter (it seems like a lifetime ago now), I was staying in nearby Salerno and had planned a trip to Napoli for the day, with a group of Salernese friends. A couple of days prior to the big day, one of my friends wound up in hospital, and the day trip was understandably cancelled. (Don't worry, he survived and thrived, but it was a scary few days.)

INTRODUCTION

In those days Naples still had, if not a bad reputation, then an exceedingly murky one, so while my heart was set on going, I had a little trepidation about venturing there alone. As I didn't know anyone living there in real life, I looked to (then fledgling) Facebook. There I found a 'friend' who was a doctor in Naples, so I sent him a quick message asking if he might meet me for a coffee the next morning. Unfortunately, he was busy until 3pm, but then I remembered another Facebook 'friend' – someone I only knew because we tended to comment on the same of this doctor's posts, and they would both comment on mine. (I had never met either of them in real life and in all honesty would have walked right past them in the street.) But I messaged him anyway: *Hey, I'm going to be in Naples tomorrow – would you like to grab a coffee in the morning?*

He was online and replied immediately. He asked which train I was coming in on and, realizing that I was going to be on my own and was a little nervous about it, he said: *I'll take the day off work. Meet me on platform 14 – it will be like the movies!*

When my train rolled into the station, I wasn't sure if I was meeting a serial killer, a madman or possibly just a really wonderful human. He stood at the end of the platform, his scarf wrapped in a style known only to Italian men and movie stars. 'We start with coffee,' he said as we linked arms and marched out of the station.

The first things he told me about himself were that he loved Depeche Mode and had a dog named Doyle. We strutted along the busy streets of Naples, singing 'Personal Jesus' all the way to his favorite coffee shop. And here I learned an important life lesson. Always ask a Neapolitan for his favorite coffee spot, and make sure you go there. They will never, ever guide you wrong.

The second thing I learned (the hard way) was to **only have one cup**. Against Mr Mode's advice, I insisted on ordering a second espresso – after all, this was the best coffee I had ever tasted in my life. The uniformed barista raised his eyebrows momentarily, then slid a second scalding cup of espresso my way. Ten minutes later I understood.

As we wandered into Piazza Plebiscito, I became acutely aware of every hair on my scalp standing on end in the Neapolitan breeze, and felt as though a parade of phantom ants was crawling over my face. Neapolitan coffee is *really* strong.

'I warned you,' Mr. Mode uttered, before telling me we were going to play a game. 'See these two horse statues? Close your eyes and walk up there between them.'

Even caffeinated to the eyeballs as I was, I figured it wasn't much of a game, how difficult could this be? Within moments Mr. Mode was cracking up laughing and calling out for me to open my eyes. Thinking I was walking a straight line, I had instead veered off to the left like an old drunk.

Turns out it wasn't the coffee, though. This is a real thing in the Piazza Plebiscito. The design of the piazza with its non-conforming cobblestones makes it almost impossible to walk a straight line. 'Blame Queen Marguerita,' he said, blowing smoke rings to the heavens. 'She offered a pardon to any blindfolded prisoner who could pass this test, and then cast a spell to stop anyone from achieving it.' And so, I had my introduction to Neapolitan superstitions. And all these years later I still do it, even dressed to the nines after an evening at the opera house across the street.

INTRODUCTION

A few minutes later walking into a chic clothing store in the Galleria Umberto, Mr. Mode whispered, 'Pretend we are lovers. The girl you're about to meet is the biggest gossip in Napoli. My ex-girlfriend will hear about it in five minutes and will be jealous!' I am *always* up for a little chicanery so of course I went all in, and as promised, five short minutes after exiting the shop his phone lit up like a Christmas tree. I knew Mr. Mode and I were destined to become great friends!

He introduced me to *babà*, a rum-soaked sponge dessert. We snacked on *pizza fritta* and brown paper cones of fried seafood. He introduced me to artisan friends on Via San Gregorio Armeno, one of whom gave me my first Neapolitan good luck charm, a *cornicello* I still carry with me today.

That day wandering Naples with Mr. Mode was one of the most fun days of my life. He is the epitome of a hilarious, gregarious, delightful Neapolitan, and the experience not only made me fall in love with this city but also its people. For years, when I brought my Glam Italia Tour groups through Naples after a day on Capri, Mr. Mode and his friends met us at the port and whisked us off to the *lungomare* by Castel dell 'Ovo for an evening of pizza and mad fun, before dropping us back at the train.

I have always believed that quality travel is not about taking photos while running from one monument to the next. It is about meeting people, experiencing their culture and their way of life. During these pizza-filled, limoncello-soaked evenings of laughter, and the boisterous noise and hilarity of any Neapolitan pizzeria, my tour clients saw the soul of Naples. Ten years later they still ask me, 'Do you remember that night in Naples? How is Mr. Mode?' He has absolutely no idea that while cruising through his life, smoking cigarettes, riding a Vespa, humming 'The Policy of Truth' and minding his own business while being his delightful self, he is also imprinting the very best of memories onto people's souls. But that's Naples for you.

I tell you this because, while in some places you still need to keep your wits about you, most of your time in Naples will include amazing interactions with some of the warmest, friendliest, most fun-loving people on the planet. Don't be surprised if within five minutes of meeting someone they invite you for a coffee or take you home to meet Mamma and feast on a giant, soul-nourishing Neapolitan lunch or dinner.

Take my personal obsession out of the mix and we arrive to another truth most tourists don't realize: **after Rome, Naples is historically the most important city in all of Italy**. It is also the most vital and the most urgent. Naples holds the key to understanding the history of this whole glorious country. I would argue it holds more visible, touchable history over a 3000-year span than any other city. In a short 100 meters from Piazza Bellini and up the Via Tribunali, you can see, touch and breathe Ancient Greece, Ancient Rome, the Middle Ages, the Renaissance, and the Baroque, along with modern day Napoli. Along the way you'll encounter faith, superstition and magic, street art, mayhem and the best coffee in the world.

Your first couple of forays into Naples can feel like *pandemonium*. One of my friends describes it as 'functioning anarchy'. What seems like complete chaos to the novice resonates like an expertly choreographed dance to the connoisseur. It's important to take a moment, breathe, and understand *this all makes complete sense to them*. Just sit back and watch a Neapolitan expertly parallel park his car uphill on a spastically busy street, while cars and scooters whizz by, people crisscross in front and behind him, vendors yell and friends shout greetings. The driver not only isn't remotely fazed by it

INTRODUCTION

all, but in two or three smooth one-handed moves (the other hand gesturing to friends on the street with a burning cigarette between stained fingers), he glides into an impossibly small parking space with just inches spare on either side. This to them is normal, and how lucky are we to be able to visit here, and live and breathe this craziness for just a day, a week or a lifetime?

My Neapolitan Amalfi Coast driver (and super good friend) Pasquale explained that they all grew up riding scooters/Vespas from when they were young – arms wrapped around their father's waists as kiddos, their first taste of mobile freedom as teens. Pasquale shrugs and says every Neapolitan driver instinctively knows what the scooter driver up ahead is going to do next, perhaps before the scooter driver does. To me it's as if an invisible conductor is directing a mad symphony where each individual part is lunacy but when melded together becomes the most beautiful melody in the world.

Speaking of melodies, you will learn that Naples is all music and fiery passion. Home to the first opera house in the world, it was also the center of the universe for musical genius. After Florence, it was the other vital center of Renaissance art. On top of that, Naples is the greatest archaeological center in the world.

Before we take this ride through Napoli together, you and me, I just want to tell you about the city's staggering beauty. As you explore this wild metropolis, pay attention to Vesuvius slipping in and out of view, teasing you between buildings and narrow streets. Always there, yet sometimes not, menacing to the fearful, magical to the enthralled. A game of cat and mouse with a live volcano that theoretically could fire back up at any time. Do everything you can to get up high and experience a Neapolitan sunrise and sunset. Let the colors imprint on you. Nowhere is this beautiful, which is why over a span of 800 years, wealthy Romans built opulent villas and devoted their summers to the Vesuvian Coast. The region was known as *Campania Felix* – happy, lucky Campania. For millennia this place has bewitched ordinary folk and emperors, artists and eccentrics.

Although Rome is the most important city in Italy (and for centuries was the most important city on Earth) and will always be my favorite city in the world, slamming in hard like a runaway freight train, Naples is in second place. I *love* Naples with an obsession that borders on unhealthy.

But who am I to tell you about Naples? If you've read the other Glam Italia books in this series, you'll already know I'm not a historian or art historian. I have no degree in Roman history nor in archaeology. I don't even live in Naples. I am, however, a professional traveler of sorts. While living out my never-ending wanderlust, I approach every new place with the eyes of a traveler. I know what you and I want to see and what we prefer to avoid. I see what the mass tourism folks miss, and know a million ways to escape their crowds, finding oddities and rarities along the way. Whether in the busiest cities or the most remote villages, I know how to find the moments and the places that turn an average trip into the best travel experience you've ever had.

For more than a decade I've been curating dream trips for my Glam Italia Tour travelers – normal people who crave more than the normal mass tourism experience when they come to Italy. And that's what I want to do for you here – introduce you to the pure magic of Napoli.

It is my hope that within the pages of this book you'll find places that excite you, experiences that thrill you and a siren song that calls you.

INTRODUCTION

Let your guard down for a moment, open yourself to the panoramas and the art, the dusty elegance and the extraordinary wealth of culture, and maybe Naples will bewitch you too.

Let's go…

2.
How To Use This Book

The most important things in life are our thoughts, feelings, actions and experiences.

~ Pythagorus

I am not a fan of the type of travel that has you stuck in the middle of hordes of tourists, stomping your way to the next attraction on a list you neither curated nor care about. So don't expect to find daily itineraries in this book.

Instead, I will tell you the stories behind a series of endlessly fascinating places here in Naples. I always want to know the *why* behind everything I'm looking at. Sure, it's a great building, but *why* do I need to see it? There is more to each place than the year it was built and what it was used for, so where possible I like to give you a little context. Over the decade-plus of my Glam Italia Tours, I've noticed most travelers won't remember the names of the buildings we see, but they invariably remember the stories that go with them. Knowing that a building is where the royal family lived from year X to year Y is moderately interesting, but it's vastly more interesting to hear that this is where the mad king staged a fake wedding to lure in the enemy barons. (The barons would never miss a fabulous fete, and once they had entered his circular salon, all decked out in their finest celebratory attire, the king's archers popped out from the rafters and shot them all. Then he threw their bodies in the basement where, today, you can still see their bones and the remnants of their party clothes.) To me, this is the difference between just noticing a castle near the waterfront and being compelled to look inside it.

There will be places in this book you'll think sound interesting, but you'll choose not to add to this trip's itinerary. Other places will make their way onto your own unique **must-see** list (I recommend creating create a **must-see** list as you read this book). This is how you maximize your travel time and dollars. Fill your Naples itinerary with the places and experiences that fascinate *you*. Jot down other spots that are close by so you can drop in on them as you walk past, if you have time. This approach will keep you away from the crowds and will reveal a Naples you'll fall in love with. You'll have a thrilling visit, and you'll leave the city as exhilarated as I always do.

The chapters are broken up by category, not geography. Find things that fascinate *you*. The heart of Naples is quite small and very walkable. You can walk to most of the places I tell you about, soaking up the city as you go. Within some of the chapters, multiple items of interest might seem to be at cross purposes –you can find representations of faith alongside some of the trippiest superstitions, magnificent art, doorways down to Ancient Rome and further down to Ancient Greece. That's just Naples – intoxicating layers of glorious history and madness, beauty and excess, one incredible site followed by another.

Before we begin, I want to draw your attention to the **Churches** chapter. Many of you are not religious/not Catholic/not interested in churches, but bear with me. Along with spectacular interiors and mind-bending architecture and art, inside the churches of Naples you'll find some of the most astounding, weird, quirky and crazy stuff

HOW TO USE THIS BOOK

you never even knew you could imagine. These days, I go inside every church I pass in any part of Italy, because more often than not there will be priceless treasures just sitting there with no one to show off to. But holy moly – in *Naples?* The curiosities in these churches will have something to fascinate and intrigue everyone. So, make sure you read everything in this chapter – you are bound to learn about places you've not heard of before and I can guarantee there will be things in here you will be dying to see.

Some of the better-known attractions inside churches have their own chapters, like the **Caravaggio** chapter and *The Veiled Christ* chapter. This is just to make it easier for you to find them, without knowing the names of the churches they live inside.

Make sure you read the chapters about **What to Eat, Which Wines to Drink,** and **The Best Coffee in the World.** There is so much more to Neapolitan cuisine than just pizza. (However, you must try pizza while you're here.) In fact, Naples is one of Italy's culinary capitals and Italians travel here from all over the country just to indulge in the food. Naples is a port city and port cities always have a tremendous street food culture. You need to know the specific Neapolitan street foods to seek out and try.

As you make your way through this book, make a list of places you'd like to see, then map them out once your list is complete. They're almost all very close to one another. You'll find you can see an enormous amount in a very short time here, easily and with no rush. That may be one of the most surprising things about Naples – it's enormous yet quite small, overwhelming, but completely manageable.

I also recommend walking the city with a local, licensed private guide, whether by yourself or with a small group. Apart from being

100% sustainable (your travel dollars go directly into the local economy, to people who are working hard to preserve their city and its history), it is also a brilliant introduction to Naples. Tell your guide about some of the things you want to see, and they'll tailor the experience to it, which is even more reason to become acquainted with the places I tell you about in this book. You'll discover as you read, that there are several cool places you can *only* access with a guide, so it doesn't hurt to already have one up your sleeve. You'll hear me mention various guides in the stories I tell. These are people I've worked with for years and who have become dear friends along the way. (There are links to a free PDF you can download with the contact details of the private guides I personally work with, so you too can craft your perfect Neapolitan experience.)

But first, let's learn a little bit about the staggering history of this amazing city.

3.
A Very Brief History of Naples

Small opportunities are often the beginning of great enterprises

~ Pericles, 5th century BC

Along with being one of the coolest, most exciting cities in the world, Naples is also one of the oldest cities in Europe.

Let's take a whirlwind whip through the city's history, mostly focusing on eras that appear in this book and leaving out massive chunks in between. With nearly 3000 years of history, there is far too much to squish into a single chapter, but with just this brief synopsis you'll start to realize just how much there is to see and experience here, and why this sensational city is so incredibly important.

Our story begins in around the 8th century BC, when the Greeks created the first cities of Magna Grecia, or greater Greece. At that time, this new city was called Paleopolis, or Parthenope, named for the Greek siren. This was a strategically important city in the Mediterranean, and quickly became a busy and important port. Paleopolis/Parthenope was built from tufa stone, the remains of a volcanic eruption in the Camp Flagrei 44,000 years prior.

In roughly 470 BC, the Greeks moved ever so slightly inland to a more defendable spot, which they walled and built on a grid system still in use today. They renamed the new metropolis *Neo–polis*, or New City. Neopolis gradually contracted down to Napoli, the name we know today. (You can see part of this original Greek wall and learn more about it in the chapter **Piazza Bellini**.)

As we move through this book and begin exploring Naples, we'll visit places that date all the way back to this time. You can still see (and touch) parts of ancient Magna Grecia. When we go up high in the city, such as to the Vomero neighborhood, you can look out over the original street pattern created by the Greeks. This original city, now called the Historic Center of Naples, is designated a UNESCO World Heritage Site.

As one of the most important cities of Magna Grecia, Naples played a key role in bringing Greek culture to Roman society. Ancient Romans loved all things Greek. They loved the architecture, the art, the language and the philosophy. For several centuries, wealthy and important Romans – including those who would become emperors – were educated in Greece. All things Greek became wickedly fashionable and, as such, early Naples was a major cultural center.

In 326 BC, the Roman army marched on Naples and took over. (I'm skipping over a bunch of wars here.) Rome did however let Naples keep its Greek customs, language and traditions, and allowed the people broad autonomy. Despite further wars, ultimately Naples not only survived, but thrived. Wealthy Romans built massive summer villas along what became known as the Erotica Coast. This was the place to be. Although portions of the old Greek architecture remain, over time the Romans had to modify and expand the city. There are places, especially in the historic center, where from street level you can go down 10 meters and walk through ancient Roman market streets, and then go down 30 meters into the ancient Greek world. There is always something more beneath your feet in Naples.

In 79 AD, Mount Vesuvius erupted, completely changing the coastline. Towns and villages disappeared beneath layers of pumice and ash that fell meters deep in just 24 hours. Towns were there one day, and had disappeared the next, not to be rediscovered for 1700 years. Eventually life in this area settled back down and it remained a hugely popular summer retreat for the upper classes.

By the 4th century AD, the Roman Empire had become vast and unwieldy and had split in two. The Empire of the East and the Western Empire. In the 5th century AD, the western Roman Empire was invaded and crumbled, ending in 476 AD or thereabouts. To keep up with the revolving door of who was running Naples over the next few centuries, you'd need a whiteboard and a variety of colored pens. The Ostrogoths were there for a while, as were the Lombards, and there was Byzantine rule, there was a duchy for a while, and a sacking by the Saracens. In 1139, the Normans (Vikings) conquered Naples. They began their conquest of southern Italy around the year 999 AD and by roughly 1154 ran essentially everything from Abruzzo south (think Abruzzo, Molise, Puglia, Basilicata, Calabria, Campania and Sicily).

Skipping ahead the next period of history you'll find significant to this book is that of the Angevin Dynasty (French). Charles I d'Anjou established the Neapolitan Angevin Dynasty, which ruled Naples from 1266 to 1435. Charles understood the power and importance of commissioning great works of art in Naples. He invited the best artists from France and Italy to join his royal court. This became a tradition followed by subsequent kings of Naples, using artistic patronage to validate themselves, and in the process, secure Naples' identity as a European cultural center. Naples became a symbol of dignity and prestige. And power. For you and me, this means loads of fascinating art to enjoy and a visual roadmap of centuries of Neapolitan life. Some of the places we'll visit in this book from this era include the **Cloisters at Santa Chiara, San Lorenzo Maggiore, San Domenico Maggiore, Donnaregina**, and the **Duomo**.

Two lines of the Angevin family fought for control of Naples, and Charles III killed Joanna I (Queen of Naples) and his daughter Joanna II adopted Spanish King Alfonso V of Aragon, which brings us to the next dynasty to rule Naples. In 1442 Naples became part of the Spanish Aragonese Dynasty. Spain controlled Naples until the late 17th century, using it to boost Spain's own economy and military prowess. (We touch on some of this in the **Caravaggio** chapter.) People who worked the land around Naples had to give almost everything to Spain, leaving them starving to the point where they abandoned their farm holdings and moved into the city of Naples in the hope of finding food.

During this time, the Spanish built **Castel Nuovo**, the **Royal Palace** and also **Capodimonte**, along with masses more. Naples was an important military center for Spain, and the Spanish army played a big role in day-to-day life in the city during this time. Spain needed to build housing for its soldiers and their families. Below Castel Sant' Elmo on the Vomero hill, they built a maze-like labyrinth of narrow alleys with tall apartment buildings to accommodate them. This area became known as the **Spanish Quarter**, one of the most iconic neighborhoods in Naples.

By 1701 Spain was no longer the super-power of Europe. After a 13-year fight for the spoils (known as War of Spanish Succession), in 1714 Naples came under the rule of the Austrian Hapsburgs. But not for long. Charles, Duke of Parma (of the Spanish Bourbons) conquered Naples and Sicily in 1743, becoming King of Naples and Sicily in 1735. From 1734 to 1861 Naples was under Bourbon rule. After a couple of centuries of Spanish domination, the city had become run down and dilapidated. The Bourbons not only brought political stability, they also modernized Naples and infused it with opulence. Charles of Bourbon lead Naples into the Age of Enlightenment, surrounding himself with politicians, artists and intellectuals. Under his rule, Naples became one of the two major cities of Europe. The two most important cities in Europe, and the two cultural centers, were Paris and Naples. This was a time of enormous architectural heritage for the city as well as a time of spectacular interior design for the ruling classes.

It was at this time that **Pompeii** and **Herculaneum** were discovered. The oldest opera house in Europe was built, the **Teatro San Carlo**, elevating Naples to the European center of musical genius. This was also when Goethe came and famously said 'See Naples and die', because once you had been to Naples, nothing and nowhere else could compare. It was also during this age of opulence that the incredible **Caserta Palace** was built.

Things went a little off course with the French Revolution (1789–1799). Bourbon King Ferdinand IV worried that his own people would stage a revolution (more about this in the **Caserta** chapter). Ultimately, he fled to Sicily and the French briefly seized Naples. There was some to'ing and fro'ing with Ferdinand coming and going, until in 1806 Napoleon sent his brother Joseph to conquer Naples. Naples was annexed to France and Joseph was made King. Two years later, Joseph was moved to Spain and Napoleon inserted his brother-in-law Joachim Murat. Under Murat's rule, feudalism was abolished, and the French legal code was implemented. Murat is often referred to as 'the Good King'. One of his achievements was the creation of **Piazza del Plebiscito**, next to the royal palace. Murat didn't last too long though. He ran afoul of Napoleon, was court-martialed and died by firing squad in 1815.

With the Good King now gone, in 1816 Naples unified with Sicily and they became the Kingdom of the Two Sicilies. In 1861, the kingdom was defeated by Garibaldi who arrived in Naples by train, right into the square that still bears his name. The Kingdom of Sicily was no more, and Naples became part of the brand-new unified Kingdom of Italy.

Which Italian Language?

One random fact that I find fascinating is that at the time of the Unification, the Tuscan intellectual class was considered the most sophisticated, so their version of the Italian language was the one adopted to be the national language of the new Kingdom of Italy. However, at that time Neapolitan Italian was spoken by more people than any other dialect or Italian-based language in Italy.

During World War II, Naples was occupied by the Nazis and bombed relentlessly by the allies. You can still visit churches that haven't been fully repaired after the destruction suffered from allied bombs. The extensive tunnel network below the city was used as bomb shelters for Neapolitans, the ancient world saving the new one.

You can delve into any moment in time in Naples' history and find endless fascinating, quirky, crazy and brilliant characters. I fell down the rabbit hole with one of the Joannas of Naples when I listened to *The Rest is History* podcast. My favorite wayward Pope was a Neapolitan pirate from Procida – I go into great detail on him and his absolutely nutty story in my book *Glam Italia! 101 Fabulous Things To Do In Florence*. Years ago on a trip to Caserta, I was intrigued to learn about Maria Carolina, the vastly more interesting sister of Marie Antoinette. Her husband Ferdinand IV was also an interesting character, known for eating pasta with his fingers.

Beware of the Ferdinands in Neapolitan history. There were multiple kings named Ferdinand and the numbers following their names don't always make sense. This is largely due to the dynasty from which each of them heralded. For example, in the 15th century crazy King Ferrante was also called Ferdinand I. Fast forward to the 18th century to Maria Carolina's husband – he was King Ferdinand I of the Two Sicilies, but before that, he was Ferdinand IV, King of Naples and Ferdinand III King of Sicily. Moving through this book you'll meet both Ferrante and Maria Carolina's husband, whose lives were 300 years apart. Don't be confused when you see them each referred to as Ferdinand I.

Just spending a morning walking the historic center with a guide, and you will learn about more and more intriguing personalities peppered throughout the long story of Naples. To this day whenever I'm in Naples, I hire local guides as often as I can. They always point out interesting things I never knew (even on streets I've walked 100 times) and amaze me with new stories of mercurial, brilliant, debauched or lunatic *dramatis personae*.

4.
Getting Around

*The universe is like a great book,
and those who do not travel read only a page.*

~ Pythagoras

Looking at a map of Naples can be a little overwhelming. The city looks massive. However, most of the places you will want to see are remarkably easy to get to and are easily walkable.

My first choice is always to walk wherever possible – you'll experience so much more, get a great understanding of the city, and will spot things you'd miss using other forms of transport.

On the other hand, I loathe being out in the rain, so during a December visit not too long ago I made sure to get super well acquainted with Naples' public transport. The public transport here really is fantastic. It is inexpensive, incredibly efficient, and clean and safe.

During busy times (high season for tourism) or in places when anyone is getting physically close, I advise being extra careful with your belongings. As with anywhere in Europe, I believe in always assuming there are pickpockets right up next to you – that way you will be hyper-vigilant.

The Metro

There are plenty of European cities where I would avoid using the subway, but I love using the metro in Naples. The stations tend to be incredibly deep below street level, which is oddly exciting.

Most of the trains are modern and new and in great shape. Some of the stations may look a little hinky from the outside, but inside they are clean and safe. Check out the chapter on **The Metro Station Art** – you'll want to visit several of them. They're incredibly cool, and in my opinion, a fantastic and inspiring idea.

On my most recent jaunt to Naples a one-way ticket on the underground cost €1.20

The Funiculare

Until you get there, you don't realize just how steep and hilly Naples is. Traditionally Neapolitans living *alto* had to finish a hard day at work and then climb huge staircases to get home. (As in 400+ steep steps.) So a series of funiculars were created, quickly zooming people up and down the hill.

The **Chiaia** and **Montesanto** funiculars came first, then in October 1928 the **Funiculare Centrale** opened. This one runs between Piazza Fugo in Vomero and Via Toledo in the historic center. It has since become one of the world's most used and highly trafficked funiculars. Serving four stations and running 1270 meters (4167 feet) within around 5 minutes, the Funiculare Centrale moves 28,000 people up and down the hill per day.

Take the funicular up to **Vomero**, visit **Castel Sant' Elmo** – the views are incredible – then walk down either the **Pedimentina** to the

Spanish Quarter or the Calata San Francesco to Chiaia. (Both are detailed in the **Stairways** chapter.)

Taxis

Taxi service in Naples is excellent too. Everyone warned me that I would be overcharged by deceitful drivers in filthy cabs, but in reality, the cars are modern and clean and each ride I've taken has cost less than the estimate. I've found the drivers to be super fun and very chatty too.

Late at night after the opera (**Teatro San Carlo** chapter) I had a taxi driver with tattoos all up his throat and neck and around the backs of his ears, as well as a few bits on his face. It was winter so I couldn't see where else he was inked, but I assume all over. He drove slowly all the winding way back up the hill to the Vomero, pausing along the way to point out the best views, and giving me a running commentary on the various operas he had been to at the San Carlo, as well as the ballets he had enjoyed there. He also wanted to know all about the new interpretation of Turandot that I had just seen. I don't know why I assumed someone so heavily inked and pierced wouldn't enjoy the opera, but that's Naples for you. Endless fantastic surprises.

Later that same trip, when the taxi picked me up to go to the train station, I had tears rolling down my face because I really, truly was *heartbroken* to be leaving Naples. The driver (this one was without throat tattoos) asked me why I was crying and then asked me what time my train was. He then switched off the fare counter and we took a long, scenic drive around Napoli, talking about why we each loved the city and sometimes just silently looking out the window. When we eventually pulled up at the train station, he would only take the originally quoted €15, even though we'd been driving and talking for a half hour.

Buses

Naples has a decent bus system too. For the most part, if you're not walking, you'll probably jump on the metro, but some places like the **Capodimonte** museum or the beautiful **Posillipo** neighborhood require a bus ride. The Capodimonte bus schedule runs like clockwork. The Posillipo schedule in my personal experience has been more conceptual – the bus arrives when it arrives.

Walk

Cities like Naples are best experienced on foot. Although, in saying that, I will never walk *up* the staircases to Vomero (I only ever walk down), and if it's raining or boiling hot you'll find me hightailing my way down to the metro. But life happens on the streets of cities like Naples and Rome, so you'll maximize your experience by walking as much as you can. This is when you'll find the details, from street art to random sculpted pieces of Greek history, from the superstitious rubbing of bronze skulls to the street stands selling exploding lemon drinks. Walking the city, you'll discover the famous *basso* apartments, small, iconic street-level apartments with nonnas hanging out the window watching the world go by.

Naples is also all about the noise, from vendors shouting out their wares, Vespas whizzing by, car horns blasting, and the never ending high volume chatter of the Neapolitani. This is the experience you came here for, so walk whenever you can.

CROSSING THE STREET

I am all about applying some strategy when you travel and, believe me, crossing any busy street in Naples requires some serious strategy. Here, the traffic rules we have at home don't apply. If you stand at a zebra crossing waiting for cars to stop, I hope you have a good book with you to occupy your time. Most cars won't notice you and, if they do, they'll most likely just ignore you. The traffic light crosswalks work well though, and the cars will have stopped for the traffic light. Probably. But there's not always a traffic light near where you need to cross. So, what to do when, like the chicken, you need to cross the road?

My first strategy is to look for old people and cross with them. It's a double win, because they understand the system and Neapolitans prefer not to run over old folks.

Strategy number two is to look for small children and mothers with babies. As with the elderly, they understand how the traffic works here and Neapolitans really, really don't want to run over moms and babies, so if you stick with them, you will safely saunter across the road and reach the other side in one piece. Win/win. Nuns are always a good option too.

Strategy number three is to watch how the Neapolitans do it and do what they do. It's a little hair-raising, but it is possible. Over time, I've become much better at this, and I always get to the other side just fine, but my friend Pina tells me I need a little more finesse. (She and I normally meet at the end of the day for a spritz and a gossip.) Pina tells me to just walk out into the traffic, make eye contact with the driver (telling him *I see you and I know you see me*), and then rather than stopping and waiting, just weave through the cars like you own the road. When I do this with her, miraculously, no one runs us over. I'll probably never have Pina levels of self-assuredness, but I can spot a nun or a nonna from a mile away.

I've discussed this approach with taxi drivers in Naples and each time they just shrug their shoulders and say, 'But of course! If you gave me the evil eye and walked across the road, I'd assume you were from Napoli!' Then they invariably honk their horns at people, tell me other strategies for crossing the road, advise me where to get the best coffee, and talk about the Napoli football team.

Arriving in Naples

BY FERRY

My preferred way to arrive in Naples is by sea. I have taken the ferry to Sicily from Naples many times and vice versa, and you cannot beat the beauty of this approach. However, we can't always do that, so let's look at other options.

BY TRAIN

I usually come and go by high-speed train. Extremely efficient and convenient, I think this is the most practical way to arrive/depart. You do, however, spend about 15 minutes cruising through the projects/less desirable parts of town.

BY CAR

And by 'car', I mean have a professional NCC driver bring you here. You do not want to be driving in Naples unless you are Neapolitan (or maybe Sicilian). You won't understand the rhythm of the traffic here, nor the insanity of the parking. And you seriously do not need that level of stress in your life.

As when arriving by train, you've got a good 15 minutes of projects to drive through before entering the heart of the city.

BY PLANE

Naples-Capodichino Airport is just outside the city. From there you can take the Alibus into the center for €5. The trip takes 15 minutes. Alternatively, a taxi runs around €20. Be sure to get the driver to tell you *the exact amount* before getting in the taxi. I've never had a problem with taxis in Naples, but they have had a reputation for trickery in the past.

5.
The Naples Pass

If you're spending a few days in Naples (highly recommended) you may want to buy a Naples Pass.

You can purchase a pass for 1 day, 3 days, 5 days or 7 days, with the 7-day pass being the most popular. Each pass allows you entry into more tourist attractions, with the 7-day pass having the most. The 7-day includes entrance to*:

- Pompeii
- Herculaneum
- The Archaeological Museum
- The Capodimonte Museum
- The Royal Palace of Naples
- The Royal Palace of Caserta
- Castel Sant' Elmo
- The Filangeri Museum
- The San Gennaro Museum
- The Sotterata Neapolis (underground) and the Complex of San Lorenzo Maggiore
- The Museo Divino
- Entry and Guided Tour of the Bourbon Gallery (and underground tunnels)
- Entry and Guided Tour to the Catacombs of San Gennaro and San Gaudioso

- The Complex of Sant'Anna dei Lombardi
- Discounts at 100 attractions in town
- Unlimited free transport on trains and funiculare.

* I recommend going to the NaplesPass.eu website first and checking which sites you can enter with which day pass, as it changes. From there you can decide which pass is best for you. Also check the days each place is open. You don't want to buy a pass and then find most things are closed on the days you'll be there.

How Does It Work

Download the Naples Pass app to your smartphone. From there you choose the number of days you want and whether you want the transportation option or not.

Once you activate your pass you can use it for the appropriate number of days. Don't activate it until you arrive in Naples, on the first day you want to use it.

At the time of writing this book in 2024, the transport feature is €27.50 for 7 days. The average metro ride one way is €1.20. A day pass for the metro + funiculare is €4,50.

If you are staying above one of the funiculare (I stay in Vomero, so the funicular is my way up and down the hill), you can scan your pass each time you go up and down, as well as whenever you use the metro. I doubt I would ever use the transport pass enough to make a financial saving on transport alone, but to me, the convenience of being able to just scan the turnstile with my phone and not have to wait to buy tickets makes the transportation pass worthwhile. On a recent sojourn in Naples (while writing this book), I bought a 7-day

Naples pass just to see how much I would use it, and to evaluate whether it was value for money or not. I didn't get through all the available attractions (mostly because I tend to spend hours wandering, exploring, drinking coffees and spritzes and socializing), however, I did think it was good value. You may want to check how many attractions from your **must-see** list are on the pass.

6.
A City of Staircases

He who doesn't love Naples has yet to learn how to love life.

-Anonymous

Naples is a vertical city, settled into the curved embrace of the hills behind it. It looks like nature's own giant amphitheater, with tiers of stadium seating swooshing around the arc of the mountains, offering views all the way out to the realms of the gods. So, you may be wondering, before the funiculare, buses and metro, how did people scale these steep heights each day? The answer is staircases.

Throughout history, Neapolitans have needed functional and fast means to get up and down the slopes, connecting the historic center and the port with the hills above. Over its 3000-year history Naples built more than 200 stairways or staircases connecting the slopes to the city and the sea. Considered masterpieces of urban planning, these ancient pedestrian paths are still in daily use, and several of them need to be on your travel radar. They are not merely a tangible, touchable link to the past and a wonder to behold. Some of these staircases have some of the most dramatic, thrilling views of this dynamic city.

Let's look at three staircases on the hills – you need to scale at least one of these – and one more hidden inside a palace that is not-to-be-missed.

Up or Down?

I recommend going *down* the staircases rather than up. These stairways are steep, so if you're not a fitness maniac or a triathlete, climbing the stairs is not going to be fun. Especially in the heat.

More importantly, **you only get the view on the way down**. And this experience is all about the glorious, panoramic views.

Vomero

THE SALITA DELLA PEDAMENTINA

The Pedamentina connects the Vomero neighborhood on the hill with the Spanish Quarter at the bottom.

It starts at the Piazzale San Martino (the pretty piazza in front of the Certosa San Martino), just below the Sant' Elmo castle. From the piazzale you look out over the entire eastern side of Naples. The view stretches across the historic center in a patchwork of yellows, Pompeii reds, whites and greens, with the brilliant blue of the bay to your right. Not only can you identify the large buildings from here, you also get an (almost) bird's eye view over Spaccanapoli, the Naples splitter, slicing its way through the city center. Your eye races across the city and ends with Mount Vesuvius, dominating the skyline in the near distance. From up here you can get a fantastic concept of where you are, where you've been, and where you're going.

The *Salita della Pedamentina* was built when work began on the Certosa di San Martino (1325). A contraction of the Italian *piedi del monte* (feet/foot of the mountain), this path was used to take building materials up the hill. It also provided access to Castel Sant' Elmo, built in 1329 by Robert the Wise. The Pedamentina is still considered an urban masterpiece.

Interestingly, it is still used by the Vomerese as a way to travel to and from the Corso below. Don't be surprised to see old folk walking their way up the hill toward you. Recently I encountered a man who had to be in his 80s, steadfastly making his way up the hill. He was at least three quarters of the way up and wasn't even slightly out of breath. No doubt he has been walking it most of his life.

The staircase zigzags down the hill, winding its way down 414 elongated steps. Parts of it are a tad rough around the edges, some parts are a little steep, some parts stretch along narrow streets where you need to walk in single file.

But Lordy, the views! They're gorgeous and give you even more reason to fall in love with Naples. So, as long as it's not too hot out and it's not raining, I often take the winding Pedamentina (*down*!). It takes around 30 minutes to get from the piazzale at the top, to the hustling, bustling madness at the bottom. When you do reach the bottom, look back up and imagine how much fun enemy soldiers must have had trying to get up the hill to attack the castle!

THE CALATA SAN FRANCESCO

This staircase connects Vomero to the beautiful seafront neighborhoods of Chiaia and Mergellina. This walk is vibrantly colorful and absolutely *stunning*.

The passage ends at the Chiaia beachfront, a super chic neighborhood full of lovely bars and restaurants and wonderful shopping. Allow time to wander along the waterfront and check out the private yachts and pleasure crafts moored in the marina. You'll get amazing photos here with the gleaming white boats, colorful houses, intense blue sea and azure skies all watched over by Mount Vesuvius.

Calata San Francesco begins at Via Belvedere in Vomero. The first stretch of the walk is stair-less and not overly steep. From Via Aniello Falcone, the entrance to the Calata looks private, but just cross the road and keep walking. At the base of the first set of stairs the Calata San Francesco comes into view. From here, it zigzags down a series of steep stairways bordered by brightly colored buildings until it reaches Via Tasso, where it changes name and becomes the *Salita Tasso*.

Stop at every opportunity to take in the view across to the Sorrento Peninsula and Capri. It really is fantastic, especially on a sunny day. Once you get to the Corso Vittorio Emanuele, the name changes again and becomes *Via Arco Mirelli*, a narrow, steep and busy street that ends at the Riviera di Chiaia. Keep your elbows in and your wits about you as you make your way through this final section of the walk. Cars and scooters whizz by fast, so you need to pay attention. It really is worth it though, and after all the gorgeous views, you end up in the Beverly Hills of Naples. This staircase experience is fantastic.

Posillipo

A little further along the waterfront from Chiaia and Mergellina, you reach the achingly beautiful Posillipo neighborhood. Apart from being gorgeous itself, it's from here that you get the most iconic views of Naples, the views you've seen in a hundred postcards and picture books. There is a staircase and a wild, winding road for you to see here, and both are just breathtaking.

The Salita Villanova

This is one of the least well-known staircases in Naples, but the Villanova Staircase is one of the most scenic. And chances are you won't know anyone else who has been here.

The Salita Villanova takes you down 652 stairs from Via Manzoni in Posillipo to Via Posillipo at the seafront. Also known as *O' Canalone*, this ancient pedestrian passage was built into the volcanic tufa stone centuries – if not millenia – ago by local farmers. They used this route to bring their wares down the hill to the old seaport. This entire area was once populated with enormous Roman villas, which I talk about in the **Other Archaeological Sites** chapter.

For many years the stairway was abandoned and impassable, blocked by trash and overgrown vegetation. Then in 2020 a group of local residents and volunteers stepped in and cleaned the entire staircase. Their work, paired with structural renovations, enabled the passage to be reopened. The panoramic route is sensational, bordered by small streets of sumptuous villas and gardens, with sparkling blue views across the bay and Vesuvius menacing away in the distance. The staircase ends close to one of Naples' haunted houses, the 17th century Palazzo Donn'Anna.

From here, either stop along the waterfront on Via Posillipo for lunch or walk 10 minutes to the marina in Mergellina and the multitude of eateries along the lungomare between the marina and Castel dell' Ovo. (It's all much closer than you realize.)

Getting there: Take the Mergellina funicular to the Manzoni stop. From there, look for the entrance which is close to number 143.

THE THIRTEEN DESCENTS OF SANT' ANTONIO/ *LE TREDICI DISCESE*

One of the most beguiling viewpoints in Posillipo is the terrace of the Sant' Antonio church. This massive viewing deck is a photographer's dream. Expect to find the camera shutters of hobbyists and professionals capturing breathtaking blue hours and dreamy golden hours from up here. You'll find night photographers and those capturing every moment throughout the day – this is the most iconic view of Naples. It's also a hotspot for wedding photos.

The getting there part is quite interesting, if not a tad perilous. A series of 13 gear-box-grinding, hairpin turns called *the ramps* bring you from Piazza Sannazzaro up to the 17th century baroque church. The ramps were built over an ancient Greco/Roman road that connected Mergellina with the hillside community of Posillipo. In 1643, the Duke of Medina had them enlarged and reconfigured to improve access to the church. He immortalized his handiwork with a plaque in Piazza Sannazzaro at the first of the ramps. The ramps themselves are definitely photo-worthy, cutting their way up the hill. They're steep, so I recommend coming down, not walking up. Listen out for cars and stay against the wall in single file.

Getting there: The church and belvedere/terrace are a short walk from the S. Antonio funiculare station. If you walk down the 13 ramps, you'll end up close to the sea in Margellina. As with the Salita Villanova, stop for lunch along the waterfront. Before you leave, drop in on the next staircase, which is 5 minutes away inside a palazzo in the Chiaia shopping streets.

Palazzo Mannajuolo

In the heart of Chiaia's elegant shopping streets, you can find one of the city's finest examples of art nouveau architecture, the Palazzo Mannajuolo.

Although the ground floor is now entirely made up of chic storefronts, the western facade of the building (as seen from Via dei Mille) is still impressive with its armored concrete in stunning convex and concave sections and dome on top. Built in 1910 by entrepreneurial engineer

Giuseppe Mannajuolo (who owned the land) and Gioacchino Melluci, the building is most famous for its incredible internal staircase.

This jaw dropping elliptical staircase twirling its way up to Heaven looks like the brainchild of a movie set designer. It really is sensational. When you photograph it from the bottom looking up, the image looks reversed, as though you were at the top looking down. It also looks impossibly high, much higher than the building itself. It really is a marvel and, for geeks like me, the marble steps and iron parapets swirling upwards in impossible decreasing ovals has to be on my Naples **must-see** list. You must visit Chiaia anyway, and although visitors are allowed to view the staircase, we are not permitted to climb it. A visit here only takes 10 minutes out of your day, so drop in if you can.

The entrance is on Via Gaetano Filangieri through the arched doorway between Banca Mediolanum and Versace.

Address: Via Filangieri, 36
What's nearby: All the chic shops, and Insta-worthy Sant' Arpino.*
* Before you leave Chiaia stop by one of the most Instagrammable corners in Naples, The **Vicoletto Sant' Arpino.** This narrow street is made of a single, steep staircase that just screams for photos! Legend says a secret tunnel runs below the stairs to the Piazza del Plebiscito.
Getting there: From Palazzo Mannajuolo, walk one block along via Filangieri then turn right on Via Chiaia. Vicoletto Sant' Arpino is on your right, behind the Tabacchiere Scialo Mario.

7.
The Fabulous Metro Art Stations

The noblest motive is the public good.

~ Virgil

Remember when subway stations used to be gross and dirty? When I lived in London, subway stations were the filthy breeding grounds of the mega rats. Standing on the platform waiting for the tube, you could spot them scurrying along the tracks, sniffing at trash, their evil eyes piercing red in the semi-darkness. That was the era of the super rats, giant rats that built up insane levels of immunity living in the hospitals, then made their way into the outside world to terrorize the public. In my memory they were the size of the Queen's corgis, but in reality they were in all likelihood merely the size of enormous rabbits. The New York subway wasn't much better. It too was filthy, and smelled like a combination of vomit, urine and death. The tracks were typically full of trash and rodents with ADHD. (To be fair, I haven't been on the subway in New York or the tube in London for years, but they were always kind of icky.)

Until quite recently, I didn't use the subway in Naples either. I assumed it would be another dirty, trash laden, rat infested underground, full of beggars and thieves, foul air and things that make you itchy. After all, if the subway of a wealthy city like NYC was so disgusting, how could a relatively poor southern Italian city like Naples be any better? You can imagine my surprise when I *did* finally go down there and found a clean, safe, modern and highly efficient subway system. Seriously, New York politicians need to come ride the Naples subway so they can see how it's really done!

Walking is always my first choice when I'm in Naples, but when the weather's not working with me or when I need to get places quickly, I use the metro. And it's fantastic. It is more than just clean, efficient and modern though. As part of a city government initiative to clean up public transport centers and make them more attractive, the city of Naples decided to make some of the metro stations *art stations*.

The Metro dell' Arte project redeveloped several stations into catacombs of contemporary art, commissioning contemporary artists and architects to infuse the everyday life of local commuters with beauty and color. The concept is brilliant and has turned some of the metro stations along Line 1 into an open-air museums of sorts. It is further proof that this modern, vibrant city is also a European cultural center and is yet another reason I am so passionate about Naples.

The following art stations are some of my favorites. Make an effort to get to some of them and keep an eye out if you're passing through others. Be sure to ride the metro while you're here in Naples!

1. The Toledo Station

This one is the crown jewel of the Naples Metro art stations. It is so different and so spectacular; I often use this station even though it's not the closest to my destination – I just love seeing it. But I'm not alone, the Toledo station was nominated as the most beautiful train station in all of Europe.

As you ride the escalators 130 feet below ground into Naples' deepest metro station, thousands of Bisazza tiles above and around you change from pale to the deepest of blues, more inky the lower you go. It's as if you are descending to the bottom of the sea, or maybe the deepest reaches of the Ancient Greek cisterns below the Via Tribunali. An 80-foot-long LED installation produces images of the sea, rippling with the continuous momentum of the waves. Meanwhile, way up above you, Blanca's Crater de Luz (a cone-shaped mosaic void) reaches up to the topmost point of the station, with an oculus letting in natural light. You truly feel you are below the sea. On the upper level, remnants of the original Aragonese walls are integrated into the mosaic adorned atrium. You'd be hard pressed to find a more spectacular train station anywhere in the world.

Toledo Station is on the main shopping street, the Via Toledo. **What's nearby:** From here, walk to the Piazza del Plebiscito, the Teatro San Carlo, the Galleria Umberto I, and the Royal Palace in one direction, and into the heart of the Spanish Quarter in the other. Also close by is the Funicolare Centrale to whizz you up the Vomero Hill.

2. The Garibaldi Station

The main train station of Naples has a hyper-modern, futuristic vibe. Crisscrossing escalators covered in mirrors look like angular helixes, reflecting the natural light from the glass ceiling above. At the bottom, a mirrored wall has photos of passengers that blur as real people pass through.

Chances are you'll come through here either from your fast train to Rome or on your way to catching a circumvesuviana train to Pompeii. Give yourself a few minutes to wander, grab a *creme al caffè* and a *sfogliatella*, or if you're in the mood for something more substantial, visit the food hall inside the station.

3. The Università Station

Different yet again, the Università station is an explosion of shapes and colors and cutting edge modern, *digipop* design. Trafficked by thousands of multi-cultural academics (and regular folk) every day, this station is a story about communication, from the old world to the new high-tech world.

Arriving from the piazza, you pass through modern high gloss black columns cut into the profiles of faces, towards an LED wall of shifting colors and patterns. Vibrant fuchsia, lime green and intense lemon-yellow spark the brain. The intention as you pass from ground level to underground is to take you from the conscious brain into the spiritual mind (or busy brain to focused mind). Rolling LED displays show universally recognized words, again referencing the university setting: knowledge and modern technology in a multi-cultural setting. Paired with this hyper-modern communication, the stairs on either side have abstract paintings of Italy's most famous writer, Dante Alighieri (in the Piscinola direction) and his great love Beatrice (in the Garibaldi direction). I love paintings that roll down stairs. At the bottom of the escalator, you step into a world of digital art with bright pinks and greens indicating the directions, digital floors and LED ceilings making you feel as though you've stepped into a modern digital painting.

I wouldn't want to come down here with a migraine, but otherwise this has to be the coolest, most modern train station I have ever seen. It's fun to think that college students' brains are getting fired up every day as they make their way to and from school.

4. Municipio Station

It seems that any time you dig in Italy, whether to re-floor your house or to build a metro station, some form of historic treasure is going to pop up. From amphorae and mosaic floors to statues and even, on occasion, massive archaeological sites. So, when you're digging in one of the oldest cities in all of Europe, you can expect some insanely amazing stuff to emerge. This was the case when Naples began excavating the subway station in Piazza Municipio, near Castel Nuovo. Except, instead of just finding cool artifacts, they also discovered *the ancient port of Neapolis.*

Through this discovery, archaeologists learned about changes in the original Hellenic/Roman coastal landscape and found the original ancient port infrastructure. In particular, they learned that in antiquity (the Ancient Greek and Roman eras), a large man-made bay lay between what would centuries later become Castel Nuovo in the west and the church of Santa Maria di Porto Salvo in the east. Geological coring provided sediment data allowing them to date the structures they found to around 326 BC. They also learned the construction of the artificial harbor began in the 3rd century BC with dredging works that removed marine sediment until they reached a hard layer of Tufa stone. They found original channels and pits dug for larger ships to enter the harbor, slipways and terraced walls. Then in the 1st century AD, new structures were built including buildings (maybe for warehousing?) jetties, quays and a road. This part of the port was in use until the 5th century AD. At some point a mudslide buried parts of the port, and by the 5th century AD, the basin had become marshland.

In 2003, construction workers working on the Municipio metro station unearthed two Roman ships. By 2005, they had uncovered a total of *seven* ships. Two were from the 1st century AD. Another was wrecked sometime in the late 2nd century. The remaining boats are thought to date back as far as the late Hellenistic period. Paintings from Pompeii show these exact types of boats. We know from the paintings that the boats were painted in bright colors and were quite spectacular. From the specific materials used in construction, to the conventional mortise and tenon method of joining a ship's beams, the information gathered from the discovery of these ships has been incredible.

Some of the boats were used to transport goods to and from bigger ships moored in the harbor, while others were used for longer trips along the coast to the port of Ostia. Two had hulls 11 meters long, while the other five were 15 meters in length. Along with the ships, they found personal belongings: shoes, jewelry, dice, ropes and ceramics. There were also glass bottles and sealed amphorae.

Who wants to know more?

If, like me, you want more details about all of this, I recommend going to www.she.hal.science and searching for "The Remains of Four Vessels Found In The Ancient Harbor Of Naples". The document is a bit sciencey, but fascinating, and it has diagrams of where everything was found.

At the time of researching and writing this book in 2024, the ships are submerged in cold water in a specially designed, temperature-controlled space in the Piscinola neighborhood. After all, how do you make the ships and the roughly 3.3 million artifacts housed in Piscinola accessible to the general public? The plan is to make the corridor connecting Piazza Municipio to the Beverello dock a permanent museum and move as much as they can here. Depending on when you are reading this book, the boats and museum may/may not be completed/open to the public.

Meanwhile, the interior of the Municipio metro station is beautiful. As you move through the corridor, one wall has cream and tufa colored dreamy artwork in the form of a hallway-length video installation showing ancient Naples with people in the foreground, while the opposite wall has yet another treasure. Here you'll find the original footing of Castle Nuovo towers. The castle footing takes up the entire floor to ceiling space as you enter the station. It's quite incredible to walk along the length of the space – from street level you don't think about how much of the castle structure is actually below ground.

I recommend visiting Castel Nuovo (see the **Castles and Palaces** chapter) and either using the metro to get here or coming down for a look while you're in the vicinity.
What's nearby: Castel Nuovo, Piazza Municipio.

5. Dante Station

I use this station often when the weather is too hot or rainy. It is the access point to get to Piazza Bellini (see **Piazza Bellini** chapter) where I love to visit the Greek walls and have a coffee or a spritz. Dante is the closest metro stop to the bottom end of the Via Tribunali, so it's a great place to start a tourist day. Immediately outside the metro station, you can grab the bus up to the Capodimonte Museum, which is too far to walk to. In December, Piazza Dante is full of Christmas stalls, which are fun to visit too.

Above the stairs leading down to the lower level, in bright white neon script, a beautiful passage from Dante's *Convivio* tells the reader that color and light are wonderful because we only know them with our face (eyes) and no other senses. Further inside the station, steel-studded white glass panels feature work from contemporary artists. Paintings by Carlo Alfano in the entrance area, objects on a steel panel the wall of the lower area by Jannis Kounellis, and on the second floor Michelangelo Pistoletto's *Intermediterraneo* features a mirrored surface simulating the Mediterranean.

6. Museo Station

The Museo station is next to the MANN (Archeological Museum of Naples), the greatest archaeological museum in the world. So it is fitting that inside the station you are greeted by some well-known ancient Roman statues. There is a replica of *The Laocoön and His Sons* (the original is in the Vatican museums). There is also a replica of the Farnese *Hercules*.

Steel-studded white glass panels give a slightly antiseptic feel to your descent to the tracks. On occasion when I've been here, there have been fabulous black and white photography displays behind the white glass panels along the tracks, including photography of ancient Roman statues. I don't remember seeing these the last time I used the station, so they may be part of a revolving exhibit, or perhaps I was just on a different line?

A special area of the Museo station hosts a mini museum display from the MANN called the *Stazione Neapolis*. Here you can see a variety of relics discovered during the excavation of the subway. Some are from as far back as the Ancient Greek and Roman periods, others as recent as the 17th century. I still find it exciting that Neapolitans get to walk past all of this every day on their commute to and from work! **What's nearby:** This is the station for the National Archaeological Museum but is also only a couple of blocks' walk to Piazza Bellini in one direction and my favorite eateries in Sanità in the other.

7. Materdei Station

The Materdei station features artwork from Domenico Bianchi, Sandro Chia and Luigi Serafini. The stairways to the lower floors are full of cool, modern mosaics.

The highlight of this art station is the central corridor, covered in Sol LeWitt's vibrant *Wall Drawings*. He also has a fiberglass sculpture at the end of the corridor. Known as the father of minimal art, American LeWitt lived in Spoleto in the 1980s and maintained a close bond with Italy. His work at the Materdei station was one of his final projects. He died from cancer shortly thereafter.

The Daily Telegraph rated Materdei as the 16th most beautiful metro station in Europe.

8. Salvatore Rosa Station

Salvatore Rosa on the east side of Vomero is one of the most distinctive metro art stations. The exterior and the park outside feature modern sculptures and mosaics which complement the art inside the station. Inside the station, clean, dramatic lines are offset by a variety of sleek, modern art pieces from Neapolitan and Italian artists including Raffaella Nappo, LuCa, Enzo Cucchi, Quintino Scolavino and Natalino Zullo. It all feels quite chic and very cool.

The entrance to the station is through a huge glass pyramid.

9. Quattro Giornate

Quattro Giornate or *Four Days* station commemorates the four-day uprising that freed Naples from Nazi occupation in September 1943. Resistance-inspired bronze reliefs occupy the entrance. Descending to the platforms below, four silver sculptures represent the Neapolitan women who made it happen. There is also text that speaks to the passion of the fearless who took up arms to defend Naples.

10. Vanvitelli

The most interesting art component of this station is a blue neon spiral on the ceiling in the central hall. The spiral features numbers in the Fibonacci Sequence. Fibbonaci was an Italian mathematician who invented/re-invented a sequence of numbers where each number is the sum of the two preceding numbers. There are also some contemporary artworks, floors with stars and metallic cylinders, mosaics and an exhibit called *Off Limits*, involving a rock in a glass cage.

The Art Stations of Naples are a brilliant concept and a modern addition to a city steeped in art and culture. They definitely make using the metro even more fun and need to be on your travel radar.

8.
The Neighborhoods of Naples

Naples is the flower of paradise. The last adventure of my life.

~ Alexandre Dumas

On a map or from a bird's eye view, Naples seems overwhelmingly enormous – almost Los Angeles-levels of never-ending sprawl. Even to me, the vastness of Naples sometimes overwhelms. But here's the thing, almost everything you will want to see (and almost everything in this book) is actually quite centralized and within walking distance.

So let's have a look at the main neighborhoods I'm going to discuss in this book, get an idea of where they are, what's going on there, how to get to and from them, and maybe get an idea of where to stay in this exciting city.

Vomero

I'm starting with the Vomero neighborhood because that's where I love to stay. I'm a creature of habit. When I find a neighborhood I love, I make it my home base and keep coming back to it over and over, so this neighborhood feels like home to me in Naples.

If Rome and Paris had a baby, it would be the Vomero. Vomero takes pride of position up on the hill, looking out over the Gulf of Naples. Its airy, tree-lined boulevards full of outdoor cafes and shops feel a world away from the mayhem of the city below, yet they are close enough to all the action that you still feel you are living and breathing Naples.

This neighborhood was once farmland and woods. In fact, a map from 1630 indicated everything west of Castel Sant' Elmo was empty land, forest and farms. In the 1500s, around 1200 people lived up here – roughly 300 families. Pathways and stairways existed but were largely overgrown and unused. The 1700s saw the construction of several large estates and some churches of varying sizes. Then, around the turn of the century multiple large pieces of property, like the **Villa Floridiana** were built.

After the Unification of Italy, an urban renewal scheme called the *Risanamento* created new growth in the neighborhood. The increased population inspired construction of the first funicular to get people to and from Naples at the bottom of the hill. There are three main funiculare: the Chiaia was built first in 1889 and runs from Vomero to Chiaia. The Montesanto line opened in 1891 (Vomero to Piazza Montesanto in the Spanish Quarter). In 1928, the Centrale line funicular opened (from Vomero to Via Toledo).

By 1900, the city of Naples was undergoing massive rebuilding, and the Vomero and Camoldoli neighborhoods on the hill became part of greater Naples, and as such, you'll notice the architecture up here is different to that down below. The Vomero streets are lined with huge, Liberty-style houses. (Unfortunately, there later came some overbuilding, but the heart of the zone from Vanvitelli to the edges of the hill is absolutely gorgeous, resplendent with stunning views.)

My friend Veronique, a transplant from France who now cringes in horror at the thought of ever leaving Naples, lives in a massive apartment in a subdivided palazzo (built in 1743, according to the plaque in the courtyard). This palazzo is everything I have ever dreamed of. Historic and beautiful, no doubt with a messy yet fascinating history, the palazzo is now 15 huge apartments, each riddled with frescos and floor-to-ceiling *portafinestra* windows, looking out over the bay. The courtyard has a huge garden that ends in a low wall overlooking the sea. There is a massive old lemon tree in the courtyard, heavily pregnant with luscious fruit. Veronique holds lemons under my nose and tells me they smell this good because they spend their lives looking out at Capri. Then she plucks a half dozen for me to keep in my apartment because she says I need them. And I do. If one of the other 14 apartments in this building ever becomes vacant, I will hijack my entire life to live here.

The Vomero is fantastic, and you need to make wandering up here part of your Neapolitan experience. Come up on one of the funiculare (because it's fun), visit the Certosa San Martino and Castel Sant' Elmo, sip coffee in the garden at the Villa Floridiana, soak up the street musicians, the outdoor produce market stands, the cool shopping streets, and then (knees and hips willing), take one of the staircases down. (the **Staircases** chapter will give you all the details) One of them leads you to the Beverly Hills of Naples: Chiaia. It has views beautiful enough to cry over all the way down to the sea.

Chiaia

Had I stayed here first, this would have become my neighborhood. But by the time I really explored it, I was too deeply entwined with Vomero to consider staying anywhere else. But Chiaia is simply beautiful. Wedged between Piazza Vittoria on the east and Mergellina at the west, this colorful seafront neighborhood is one of the most affluent in Naples. Along with luxury stores and chic dining options, it is also home to the medical school and the business school.

Between the hillside houses and the sea, the Villa Comunale public park offers shade from the hot Neapolitan sun and is also home to the **Naples Aquarium**. Built in 1874, the dream of German zoologist Anton Dohrn was to have fresh sea water circulating through tanks where sea creatures 'could expose themselves to the eye of science'. It is now also home to the National Biology, Ecology and Marine Biotech Institute and is one of the most important marine observation and research institutes *in the world*. Definitely worth a visit.

I love taking the **Calata San Francesco** staircase down from Vomero, crossing the street to the sea, and then walking along the lungomare to Mergellina. Or close to it anyway. This gives you yet another perspective of Naples and its completely ridiculous beauty. Under Vesuvius' watchful gaze, pass through the marina with its luxury boats, pick up hot taralli from the kiosks along the waterfront, and enjoy their nutty, peppery magnificence as you look out at Capri and the Sorrento peninsula in the distance.

What's nearby: While you're here, along with eating and drinking and enjoying the shops and the views, you can drop in on the Museo Pignatelli house museum as you wander back toward Via Toledo. Be sure to stop in at Palazzo Mannajuolo to see the magnificent art deco helical staircase. You are mere minutes' walk from the entrance to the Bourbon Galleries underground site if you veer left, or the Castel dell'Ovo and the Fontana Gigante if you veer right. The eastern edge of Chiaia is the gateway into the historic center – as if this neighborhood wasn't engaging enough, most of the things you want to see in Naples are walking distance from here.

The Historic Center

From Vomero, another option is to take the funicular from Fuga station down to Via Toledo at the western edge of Naples' historic center. From here to your right, you immediately encounter the Galleria Umberto, the Teatro San Carlo, Piazza Plebiscito, the Palazzo Reale and Castel Nuovo/Maschio Angiono. Turn left instead and all the glories of the historic center await you. The bulk of this book is tightly packed into the streets immediately in front of you. Walk one city block to Piazza Dante and catch the bus up to Capodimonte or walk through the Porta Alba to Piazza Bellini and up along the Via Tribunali.

Ever the creature of habit, I do this all the time. I start with the Ancient Greeks at Piazza Bellini then lose myself amongst the treasures lining every inch of the Via Tribunali for hours on end.

Spaccanapoli – the Naples splitter – is a long, straight road that slices through Naples from the bottom of Vomero, through the historic center, all the way to the train station. It changes names several times along the way (Via Benedetto Croce becomes Via San Biagio dei Libra which then becomes Via Vicaria Vecchia), so if you ask your GPS to take you to Spaccanapoli it will probably get lost. When the Greeks moved their colony inland from Megaride they created the first master planned community. They based their new city along three large parallel boulevards called *decumani*, and then built intersecting streets at 90-degree angles. The lowest of the decumani, the one closest to the sea, is Spaccanapoli. It runs roughly parallel to the main street I talk about in this book, the Via Tribunali (the middle street of the three).

You get a fantastic view of Spaccanapoli, literally cutting its way through the heart of the city, from the belvedere by Certosa San Martino up in the Vomero neighborhood. (In the **Staircases** chapter we talk about taking the **Pedimentina** stairs from here to piazza Montesanto, from where a quick zigzag puts you onto via Benedetto Croce.)

The Spanish Quarter

The third option from Vomero is to either take the Montesanto funicular or the Pedamentina staircase down to the most evocative neighborhood in Naples, **The Quartieri Spagnol**i, or Spanish Quarter.

In the 16th century, this neighborhood was built to house the Spanish soldiers occupying the city (Naples was under Spanish rule at this point). Tall buildings on either side of narrow roads blocked out the sunshine, creating a dusky labyrinth rife with crime and prostitution. Now it's one of the most characteristic neighborhoods in all of Naples. If current me loves staying in Vomero, me in my 30s would have beelined straight to the Spanish Quarter and stayed almost anywhere there. Here is the mayhem and the action you instantly associate with Naples. Narrow streets and alleys all begging you to explore them, Vespas whizzing by, laundry hanging in the sun, food stands, bars and eateries everywhere you look. To me this neighborhood is the soul of Naples – the chaos and the madness and the excitement. Here you feel the blood pumping through your veins – I just *love* it!

The paradox of one of the sunniest cities in all of Europe being filled with streets in perpetual grades of twilight is a perfect metaphor for the Spanish Quarter. The combination of history, intrigue, exhilarating madness and a complete lack of reason is spellbinding. There is no rationalizing the Quartieri Spagnoli (or most of Naples for that matter.) It's never going to make sense. So, all you can do is stop being judgmental, let it be everything that it is, and soak up the excitement of this brilliant yet crazy neighborhood.

Lost in the Spanish Quarter, **by Heddi Goodrich**

In the **Reading List** chapter of recommended books, I've included a tremendous book by Heddi Goodrich. At 16, she came to Naples as a foreign exchange student, then stayed on to go to college here. She lived right here in the Spanish Quarter. Reading her book, I always feel this profound sense of loss that I didn't live in the quarter in my late teens and baby twenties and go to college in Naples.

Bordered between the Vomero and Via Toledo (from where things feel a little calmer), this neighborhood is small but vital, and you haven't really experienced Naples without wandering through here at least once. I find ways to weave the Spanish Quarter into most days I spend in Naples, which is made easier by taking advantage of the Pedimentina and the funicular to and from Vomero.

Via Pignasecca cuts a diagonal line from Piazza Montesanto to Via Toledo. This outdoor market street, **Mercato Pignasecca**, feels like a movie set. You almost expect Marcello Mastroianni to step out of an alleyway, light a cigarette, and make his way to Sophia Loren's door. It's loud and gritty, peppered with folks from every walk of life doing their sidewalk shopping, the shouts of the fish market vendors providing the soundtrack. Mercato Pignasecca is fantastic for people watching, as well as for filling your belly with Naples' calorie dense street food. I love picking up a *cuoppo pesce fritto* (fried seafood pieces in a brown paper cone) kicking back and watching Naples happen all around me. It is, of course, also the perfect place to buy fresh fruits and vegetables. *Remember not to touch the alluring piles of produce – the vendor will grab and bag you everything you ask for.* Take a moment while here to soak up the history of the buildings and alleyways around you. This is exactly how life has been pounding out here at full volume for centuries.

There is some tremendous street art to get involved with in this neighborhood. From the blue baby in Pignasecca to the Maradona mural and all the Maradona inspired art leading up to it. You *must* walk along **Vico Totò** (via Portacarrese), the street devoted to street art capturing the beloved Neapolitan actor and comedian Antonio "Totò" de Curtis. I just love how the walls of Naples celebrate both the city's identity and its most cherished characters. You'll find Sophia Loren gazing out at you too, like the world's most beautiful siren.

The energy on the streets in the Spanish Quarter feels like the lifeblood of the city: vital, exciting and overwhelming all at once. It's also a street photographer's paradise.

Sanità

In my 30s I would have gravitated to the Spanish Quarter, but the version of Corinna who spent much of her 20s exploring Europe would have hightailed it to this neighborhood, the Sanità (just not back in those days – until ten or fifteen years ago this was a really dangerous/scary neighborhood and, in reality, I wouldn't have gone anywhere near it. But now it is one of the coolest, most vibey neighborhoods in Naples).

During the past decade-plus of re-gentrification, Sanità became a zone that celebrated its youth. In the **Underground Sites** chapter, we talk about La Paranza, the organization that trains and employs the youth of Sanità to run the catacombs and other historic sites in the area. In the **Museums** chapter, I introduce you to the most exciting new artist of my lifetime, a sculptor called Jago who moved his exhibition space, the Jago Museum, into an abandoned church here in Sanità, and whose employees are all from La Paranza.

As with the Spanish Quarter, the street history here reads like a movie set, albeit one with Vespas whizzing past you at breakneck speeds and street vendors calling out the enticements of their wares. In the middle of it all, you have historical sites like the **Palazzo della Spagnolo**, street art like the **Basilica Santa Maria della Sanità** mural, and some of the best eateries in Naples, including my favorite, **Isabella de Cham**.

Sanità reminds me of Berlin in the late 80s and early 90s. Still incredibly affordable, it is a magnet to artists and musicians and is undeniably cool.

Getting there: From Via Tribunali take a left at Via Duomo and walk two city blocks to Via Foria, the street that is home to the **MANN (archeological museum)** just a couple of blocks to your left. Crossing Via Foria you are now in Sanità. The metro stops here are Museo and Cavour, with the Materdei stop at the neighborhood's edge just a little further along.

Posillipo

If Chiaia is the Beverly Hills of Naples, then Posillipo must be the Malibu of Naples. This neighborhood, on the hill just beyond Mergellina, is elegant, chic and ridiculously beautiful. Here you'll find the most iconic views of Naples and Vesuvius across the bay. From the **Terrazzo Sant' Antonio** and the **Salita Villanova** you can snap your own amazing photos – the ones you've seen in a million postcards and picture books.

For several centuries, Posillipo was also home to Roman elites. From here through Baiae (a town we'll meet in the **Other Archeaological Sites** chapter), massive villas lined the waterfront, each more stupendous than the next. You can still visit one of them, **Villa Pausilypon**. From the city center, pack a picnic and grab the C31 bus to **Parco Virgiliano**, a gorgeous park perched above the cliffs of Posillipo. From here you can enjoy stunning views over the water, and it is one of the few places where you can see all three islands, Procida, Ischia and Capri, in a single glorious panorama.

Meanwhile the stretch of Posillipo that runs along the waterfront is peppered with quaint cafes and *trattorie,* their delicious aromas mingling with the salty breeze coming off the water. A 10-minute stroll along the seafront from the center of Via Posillipo brings you to Mergellina and Chiaia. Everything here is easy and accessible.

Walking the Neighborhoods

If you look at a map of Naples, you'll see all these neighborhoods fall into one another across a very small space. All of it is walkable, and you'll find it easy to see an enormous amount here in a single day, all at a comfortable pace, eating your way into a food coma in the process.

Now that we have an idea of where the various neighborhoods are in Naples, let's take a look at where I recommend starting your day…

9.
Piazza Bellini

What you leave behind is not what is engraved in stone monuments, but what is woven into the lives of others.

~ Pericles

Were you and I to spend a day together in Naples (or if we were plotting out an itinerary for you), it would begin here at Piazza Bellini – or to be exact, a block away in Piazza Dante.

Piazza Bellini is not only a great geographical beginning, historically it also takes us back to the very beginning, back to the days when this town was called Nea-Polis, or *new city*.

Via Tribunali

As we explore this fantastic city together you will see non-stop references to the **Via Tribunali**, one of the main east-west streets running through the center of Naples. I find Tribunali to be an easier landmark than **Spaccanapoli**, the other main *decumanus*, or artery, running a block or so below. This is largely because Spaccanapoli is actually three streets linked together. If you're anything like me, finding your way through a hustling bustling city with a constantly changing street name can be a bit navigationally challenging. So Tribunali it is.

Parthenope's Tears

The story begins with a Greek siren named Parthenope. Roughly 3000 years ago Greece decided it needed to expand its holdings, so it sent boats of young men out to discover and conquer new lands. The first place they discovered was southern Italy. The first place they settled was just outside of Naples in Cumae, in the 8th century BC. The sailors dug out tufa stone, from an eruption in the Campi Flagrei 44,000 years prior, and built their new city. Cumae was an ideal place to begin. It offered incredibly fertile land and was geographically advantageous for trade. From Cumae on the coast, they then built a new town on the hill of Pizzofalcone promontory and named it after a Greek siren, Parthenope.

I have heard two legends about Parthenope. The first says she tried to lure Ulysses from her promontory as he was sailing by, and when he wasn't beguiled by her singing, she drowned herself. Her body washed ashore at Megaride, where Castel Ovo now stands.

The story I prefer was told to me by a local guide, who said that when Ulysses ignored her singing, Parthenope's tears created the Bay of Naples. Either way this new city-state or *poleis* was called Parthenope.

Before too long, the Greeks built another new city or *polis*, slightly inland from Parthenope. This one was built on a rectangular grid running east-west and was protected by a huge city wall built from giant blocks of tufa. They called this *Nea–polis,* or New Town. We call it Napoli, or Naples.

Piazza Bellini

From the Piazza Dante metro stop (a good landmark to keep up your sleeve as the entry point to many of the places you want to visit in

Naples), walk a half block through the Port Alba, past the booksellers and the street musicians, cross the Via Costantinopoli and into Piazza Bellini. (This will take you all of four minutes, assuming you do stop to look at things along the way.)

Piazza Bellini is the first place where we come face to face with the ancient Greeks. The piazza is lined with eateries and bars, all of which look onto a set of ruins. Not just any ruins though, these are the remains of the original ancient Greek walls built to contain *Neapolis*.

Now I don't know how often you've started your day looking at a 3000-ish year old Greek wall or ended it with an aperitivo hour overlooking the same said wall, but I do it all the time when I'm here and it *still* thrills me. From this moment, Naples' Ancient Greek history is no longer some abstract concept. It is real. Right there for you to see.

This piazza is close to the university and to the art academy, so early evenings tend to be filled with students nursing a drink, leaning against the low fences that stop them falling into the Greek ruins. I always think this is part of why Neapolitans have such a strong sense of self, of who they are and where they fit in. Not only is every minute of every day filled with beauty and tangible proof of their history, but they can also come here, grab a spritz or a wine or a beer and subconsciously connect with their heritage from roughly 3000 years ago.

Piazza Bellini is fantastic. Don't miss it.

What's nearby: From Piazza Bellini, you have about 30 seconds walk to get to the beginning of the Via Tribunali. The MANN (Archeological Museum) is roughly two blocks up the Via

Constantinopoli. In the opposite direction you can window shop along the Via Toledo to the Galleria Umberto and on to Piazza Plebiscito in 10 to15 minutes. I normally stop at Leopoldo for a coffee on the way. Also nearby are Via Tribunali, Santa Maria in Purgatorio, the Church of Gesù Nuovo and the Cloisters at Santa Chiara.

10.
Street Art in Naples

Everything is blue in Naples. Even the melancholy is blue.

~ Libero Bovio

Everywhere you go in Naples you are surrounded by street art. It's easy to confuse this with graffiti and think you're in a bad area, but rest assured, you're not. Street art has always been part of Neapolitan self-expression. Excavations at Pompeii uncovered 2000+ year old graffiti scratched into the walls, from love notes to political ads, so there's nothing new here.

In 2018, archaeologists discovered graffiti in Pompeii's Regio V district supporting the theory that the eruption happened in October of 79 AD, not August as previously thought. (The graffiti read something along the lines of: *On October 17 he overindulged in food.*)

As you wander the streets of the historic center, you'll see Sophia Loren looking out at you, the much-loved Italian actor and comedian Totò gazing down the street, and the ever-jubilant Maradona celebrating and celebrated. Some of the biggest international names in street art and murals have their work decorating the walls of Naples, from Blu to Zed 1, Alice Pasquini to Roxy in the Box, Jarit Agoch to Chop & Kaf. Each with their own style and messaging, there has never been a better time to experience and soak up Neapolitan street art.

Naples is an exciting place for artists, and this is a great time in the Naples art scene. It feels like Berlin maybe 20 years ago, when artists from all over came and created and lived in neighborhoods they could still afford. In my opinion, the street artists in Naples are part of what is raising the modern artistic profile of the city, and part of its rebirth yet again as a cultural destination. They add to the excitement, the vitality and to the very heartbeat of this completely fantastic city.

I love street art. From the small, tucked away pieces to the big, in your face ones, this street art adds another dimension to the

Neapolitan experience. I take endless photos of it everywhere I go in Italy. If you pay attention, you'll notice much of it is beautiful and clever, and here in Naples there tends to be some incredible social commentary behind it. If you do a walking tour with a local guide – and I sincerely recommend you do – have them explain the street art as you go. (You can get a list of private guides I work with in Naples at GlamItaliaBooks.com/Naples-Private-Guides) There is a big difference between street art, political slogans, and gang-style graffiti, and sometimes you'll see them overlap.

Once you understand the messaging, it all becomes so poignant and, in my opinion, adds another layer of things to love about Naples. For example, you'll see wall art all over Naples with modern mermaids. They don't look idealized, instead they have regular Naples-girl faces, and most of them have bodies with rolls here and there. Instead of looking like Disney princesses, they have a thickness to their bodies that is incredibly real. Even their boobs come in every variety under the sun. The messaging here is that all our body shapes are just fine, and that women come in all shapes and sizes so you should love us just the way we are. Another one I love covers her boobs with skulls and has the words *memento vivi* tattooed across her collar bones. It's a play on the latin phrase *memento mori –remember we all die*. Instead, she is telling us to remember to live, to be here in the moment.

Along with the smaller pieces, you will see enormous elaborate murals taking up entire walls. Let's look at just a few highlights that need to make their way onto your **must-see** list or that you just need to know about as you're wandering around the city:

Banksy's *Madonna with a Pistol*

Remember I told you that Via Tribunali needs to be your main reference point in Naples? I swear you could spend weeks on end just seeking out minute details along Via Tribunali and the side streets feeding away from it. Towards the upper end of Tribunali, just before you turn left onto Via Duomo you'll spot a small piazza on your left. The wall on the Via Duomo side of the piazza has a Banksy. (If you didn't know to look for it, you would walk right past.)

I get a kick out of spotting Banksy's work out in the wild. In *Glam Italia! 101 Fabulous Things To Do in Venice,* we talked about his painting of the little immigrant girl holding up a pink flare as she gets submerged in the high tide. Here in Naples, his *Madonna with a Pistol* has an ethereal, Bernini-esque Madonna floating ecstatically in front of us while, above her, a luminous halo has a gun. It alludes to the city's twin reputations for both devout Catholicism and organized crime.

After another Banksy in Naples was destroyed (a reworking of Bernini's *Saint Teresa in Ecstasy*, pictured with McDonald's and a Coke), local Banksy fan Alessandro Bello organized a petition to protect *Madonna with a Pistol*. The mural now lives behind glass – apparently not paid for by the city, but by a private citizen.

Address: Piazza Girolamani, corner of Via Tribunali and Via Duomo.
What's nearby: The Girolamani Church and museum complex, the Duomo, San Gregorio in Armeno, San Lorenzo Maggiore Underground.

Jorit Agoch's *San Gennaro*

You need to know about this brilliant Neapolitan artist. Born Jorit Ciro Cerullo in 1990, the son of a Dutch mother and Neapolitan father, Jorit's incredible murals grace the walls of huge buildings all over the world. What makes them so special is their photo-like reality. You would swear you were looking at a photograph superimposed onto a wall, not the work of a street artist. Classically trained, Jorit has a first-class degree from Naples' Academy of Fine Arts, and part of what makes his work so commanding is that, like Caravaggio, he substitutes the faces of his subjects with those of people he knows in real life. (Unlike Caravaggio, he gives his subjects twin red tribal scars on their faces, making them part of Jorit's Human Tribe.)

There are several giant Jorit murals around Naples, including two huge Diego Maradonas (one is of a young Maradona, the other – my favorite – shows him middle aged with graying hair). Most of his murals are in neighborhoods you're unlikely to venture into. However, there is one right in the heart of where you're going to be. Off the Via Duomo, one city block below the Via Tribunali in the Forcella neighborhood, you find one of Jorit's most celebrated works, the enormous mural of San Gennaro. This 2015 tribute to the city's patron saint is spectacular. The face of San Gennaro is one of Jorit's friends, a young factory worker from Naples. By using the very Neapolitan face of a real person, he has added a breathtaking humanity to the saint. Rather than you having to figure out who the saint is and why he's there, the immediacy of this work says "This is us. This is Naples". Put this on your **must-see** list.

I suggest googling Jorit's works in Naples, both to see why I am so excited about this artist, and also to see how the city isn't confining incredible artwork just to the wealthy neighborhoods. Most of Jorit's work in Naples lights up the walls in tougher neighborhoods, exposing them to and including them in Naples as a cultural destination.

Address: Via Vicaria Vecchia, 33
What's nearby: The Duomo, Naples Underground, The Dolls Hospital, Via Gregorio Armeno.

Diego Maradona

It is hard to explain to a non-Neapolitan (like myself) just how deeply this football player is loved here. You see Maradona memorabilia everywhere in Naples, from souvenirs to street art all over the place. The street art encompasses everything from enormous murals to artwork not much bigger than your hand.

I'm going to tell you about some big famous pieces to look for, but while wandering Naples keep an eye out for the small pieces too. You'll see small paintings with his jersey number on them, stickers and artwork with D10S – a play on Diego 10 (first name and jersey number) that doubles up as Dio, god. To say he was and is loved here is a massive understatement.

Naples ♥ Diego Maradona

In 1984, Argentine player Diego Maradona was transferred from FC Barcelona to Napoli, which at the time was a mid-range club. Over the next seven years, Maradona helped them win two *Serie A* titles, an Italian Cup, a Super Cup title, and the UEFA Cup. When Argentina played Italy at the 1990 World Cup in Napoli's then San Paolo stadium (now called Maradona stadium), Maradona famously called on Neapolitans to cheer for his Argentinian team instead of the *Azzurri* Italy team. (Azzurri represented the broader Italy that looked down on Naples and the south.) Meanwhile Maradona was from the south (Argentina) himself and he fought for the people of the south. To be a place that was looked down on and yet to have him, the greatest player in the world, on your home team must have felt like the ultimate revenge.

Maradona memorabilia became big business for Naples. It was its own sub-economy, much of it informal (unlicensed). Maradona never took royalties on any of it, letting the people of Naples make their money.

THE ORIGINAL MARADONA MURAL

Overlooking a small piazza, this has to be the most visited Maradona mural in Naples. Painted by Napoli fan Mario Filardi in 1990, it is essentially a pilgrimage site that always seems to be packed with Diego fans. The painting is about three stories high, and shows the football player running towards us, the breeze blowing back his hair.

Deep inside the Quartieri Spagnoli/Spanish Quarter pay attention to all the street art on the way up. You'll see Maradona-related art everywhere. You'll also see loads of Maradona memorabilia for sale. And, of course, being in the Spanish Quarter there are endless cool places to stop for a drink or a bite to eat, as well as some of the most atmospheric side streets in all of Naples.

Address: Via Emanuele de Deo, 46.

JORIT'S *DIOS UMANO*

This is my favorite of the Maradonas, and it is both brilliant and enormous. The Dios Umano mural is 10 stories tall and captures Maradona later in life when he was the head coach of the Argentine soccer team. His face is mature, his hair shot with grey, and his expression is calculating. Here, we are seeing Maradona the man, as opposed to Maradona the football player. Add in the two tribal stripes on all Jorit's subjects and you have yourself an incredibly compelling work of art. Under the painting are the works Dios Umano – *God Man*.

The building on the other side of the street has another equally huge mural, this time of a local child, under which are the words *Essere Umani* – Being Human. The two messages and paintings side by side tell us that people and gods are equal. (Or perhaps that local neighborhood kids are as important and valuable as demigods? You decide.)

These two buildings are in southwest Naples in the San Giovanni a Teduccio neighborhood. You go through this area on the train when heading to Torre Annunciata (Villa Oplontis) and Ercolano (Herculaneum).

Address: Via Taverna del Ferro.

METRO STADIO MOSTRA MARADONA

I love buzzing around Naples on the metro. It's clean, modern, efficient and, in my personal experience. very safe. There are multiple metro stations full of art in Naples, one of them being Mostra Maradona, the metro station closest to the Maradona Stadium and the giant Oltremare exhibition center. Here you can see more mural art of the city's most beloved player.

Address: Metro Station Mostra Maradona.

The Blue Baby/*Cucù... Tete* (Peekaboo)

High up on the wall above the tiny Via Tre Tornesi, a giant mural of a perfect, beautiful blue baby's head watches over the market below.

It was painted in 2018 by David Vecchiato to draw attention to rare diseases that affect children. In this particular case, the painting was for Mattia Fagnoni, a little boy with a rare genetic degenerative disease called Sandhoff disease. The Mattia Fagnoni Association fundraises through art shows and exhibitions. The art is donated from artists worldwide and 100% of the money raised goes to help families and children with fatal genetic diseases.

David (Diavu) Vecchiato does incredible street art, murals and stair paintings. I recommend doing a deep dive through his Instagram before coming to Naples so that you recognize his work around town should you come across it. (Follow him on Instagram @Diavu)

Address: Pignasecca Market.

Francisco Bosoletti's *ResisTiamo*

Although formerly the poorest and most Camorra-riddled neighborhood of Naples, the newly gentrified Sanità is one of my favorites. Its citizens worked hard to elevate the neighborhood out of the bad times, in the process creating one of the vibiest, coolest parts of town. I absolutely love the Rione Sanità. Not only is it a fantastic area to eat, it also has one of my favorite museums (the Jago Museum) and it is home to some incredible street art.

Painted on the lateral wall of the Basilica Santa Maria della Sanità, this maxi mural shows two figures embracing and supporting each other as if dancing together. The mural tells a true story of two lovers who overcame terrible illness with love and care. On a separate level, its message of hope also symbolizes the neighborhood overcoming violence, disease and crime.

The name of this painting is a combination of Resistance and *Ti Amo* – I love you.

Address: Piazza Sanità, 33

Toto Everywhere

Another character you will see in street art all over Naples (but particularly around the Spanish Quarter and Sanità neighborhoods) is the beloved Neapolitan comedian Toto. Born Antonio de Curtis in 1898 (he died 1967), his career in film spanned an astounding 100 movies, 29 of which were devoted to a character named Toto. You can take Toto walking tours to see street art about him. Again, I recommend a quick Google search to familiarize yourself with his face, because like Maradona, you'll see him everywhere.

If heading to the Spanish Quarter Maradona mural, take a stroll along the Via Portacarrese where a 100-meter stretch has been transformed into an outdoor Toto street art museum. Here you can see Toto as Superman, Batman and Flash. You'll see him in drag as Lolita, as well as in other characters from his movies. It's actually very cool.

Address: Via Portacarrese.

Alice Pasquini

Signing her work Alicè, Roman artist Alice Pasquini's work graces walls all over the world. You can find her street art in New York and Marrakesh, Barcelona and Saigon, Oslo and Naples. Her art is not restricted to city walls – it is also found in galleries and museums around the world. Along with being a street artist, she is also an illustrator and a set designer. Her paintings depict strong, mysterious females and are both impactful and arresting. I suggest googling her street art so you can recognize it both here in Naples and around Lazio.

Look for her work in Piazza Carità, by Santa Chiara, near the Ciclofficina Massimo Troisi and on Via Mezzocannone near Mensa Occupata.

11.
Caravaggio in Naples

Amor Vincent Omnia

(Love Conquers All)

If you've read my book *Glam Italia! 101 Fabulous Things To Do In Rome,* you'll already know I absolutely love Caravaggio. From his artistic genius to his wild, crazy life and his untimely end, Michelangelo Marisa da Caravaggio is one of the most fascinating painters in history. He is also perhaps the most important painter since Michelangelo (Buonarotti). In fact, when he arrived in Naples, the 35-year-old painter was already the most famous painter in all of Italy.

He had spent the past decade swaggering around Rome, creating genius works of art. He was known for his use of chiaroscuro, beaming light where he wanted you to focus while cloaking everything else in varying degrees of shadow. He also brought a devastating realism and naturalism to his work. Whereas fellow painters made their subjects perfect, painting them in bright and pretty colors, separating them from the average citizen, making them wholly untouchable, Caravaggio made his subjects real. His models were prostitutes from Piazza Navona and homeless drunks he found on the street. Their faces were exciting and different, yet entirely identifiable.

On May 28 1606, Caravaggio got into a duel with Ranuccio Tomassoni. Tomassoni is thought to have been the pimp of one of the artist's favorite prostitute models, Fillide Melandroni. Whether she was the reason for the battle or whether it was to do with Tomassoni's wife Lavinia, we'll never know. But during the duel Caravaggio's sword knicked Tomossoni's femoral artery, possibly in an attempt to sever his testicles. Tomassoni died and, in a desperate bid to avoid prison, Caravaggio fled from Rome. He would spend the rest of his life trying to secure a papal pardon so he could return to the Eternal City. He was also wounded in the fight and scared, so he ran to the great protector throughout his life, Marchesa Costanza of the Colonna family. She made sure his wounds were taken care of and spirited him out of the city, initially to family holdings in Zagarolo and in Palestrina, then they headed south.

The final years of Caravaggio's turbulent and brief life were bookended by two sojourns in Naples. In the intervening years, he traveled the southern Mediterranean, getting into trouble, continuously trailed by cutthroats and assassins. Despite his increasingly erratic behavior, these years were amongst his most prolific as a painter.

Over the course of the last four centuries most of his Naples works were either lost or moved around the world, but three masterpieces remain here, and need to be on your **must-see** list.

Naples 1606–1607

At the beginning of the 17th century, Naples was the largest city in southern Europe. The population of 300,000 was three times that of Rome, and before long it grew to half a million. Naples was the center of the world – everyone was here, every country, culture, skin color and religion was represented.

Everything you could imagine was for sale in the city's bustling markets: exotic foods, wines, silks, spices, steel, iron and everything needed for building ships. Naples was an international merchant hub. Not only did the merchants trade in goods, they also traded in humans. There were 10,000 slaves in the city at that time.

Naples was under Spanish rule. Spanish soldiers manned the garrisons and Spanish navy galleons moored in the harbor. Neapolitan aristocracy, stripped of their powers and forced to forfeit their country fiefdoms, now lived in large palaces in the city, swanning around as members of the court of the Spanish viceroy. They dressed in the fashions of Spain and made their way through the city in carriages or elaborately covered hand-carried litters. Money flowed through Naples. The city was rich. Yet despite the opulence of this massive city, it seriously trailed behind Rome in the art world. None of the big names in art were working here.

Naples was a city more than ready for the arrival of the most famous painter in all of Italy: Michelangelo Merisi da Caravaggio.

On the flip side of 17th century Naples was the extreme poverty. Beggars and paupers overflowed every street and alleyway. Although the city was prosperous, there was only enough work for a fraction of the population, and the population was growing quickly. Migrants from the countryside filled the already teeming maze of narrow streets. The Spanish exacted punitive taxes on rural peasants, forcing them to abandon their holdings and flee to the city in search of an easier life, or at least some food. Instead, they wound up on the streets in abject poverty. They were called the *lazzari*, the lepers, a disdainful moniker applied to the underclass of paupers.

Fearful of more bloody rebellions (there had been two uprisings in the previous century) or a full-scale revolution, the government decided to guarantee food to the poor. They stockpiled grain and corn, making sure everyone had access to bread at state regulated prices. But this just made things worse, drawing more immigrants to the city and exacerbating the very crisis the government sought to avert. In another poorly thought-out attempt to curb the destitute population growing, construction of new buildings was prohibited outside the city walls. The hope was that if they deprived them of anywhere to live, people would stop coming. But, of course, the reverse was true. More and more people arrived every day. The new building regulations just meant living conditions became more cramped and the streets were flooded with a sea of humanity.

This poverty impacted the physical appearance of Neapolitans, many of whom were living in a permanent state of borderline starvation. Those who arrived from the countryside had to replace a diet of fruit and vegetables with one of pasta and bread. Malnutrition caused everything from goiters to scurvy, rickets to rotted teeth. Neopolitans became shorter and more prone to deformities and illnesses. Disease was rife throughout the underclasses. By day they begged in the streets. By night they slept anywhere they could find shelter – under market stalls, in porticos and courtyards. The shortage of housing meant buildings had to grow taller, frequently six stories tall, plunging the narrow streets below into a semi-permanent darkness. Meanwhile the civic buildings maintained their grand scale and the city was full of churches and monasteries. And a giant park.

The Seven Acts of Mercy

It is to this juxtaposition of extreme wealth and absolute squalor that Caravaggio arrived to Naples in October of 1606. Within a couple of weeks, he was given an extremely prestigious commission. He was to paint a massive piece for the high altar of a new church, the Chiesa del Pio Monte della Misericordia, on the Via dei Tribunali, near the cathedral. The subject of this monumental painting was the Seven Acts of Mercy.

The Pio Monte della Misericordia was a lay confraternity dedicated to actually doing something for the sick and needy. Seven young noblemen, bored with the superficial life at the court of the Spanish viceroy, created the confraternity in 1601. Their original statute emphasized 'corporal mercy', meaning hands on, sleeves rolled up, real work instead of just offering up fluffy, well-meaning prayers. These guys were the real deal. Every Friday they met at the Hospital of the Incurables to help and feed the pox-ridden, the diseased and the destitute. As their confraternity grew, they expanded their care for the sick and needy to cover all seven traditional Christian acts of mercy. Then they built a church which was consecrated just two weeks before Caravaggio came to town.

This new commission was to show all seven acts of mercy on a single canvas, with the Madonna della Misericordia (the Madonna of Mercy) descending from Heaven, giving her blessing.

Caravaggio had an uncanny sense for what sets places and people apart from one another. He responded to mood and human behavior, and would have felt the plight of the local poor on a visceral level. The dramatic real-life theater and the primal way of life taking place on the streets of Naples would have appealed to his artistic sensibilities. Others may have painted ethereal creatures in whimsical colors, whose perfection had them floating above humanity in a make-believe world. But not Caravaggio. His models were prostitutes and the homeless, with faces and expressions that were gritty and real. He painted his characters into an equally gritty world. In doing so, he made the Bible stories look real and believable to anyone who looked at his paintings. He transported heavenly legends down to earth to look and feel like the average person's world. This was part of Caravaggio's magic.

'For I was hungry and you gave me meat, I was thirsty and you gave me drink, I was a stranger and you took me in, I was naked and you clothed me, I was sick and you visited me, I was in prison and you came unto me.' St Matthew's six works of mercy, which could save you from a one-way ticket to Hell, now had a medieval seventh work added: the burial of the dead. Caravaggio depicted all seven works in magnificent and slightly disturbing detail.

The painting is set in the anarchic-looking world, at the depths of a dark street corner in Naples. Everything is in motion and feels completely frantic in a whirling desperation of pain and suffering and death. The story takes place at night, but the street is crowded with people. A naked beggar crouches in the foreground, almost falling back towards us. His skin is stretched taught across his skinny back, ribs and vertebrae popping out at us. A well-dressed young man with a feathered hat and gloves looks down at him with compassion and covers him with part of his velvet cloak. A closer look shows light glinting off his sword. He still grips the remainder of his cloak, suggesting he is about to slice off another portion. But for whom? Look down and you'll see a foot and, in the darkness, a curly head. Perhaps this represents a sick person about to be given warmth.

To his left, a sunburned man raises his head heavenward and slakes his thirst with water. Meanwhile an innkeeper acknowledges a sad faced pilgrim, allowing him shelter for the night. Look a little closer and you'll see the innkeeper's left index finger pointing behind him, as if to say, 'Go in there'.

To the right, the only source of illumination in the picture comes from the candle held aloft by a bearded priest. He turns the corner while reciting the final rites to a shroud-covered corpse, of whom we can only see a dirty pair of bare feet. The pallbearer's face is in shadow, while the light flickers across the priest's white cassock, making it look almost luminescent.

A little further to the right is the disturbing sight of an old man's face reaching between prison bars to be breast fed by a dull-eyed woman, a drop of her milk resting on his beard.

Apart from the corpse, each act of mercy is carried out by an historical figure. The man drinking water is Samson drinking from the jawbone of a donkey. The bearded man offered shelter by the innkeeper is Christ the pilgrim. The man with the velvet cloak is St Martin de Tours, his sword drawn to cut his cloak in half to cover the needy, just as the vaunted saint had done. The young woman and the old man come from ancient Roman legend – she embodies two mercies, feeding the hungry and visiting prisoners in jail. They are Cimon and Pero. A jailed Cimon was starving to death when his daughter Pero came to him and fed him breast milk.

As Caravaggio gives us a window into the dark, scary streets of 17th century Naples, a serene Virgin Mary cradling baby Jesus looks down on the scene approvingly, while two impossibly beautiful angels swirl down toward us on feathery wings. One has white wings, the other's are black. Their eyes focus on the scene below and they appear to be gripping each other, as if they are falling into the mayhem on the street beneath them. The angel on the left (with the black wings) has his arm reached out, his fingers splayed. He could be reaching out to help those below, or maybe he is pushing them away from the gates of Heaven? Or perhaps he is about to tumble into the mercies. Their manic, swirling motion adds to the sense of emergency in the picture, somehow making it all seem quite frantic.

Caravaggio completed this huge masterpiece in just over seven weeks. It was quickly realized that this work of art was one of the Pio Monte's greatest treasures. In 1613, the congregation decided the painting must never be sold, at any price. By that time, there were already offers for its purchase exceeding 2000 ducats – more than five times the original cost of the painting.

The Seven Acts of Mercy is overwhelming and brilliant. It is one of Caravaggio's masterpieces and is considered the most important painting in all of Naples.

Where to see it: Pio Monte della Misericordia, Via dei Tribunali.
Hours: Open Monday to Saturday 9:00 am – 6:00 pm, Sunday 9:00 am – 2:30 pm.
What's nearby: The Cathedral of Naples, walking distance to the Underground Naples and the Roman Theater.

THE FLAGELLATION

After the massive success of *The Seven Acts of Mercy*, more commissions flooded in. In early 1607, Caravaggio took on another altarpiece, this time for a chapel in the courtyard of a Dominican monastery in the city. The subject this time was Christ's Flagellation and, personally, I find this one quite distressing.

It marks the beginning of Christ's long, violent ordeal that will end in his martyrdom. Here he is tied to a pillar and whipped with unconstrained ferocity. Other paintings on this theme show Christ as weary, sorrowful, or withdrawn, but here Caravaggio shows us his suffering.

Alarmingly, he brings us up close to the violence. The figures are enlarged, making the space feel cramped. A single pillar centers the piece, a shaft of light illuminating Christ tied to it, wearing only a loin cloth and his crown of thorns. His torturers are thrown into varying degrees of darkness. Christ has been given a sculpture-like statuesque physicality. But rather than a commanding presence, this time we see Jesus as vulnerable and beaten down. His exhaustion shows in the line of his neck as the weight of his head drops wearily to his shoulder. He can no longer hold himself up and seems to stumble towards us as if falling from the pillar that holds him.

Meanwhile, two of the torturers are kicking and hauling him back into place. The one on the left yanks his head up by the hair, readying him for the blows we know are about to come. The one on the right, his face half hidden in the shadows, kicks Jesus as he aggressively tightens the ropes that bind him. The third torturer, on the ground, binding the twigs he will flail Christ with, looks up to assess how much longer until he can start whipping. His profile makes a shadow against Christ's leg and white loin cloth, giving him a horrifying proximity to his victim. The physical closeness of all the bodies here creates an urgency and immediacy to the violence about to happen.

Caravaggio is famed for his extreme use of chiaroscuro, light falling on a subject contrasted with deepening shadows around it. In this painting the shadows are frightening. You can't tell what other evil may lurk behind. The light that bathes Jesus is cold and harsh. The overall effect is startling, disconcerting, and brings the Bible story to life with astonishing intensity.

The Flagellation has remained in Naples ever since, but instead of the original location, it now lives at the Museo di Capodimonte. This painting has been on tour quite frequently, so check if it is in fact at home before heading up to the museum.

Where to see it: Capodimonte Museum, €8.
Hours: Open Thursday to Tuesday, 8:30 am – 7:30 pm. Closed Wednesday.
What's nearby: Capodimonte is on a hill next to the Capodimonte park.

Naples 1609–1610

Caravaggio left Naples as suddenly as he arrived, heading to Malta (possibly to help smooth the way to a potential pardon from Rome). In Malta, despite being a fugitive on the run for murder, and lacking noble birth, he somehow rose to the ranks of a Knight of St John. During his year here, he painted more masterpieces. However, the good times didn't last and a violent brawl with another knight led to Caravaggio being stripped of his knighthood and thrown into prison, from which he staged a daring escape and made his way to the Sicilian port town of Siracusa.

In Sicily an increasingly crazed Caravaggio won prestigious commissions, made and broke powerful connections, and created more powerful works of art. He moved to Palermo in the summer of 1609. (Interestingly, while there he painted an altarpiece of *The Adoration* for the Franciscans, which apparently in 1969 was ordered to be stolen by a Sicilian Mafia boss and has never been seen since.)

Fearing the enemy that was chasing him, Caravaggio moved back to Naples by the middle of September. (His fears were justified. Rome had a bounty on his head, and the Knights of St John still wanted revenge.) In Naples, word of his return got around fast, and commissions rolled in. He stayed ensconced in the protection of the Colonna family, living safely in their idyllic palazzo in Chiaia.

Negotiations for a papal pardon reopened, and an optimistic Caravaggio thought he might finally be able to return to Rome.

But trouble lay ahead.

In October 1609 he paid an ill-advised visit to a bar and brothel frequented by artists and poets of the time. When Caravaggio left the Osteria del Cerriglio (still in business today), he was ambushed by four men. Three held him down while the fourth sliced his face with a blade. This was *sfregiato*, a vendetta attack to mete out revenge for an insult. It was a premeditated hit carried out by men from Malta. Crippled and (perhaps) partially blinded by his injuries, Caravaggio spent the next six months convalescing at the Colonna palace in Chiaia. He never fully recovered. The severity of his injuries became apparent in his next two works, where it has been speculated that he may have suffered damage to his eyes and possibly even had some type of tremors.

The first of his final two paintings is *The Denial of St Peter*. Although still brilliant in my mind, it was pointed out to me that Peter's hands lack the artist's normal exemplary brushwork. This work lives in the Metropolitan Museum of Art in New York. The other painting, *The Martyrdom of Saint Ursula*, thought to be his final work, remains in Naples.

THE MARTYRDOM OF SAINT URSULA

The (abbreviated) legend of Saint Ursula says she was a chaste princess who led 11,000 virgins on a pilgrimage through Germany (11,000 seems excessive to me, but who am I to judge?). The tribe of virgins arrived at Cologne to find the city besieged by the Huns, who in turn beheaded all 11,000 virgins. Their leader, wowed by Ursula's beauty, promised to marry her. When she refused him, he shot her with an arrow and killed her.

Normally Ursula's martyrdom is painted as a huge crowd scene. Caravaggio, instead, made it intimate, zooming in on the story and telling it with just five people. The scorned Hun has just shot Ursula in the stomach at point-blank range. She looks down at the wound and seems to be pulling it further apart. He looks somewhat horrified at what he has done. Ursula's maidservant looks on in shock as she reaches forward – too late – to grab the bow with her right hand, while holding the pole of a Christian banner in her left. To Ursula's right, a soldier in black armor reaches forward as if to catch her. Now look behind her to see the last self portrait of the artist. Caravaggio paints himself open-mouthed, staring blindly into space. Maybe he realized that he too was dying – dying like Ursula, at the hand of a revenge wound administered up close. You have to wonder if the face of the Hun was that of Caravaggio's attacker. We'll never know.

The painting was finished May 10, 1610, and was all set to ship to Prince Mercantonio Doria, who had commissioned it. However, the prince's man on the ground in Naples left the work in the sunshine to dry, causing the varnish on top to liquefy. Consequently, Caravaggio had to spend another two weeks fixing it. On May 27, 1610, Caravaggio's final work set sail for Genoa. It arrived three weeks later, on June 18. Sometime in the second week of July, Caravaggio boarded a felucca piloted by the same skipper, on his way from Naples to Rome. He was carrying three paintings with him, two of St John the Baptist and one of Mary Magdalene. Enroute, the felucca docked at Palo, a fort about 20 miles from Rome. (It would have made sense to dock there to have the three heavily boxed paintings transferred to carriages to ride to Rome.)

It is not certain exactly what happened when Caravaggio disembarked the boat. Perhaps his papers weren't in order, or maybe the captain of the garrison felt slighted – who knows? Whatever happened, Caravaggio was carted off and imprisoned for two days. The felucca, with his paintings aboard, turned around and headed to its final stop, 50 miles up the coast, at Porto Ercole.

Forty-year-old Caravaggio managed to pay his way out of prison and, although gravely ill, made his way to Porto Ercole to recover his paintings. He died in Porto Ercole shortly thereafter, probably around July 18. With no friends or family to care for him, Caravaggio was buried in an unmarked grave.

The felucca with the paintings aboard arrived at Porto Ercole around the same time. Hearing of the painter's untimely death, it turned around and headed back to Naples.

Where to see it: Palazzo Zevallos Stigliano, Via Toledo 185.
Hours: Open Tuesday to Sunday, 11:00 am – 7:00 pm. Closed Monday. Entry €5.
What's nearby: The Galleria Umberto is less than 5 minutes' walk, and the Teatro San Carlo is less than 10 minutes' walk from the Palazzo Zevallos Stigliano.

12.
Amazing Underground Sites in Naples

What we do now echoes in eternity.

~ Marcus Aurelius

Naples is a city of layers. While we walk the streets of modern-day Naples, 10 meters below us there is an ancient Roman city. Thirty meters below that we can visit the world of the ancient Greeks. Who even knows what might be below them? It's probably safe to assume that were you to dig under any house or structure in Naples you'd find some ancient world or other. There is an absolute wealth of treasures beneath your feet in Naples.

My friend Gaia told me a wonderful story about her grandparents who lived in the historic center. They often dined at the home-restaurant of the janitor of the school where her grandfather worked. This was one of those deals where on the weekends the janitor and his wife would make a little extra money, with him waiting the two tables in the kitchen while she prepared the food. After dinner, the janitor would open a trap door in the kitchen floor, and they would all go down to marvel at ruins from Ancient Rome. This was also where the janitor and his wife kept their wine. Even more fascinating to me is that if you tell that story to anyone in Naples, they won't so much as raise an eyebrow. From the part-time restaurant inside that tiny house to the Roman world below, everyone living here knows or has lived stories like this. This is Naples.

No trip to Naples is complete without visiting at least one underground experience. Some of the experiences are only possible with a guide. There are multiple entrances to Naples' underground sites. Here, I am just giving you a few.

Into the Sanità

First let's venture into one of my favorite neighborhoods in Naples, the Sanità. A polar opposite to the Paris-like tree lined boulevards of the Vomero neighborhood, Sanità was, until recently, a part of Naples that most Neapolitans wouldn't venture into. Impoverished, rife with crime and run by the Camorra, the Sanità was the embodiment of every bad story you ever heard about Naples. However, the thing that often gets lost in these stories is that neighborhoods like this are home to real people – people who want to feel safe, have access to a decent education and a job. Sanità, along with being fantastic, is a story of redemption. It is the story of people who fought to hang on to their hometown roots while building a whole new world in their little patch of Napoli. And for me that is reason enough to walk all the way across town to spend my tourist dollars here.

The area now known as Sanità is one of the oldest parts of Naples. Sitting just outside the original city walls, this was where the ancient Greeks and Romans buried their dead. When the Christians came along, they built their catacombs here so that they could worship underground, out of sight. (Christianity was illegal here until the 4th century).

The area eventually became woodlands with streams, separating the historic center of Naples and the royal palace at Capodimonte up on the hill. In the 17th century, it was developed into an area for the wealthy to build glorious palazzi and was renamed *Sanità* for its healthy, clean air. In the 19th century, a major road was built, connecting the city center to the Capodimonte, annexing Sanità. The neighborhood took a downhill trajectory, soon becoming one of the most impoverished and dangerous neighborhoods in all of Italy. High unemployment, low access to quality education and overall poverty turned this lower working-class neighborhood into an ideal base for the local Mafia, the Camorra. For many/most youth of the Sanità, working for the Camorra was their only option.

Hope has two beautiful daughters, Anger and the Courage to see that things do not remain the way they are.

~ St Augustine (seen on the website catacombedinapoli.it)

In around 2000, a new parish priest, Don Antonio Loffredo, turned the situation around. He discovered frescos, chapels and catacombs below the dangerous, refuse-filled city streets, and what turned out to be a 2nd century burial ground. It was filled with decades of trash and mud and in a terrible state. These were the largest catacombs in all of southern Italy, but in the absolute worst neighborhood, an area that tourist dollars didn't want to come to. But Don Antonio saw an opportunity. He convinced local youth to help clean out the catacombs, giving the boys physical work and a sense of purpose. He encouraged them to learn about their neighborhood's rich history and to become local tour guides. In 2006, they created **La Paranza**, an organization to provide work and opportunities to the Sanità youth through cultural regeneration. The Archdiocese of Naples immediately helped fund them. Across the next 16 years they reclaimed and cleaned out 13,000 m2 of catacombs.

La Paranza created training programs and used a bottom-up management structure. They opened abandoned churches, repurposing some into B&Bs, others into music studios and community theaters. The created a Sanità youth orchestra, *Sanitansamble*, and they created safe sports spaces for local kids. Artists were engaged to paint huge murals on the buildings, evolving the neighborhood into an art hub. Rents were still reasonably cheap so artists could afford to live here. The neighborhood's upward momentum grew and eateries like Isabella de Cham, Poppella, and Ai Tre Santi not only opened but thrived. More cool artists arrived, including another of my favorites mentioned in this book, Jago. Instead of moving his studio and exhibition space into a monied part of town, Jago moved into and renovated an abandoned church in the Sanità and hires his workers through La Paranza.

As the project progressed, companies like IBM and Vodafone funded restorations of the catacombs, including high tech lighting under which the jaw droppingly gorgeous mosaics glisten and the frescos can be enjoyed without damage. The boys who were part of the clean-up project got jobs as tour guides, ticket office workers, management workers – all the positions needed to run a successful tourist attraction. Don Antonio secured exclusive rights of access to the catacombs. You can only go down there with one of the local Sanità guides.

Personally, I feel strongly about supporting Sanità. Not only does it feel like arriving in the coolest new part of town *before* the masses realize it's here, but it also melds perfectly with my sustainable travel ethos. I try to make every dollar (euro) I spend land in the town I'm in and have 100% of my dollars make a positive impact on the local economy. Even though my personal impact is too tiny to be measurable, when the tens of thousands of people who will read this book (I hope!) find their way to Sanità and drop just a few euros on food or visiting a museum or taking a tour with a local guide from the neighborhood, we have collectively changed the world and been part of the solution.

So, armed with his knowledge, let's head underground to four amazing sites in the Sanità. If you only have a day or two here, it can be hard to choose just one place to go underground in Naples so, as usual, I'll offer a little backstory to help you make your choice.

San Gaudioso Catacombs

Fascinating, a bit eerie, maybe a little gruesome, and in part at least, completely nutty. I love this.

Our story starts back in the 5th/4th century BC when the Greeks were building *Neo-polis*. Needing material to build the city walls, they dug out the tufa stone from a 44,000-year-old volcanic eruption. Across the city these digs evolved into a network of tunnels, cisterns and, at some point, burial grounds. When the Romans took over, their laws stipulated burial sites had to be outside the city walls, so this site and the neighboring area of San Gennaro became a huge necropolis. Fast forward to the 4th and 5th centuries AD and they became Christian burial sites. The most famous person buried here in the old days was a North African bishop, St Gaudioso, who built a monastery here prior to his death in 452 AD. As with catacombs everywhere, devotees wanted to be buried as close to the saints as possible, so in no time this became a burial hotspot. Sacred art popped up along with the decorated tombs of the wealthy. You can still see some of it here, including a 5th century fresco of St Peter introducing Pacentius to St Paul, and a painting of St Gaudioso over his tomb.

One super interesting fact is that, although this site is underground to us, back in the 5th century this was the actual ground level of what 1000 years later would become the Sanità.

THE LAVA OF THE VIRGINS

This area is surrounded by hills. When it rained, rocks and mud ('the lava of the virgins' – their name, not mine) slid down the hills onto this hallowed ground. By the 9th century the relics of the saints had been evacuated and the mud-covered catacombs were abandoned, buried in the virginal lava.

THE DRAINING

Eight hundred years later another mudslide pushed away parts of the previous build up, revealing a 6th century Madonna and Child painting – the oldest Madonna and Child in Southern Italy. Obviously this was a sign from God, so a church had to be built here, the basilica Santa Maria della Sanità. Ingeniously, the funding for this came from wealthy benefactors who wanted to be buried in the newly discovered catacombs. Their cadavers were placed in *cantarelle*, arched niches (similar to those in Santa' Anna dei Lombardi) to drain their bodily fluids. The undertakers came down every so often and poked new drain holes in the bodies. Once drained, the bodies were cleaned up and laid to rest in the catacombs.

Here's where it gets a bit nutty (to me). For special benefactors, once they were nicely dried out, their skull could be detached and mounted into the wall above their tomb!

A Goulish Gallery

If you were going to have your skull mounted on a wall, just hanging out there, why not paint on an outfit? I can't decide if this is hilarious, brilliant, or just wildly artsy in a macabre way.

In the 17th century, an artist named Giovanni Balducci was in town. He worked under Vasari, who built the Uffizi in Florence, frescoed Florence's Duomo, and created the masterpiece *Sistine-like Chapel* at Sant' Anna dei Lombardi here in Naples.

Balducci was commissioned to paint portraits for the Basilica Santa Maria della Sanità. It was a fabulous commission, except these portraits were below deck in the catacombs. Furthermore, all the subjects were dead. His task was to paint scenes around their skulls, which were mounted on the walls. Over the centuries these skulls have crumbled away, but the paintings survived. A gaping hole where the head should be sits above painted ribcages and nattily dressed skeletons. A pair of princesses side by side have flowing skirts below their skeleton rib cages and head holes. Another skeleton with a head hole leans against a sword. A magistrate's skeleton is revealed through the opening of his blue robes. There is an entire corridor of them.

At the end of a corridor, fixed into the wall below another head hole, is a skeleton 'frankensteined' together from spare parts of other corpses. He looks like a sentry watching over the dead. Or maybe he was the ringmaster of this crazy circus?

As if this wasn't quirky enough, our painter friend Balducci wanted to join the club. He wouldn't accept any money for this project, instead requesting the undertakers drain his body and mount his skull in the wall with his dead skeleton friends. You can see him there, (painted by someone else) holding a palette and a brush.

There is loads more to see, and endless fascinating stories to learn from the La Paranza guides. Access to the catacombs is via the crypt of the church, and for obvious reasons you can only come down here with a guide.

Address: Via Sanità, 123
What's nearby: Ai Tre Santi pizzeria, Jago Museum. From the San Glaudioso catacombs it takes about five minutes to walk to Poppella Pasticceria for a pastry – if your tummy isn't still churning, that is.

San Gennaro Catacombs

This site is sensational. These catacombs date back to the 2nd century AD when a tomb was built here for a noble family who provided burial spaces for Christians. Possibly. We don't know for sure. Regardless of the actual kick off date, this burial site is considered *the most significant paleo-Christian archaeological site south of Rome.* Even if you've been to catacombs in Paris or Rome you still need to see these – they look completely different.

This became a hotspot for Christians in the 5th century when St Gennaro was interred here. There are 2nd century frescos, spectacular mosaics and a 5th century painting of San Gennaro, the oldest in existence. If, like me, you are into ancient art, this one is a must. The frescos are staggering and there are more of them than you would expect. There are also stretches of beautiful mosaic decorations as well as portraits in mosaics. This was, after all, a place for the wealthy to celebrate themselves in death.

In the 4th century the remains of St Agrippino, the first patron saint of Naples, were brought here and a small underground basilica was dedicated to him. You can still see parts of his church. The lower floor of the catacombs was built around it, with ceilings measuring 6 meters high. The upper catacomb was the burial place of the bishops and revolves around a 3rd century tomb that has *some of the oldest Christian paintings in all of southern Italy*. When our friend San Gennaro was moved here, the upper chamber became a pilgrimage site and a super desirable place to be buried.

There are three styles of burial sites down here. Poor people were buried in floor tombs called *forme*. Middle class folk were stacked in *loculum*, rectangular receptacles cut into the walls like funereal tufa bookcases. The wealthy had arch shaped tombs called *cubiculum*, Latin for bedroom. These were tall but narrow, and frequently adorned with mosaics and frescos, and secured with gates to keep the riffraff out.

One *cubiculum* has frescos of a mother, father and young child. Narrow as a shelf, the bodies must have been drained and dried, then stacked atop each other in boxes. Archeologists discovered the painting was completed in three stages, the implication being that as they died at different times, each time another died the tomb was reopened and the painting was updated to add in the new person.

These catacombs are *enormous* and happen over two levels. After this, as you wander the streets of Naples, you'll constantly be wondering just how much is going on beneath your feet.

Once again, you'll be down here with a guide from La Paranza. The level of detail they go into explaining everything is just fantastic, and they are so passionate about what they're doing, it makes your experience even better. The tour takes an hour. You can quite easily tour both catacombs in a morning, with time for a coffee in the middle.

If you have time constraints and can only do one of the catacombs or are not sure if you want to spend the time visiting them, I suggest watching some YouTube videos. I have had plenty of people think they'll skip them, but after watching the videos on YouTube they put the catacombs at the top of their list.

Also check out the catacombs' website: www.catacombedinapoli.it. The page opens to darkness with a tiny light in the distance. Using the touchpad of your computer you can scroll to slowly light up the catacombs. It's pretty fantastic. Use their planning tool to see how to fit the catacombs into your schedule without wasting time waiting around. You can buy tickets on the website too.

Address: Via Capodimonte, 13
What's nearby: The Capodimonte Museum and Park is 1 km away, so around 10 minutes' walk. San Gaudioso Catacombs are 1 km in the other directions, 3 minutes in a taxi or roughly 15 mins on foot.

The Fontanelle Cemetery

A 5-minute taxi ride or a short walk from either of the catacombs brings you to another fascinating underground site in the Sanità. This time we're visiting a 5000 square meter ossuary cut into the Materdei Hill. The name *Fontanelle* (little fountains) comes from the streams of water that came down from the surrounding hills.

In the 16th century, Naples' rapidly dying population urgently required a new body dumping site. There were three famines, a series of epidemics, and Vesuvius kept erupting. The plague of 1656 alone saw deaths of between 150,000 and 300,000 depending on which source you're reading. Incidentally the population of Naples at the time was around 400,000. If we split the difference, we can say at least half the population died. So where did all those bodies go? This massive hole in the hill looked like a good spot.

Almost 2 centuries later, in 1837, an outbreak of cholera had the local government ordering bodies be removed from churches and stored at the Fontanella ossuary. It was abandoned until 1872, when a local priest, Don Gaetano Barbati, was tasked with cleaning and categorizing the bones. He rounded up some local women and began the work of cleaning up the site and putting the piles of bones in order. It's hard to imagine what a couple of hundred years of bones must have looked like, but you know the smell alone had to be putrid.

Regardless, they cleaned up the bones and arranged them into three sections. Bones and remains that came from the churches were placed into the Nave of the Priests. The Nave of the Afflicted was for those who died during the contagions, and the Nave of the Pezzentelli was for the poor people.

The Cult of the Anime Pezzentelle

As we explore Naples, we repeatedly see the unusual Neapolitan relationship with death and superstition. Unusual to us, normal to them. We fear death and the dead, while they see it as part of life. Since Vesuvius erupted in 79 AD, the people of Naples seem to have walked hand in hand with ongoing tragedy. From earthquakes to plagues, poverty to wars, eruptions to Mafia torment, life here is well acquainted with the immediacy and proximity of death.

If faith floats airily with mystical saints you cannot see and who don't respond to your entreaties, doesn't it make sense to also give a little juice to something tangible, like an actual skull? Something you can touch and talk to, that could maybe give you a direct link to a helper from the afterlife? If praying to a saint whose face you can't even see is bringing you no relief from the torments of life, why not also commune with the remains of earthly proof that has now departed? Frankly, what have you got to lose? And so we come to the cult of the *anime pezzentelle* – the cult of the souls of the little wretches.

The godly and the rich had easy access to Heaven, but what about the poor wretches who died without burial rites? With no priest sending them to St Peter's gate, would their souls remain tormented in Purgatory for eternity? The combined need to release the souls of the wretched and to receive help here on this mortal coil gave rise to a practice whereby families would adopt a skull, clean and polish it, give it a better position in the ossuary, bring it candles and handkerchiefs, wrap a rosary around its neck, talk to it and pray with it. (We'll revisit this in the **Churches** chapter, but the basic concept is freeing the soul from Purgatory, praying it through the pearly gates, and hopefully getting help in this life in return. The Fontanelle cemetery was the main venue for this practice.)

This became such a big deal and such a common practice, the church inevitably felt threatened. Deciding the superstition ran counter to Catholic doctrine, in 1969 Cardinal Corrado Ursi closed the Fontanelle. But don't mess with the people of Sanità. From 2002 they cleaned up and renovated the ossuary. Following peaceful protests and sit-ins, the Fontanelle reopened in 2010.

This is a tremendous site to visit, if it's open. It was closed again for a while, but at the time of writing this book you can visit the Fontanelle Cemetery as part of a Miglio Sacro/ Holy Mile Walk with La Paranza.

This fantastic tour incorporates both the catacombs above, a visit to San Severo to see Jago's *Figlio Velato* (Veiled Son), Palazzo della Spagnolo and Palazzo Sanfelice and the Fontanelle Cemetery. It takes three and a half hours and takes you through the streets of Sanitá. This tour is tremendous value for money and meets every measure of sustainable travel. I can't love it enough.

Address: Via Fontanelle, 80
Website: catacombedinapoli.it

Ipogea on Via Cristallini

In a city full of awe-inspiring historical sites, this one is truly mind boggling. Take a moment here to stop and consider that you are walking into this place more than 2300 years after its construction and are seeing it in almost original form and condition. It was built at least 300 years before Jesus turned up and wasn't re-discovered until the very end of the 19th century.

This time we head to the Via Cristallini in the Sanità neighborhood, to a once swanky palazzo. In its time, this was *the* chic neighborhood, traversed by royalty making their way to and from the palace up on the Capodimonte.

In 1899 while looking for water or tufa stone below his palazzo, Baron Donato stumbled upon some ancient art. While not an odd occurrence in Naples where Roman ruins are underfoot everywhere, this discovery was very exciting as these treasures dated back 2300+

years to the Ancient Greeks. Under his palazzo Donato found a Hypogeum, a secret underground chamber that had been the private burial tomb of a wealthy Ancient Greek family. Not just the bare bones of the walls either, the art and the sculptures were intact too. Very little Ancient Greek art has survived, so this discovery was astounding and of *extreme* historical value.

This is a very big deal. And you get to see it.

THE HYPOGEUM

The hypogeum is a complex of four main tombs, each with its own entrance. Each has two internal rooms: a vestibule at the front, and the burial room down a flight of stairs. Structurally each of the four is the same, but decoratively they are quite different.

The first room (A) originally had eight bas reliefs (all but one of which have been destroyed). The second room (B) had an incredible collection of amphorae and urns, frescos, altars and artifacts. The third room (C) has wonderful bas reliefs and is incredibly well preserved. The lower chamber has architectural reliefs on the walls along with various types of garlands. A sensational medusa head set in a lunette on the back wall has warded off evil spirits for more than two millennia. Meanwhile the entrance is frescoed with Dionysis and Ariadne, and two candelabra. The final room (D) was modified during the Roman era and has niches in the walls, a Latin inscription, and contained Roman artifacts and treasures.

Each room in the hypogeum has tomb-like beds with sculpted mattresses and double stone pillows that look real enough to fluff up. The pillows were painted blue, red, yellow and purple, and the furnishings, although carved in stone, look absolutely luxurious.

Until very recently, the only way you could experience any of this was in the ancient section at the MANN (Archaeological Museum). But as of June 2022, the Hypogeum is open to the public.

The tickets have timed entry, and each visit is only 20 minutes long. They only allow a few people down there per day, but not many people know about this place so you shouldn't have a problem getting tickets – just **book in advance**. As with most underground experiences bring a jacket or something warm to throw on – it gets really cold down here.

Tickets: Tickets are booked online at the website ipogeadeicristallini.org. There are several ticket options including a base fare, base fare + audio guide, or the one I recommend, the guided ticket. (This is one of those venues where you really want someone explaining every detail to you. There are very few places like this in existence *in the world*, so if you are lucky enough to visit this absolute jewel you should maximize your experience by going below ground with a guide.) Check out the website to see this amazing site, and to see ticket times and availability.

Address: Via Cristallini, 133, Sanità
What's nearby: This is very close to the Jago Museum and is on the street behind Isabella de Cham, Ai Tre Santi and Poppella. Palazzo Spagnolo is just around the corner too.

Of Greeks and Romans

Everywhere you walk in Naples, you can assume you are walking over Ancient Rome, and below that Ancient Greece. There are multiple entrances to go underground in Naples – more than we tourists will ever realize. Many of these entrances are below private homes and churches (like Gaia's grandparents' story at the beginning of this chapter).

The Ancient Roman Street Below San Lorenzo Maggiore

One underground site I want to direct your attention to is San Lorenzo. Heads up: this is a major tourist site. As you know, I avoid major tourist attractions where possible, but this is so astounding and so important it should be on your **must-see** list.

Yes, it is madly touristy and chances are there will be loads of people waiting here, but I still think it is an important place to see. Sometimes if the planets line up just right you can find your way here when no one else is around. I had one of those weird, fluke experiences on a Sunday afternoon in December of 2023. Naples was busy and the nearby Via San Gregorio Armeno was psychotically packed. I popped by San Lorenzo Maggiore to find out when would be the least busy time to return. As I approached the girls guarding the gates, a large tour group was forming in the waiting area. The girls told me if I was cool going down there on my own, I could race down now, *before* the big group went in. This gave me a 30-minute head start.

It was the most surreal experience heading down the stairs into ancient Rome and being *the only person down there*. I had this entire underground site to myself. My Instagram highlights for Naples show videos of long stretches of ancient Roman roads and market streets down there, without another soul in sight. I had a blast and as I came back up to earth, I saw a group of 40 or 50 people being led below ground.

The moral of this story is that sometimes you can time it just right and slip in between groups. Everything is extremely well signposted down there, so you absolutely know what you're seeing if you find yourself down there alone. A guide does give it an enormous amount of extra flavor though.

As you walk the Via Tribunali to San Lorenzo Maggiore, pay attention to the buildings on the San Lorenzo side of the street. Look at the arches and porticos with storefronts inside, the merchandise displayed under the porticos and listen to the vendors calling out to passers-by. It feels like absolute mayhem all around you, doesn't it? People and action and noise. Below ground is basically a replica of this, albeit a 2000+ year old one with the people and merchandise removed. It was the ancient Roman market built in the 1st–2nd century BC. The market was in use until around the 4th century AD, when it was buried in a mudslide. Eventually the mud hardened and became the base for the new city to be built on top.

From the internal courtyard of San Lorenzo Maggiore you take the stairs 10 meters below ground to what was street level in ancient Rome. It feels like stepping through a time portal because down here the old market is still intact. You can walk the old Roman streets and look inside all the shops. If you pay attention to the stones on the street, you'll see big white cat's-eye stones that reflected moonlight and torch light to guide nighttime shoppers. Merchants bringing their goods in from the ships at night would have relied on these original street reflectors (this technology was invented by the ancient Romans, we just copied it).

Some of the shop identifiers are still in place – the laundry where fabrics were washed, next to the shop where garments were manufactured and sold. The workshop where fabrics were dyed, water trough and channel for the water to flow down all still intact. The bakery with its oven in the corner and serving area to the front. Signs in front of each shop tell you the function of the various stores.

There is a section for shops selling more expensive merchandise, as evidenced by the mosaic floors and fresco'd walls. You can still identify the Pompeii reds in the frescos.

This was originally a two-story building. The old stone staircases lead to nowhere now, but 2000 years ago they were climbed by vendors and shoppers heading up to the second floor.

Upstairs in the cloisters, look for a large, fenced hole in the ground. From there you can look down into the ruins of a round temple that once marked the center of the market.

In another section, ancient Greek hydraulics brought water into what would become the Roman market a few centuries later. I love pairing this experience with a visit to Pompeii (not on the same day) because each site helps you understand the magnificence of the other. If you add in the mayhem at ground level, you get a really good understanding of life in 1st century Naples.

There is an enormous amount to see in the cloisters and inside the church, so allow yourself time to wander through the room with the giant *presepe* nativity scene, the chapter hall, the old refectory and the basilica itself.

When you are done here, wander around the corner to Piazza Bellini (5 mins) have a coffee or a spritz and process what you just saw and experienced. It's overwhelming, so you'll probably need a moment. The fact that you can saunter down the street, check out one of the greatest Caravaggios in existence, eat a *cuoppa* or a *pizza fritta*, and drop down below ground into Ancient Rome in the space of a couple of city blocks is just insane. Naples, my friend, is just incredible.

Address: Piazza San Gaetano, 316
Website: www.laneapolissotterrata.it
What's nearby: This is in the middle of everything on the Via Tribunali. Caravaggio is just up the street, San Domenico Maggiore is 2 minutes' walk, as is the San Severo chapel (Veiled Christ), Santa Maria dell Anime in Purgatorio is across the street.

The Ancient Greeks and The Lapis Museum

As if all this wasn't enough, now I want to tell you about the site just across the street, where we descend 30 meters into the world of the ancient Greeks and the beginning of *Neopolis*.

When the Greeks dug out quarries of tufa stone to build their temples and the defensive walls of their new city 2500 years ago (see the **Piazza Bellini** chapter), the huge caverns left behind became city water reservoirs. Then the Romans came along, added aqueducts and improved the cisterns to capture and hold the city's water. They also created a maze of tunnels feeding water from Serino, 70 km away, to the city's fountains and private homes.

This underground experience is fantastic but is definitely not for anyone with walking limitations. Of the various entrances around town, I prefer this one from within the 17th century Basilica di Pietrasanta on the Via dei Tribunali, as others have some claustrophobically narrow tunnels to walk through.

You can only enter with a licensed local guide, which is great because there are so many stories to be told down here, and you could get lost in the miles of tunnels below the city. You can walk from here to Pompeii through the network of underground tunnels. Even when you are down here in the depths it is hard to conceive of just how vast the tunnel network is, hence the need for a guide.

As you walk roughly a mile through the underground cisterns (at times along paths only wide enough for one person), a multimedia light display illuminates the water flowing all around you. My guide Chiara tells stories of the *Munacielli*, little, short men who cleaned the cisterns and transported water up into piazzas and villas above ground. Munacielli had to be short to pass through the low tunnels. Their elfin stature led to legends of sprites sneaking into homes from the underground world, causing mischief. Refusing payment to the water carrier might result in elves sneaking into your home, pilfering valuables, pulling clothes and bedding from unsuspecting family members and pinching housewives. Other fairytales told stories of benevolent Munacielli appearing in the night to help those in need, giving them valuables (stolen from other homes) and leading them to hidden treasure. As you walk the pathways, look for tiny ledges along the walls, just above the water. These were the work paths of the *Munacielli,* only wide enough for a child or a very tiny man.

On the walls, look for the millions of diagonal striations. These are the cut marks from the pickaxes of the original Greek workers and slaves, as they cut away huge blocks from the tufa to use for the city walls. There is an odd immediacy to this detail, connecting you here today to workers toiling away 2500 years ago.

Past the cisterns and Naples' original aqueduct, the paths lead you into giant underground caverns used as World War II air raid shelters. Air raid sirens would alert people to race down here from access points around the city, sometimes hiding here for weeks on end. They built walls of toilets, strung lighting and made it livable. Another interesting story Chiara tells is how the sirens might go off while parents were working across town or children were in school, separating the young from their families. The community of Naples took care of all children separated from their families until they could be reunited, which was sometimes days or weeks. A tremendous multimedia show in the air raid shelter area shows fighter bombers flying overhead and the sounds of war all around you.

You have to wonder, if a city as seismic as Naples is built on top of a rabbit warren of tunnels, caves and ancient Greek cisterns, how come it doesn't all just collapse into a giant sink hole when the earth starts shaking? This area is known for big earthquakes. It turns out all this open space below the city, with the tunnels, the cisterns and the caves, seems to absorb most of the shaking. Fingers crossed, this is keeping all those magnificent buildings and the miles of multi-storied apartment buildings from collapsing.

Before entering the church be sure to check out the remains of the temple of Diana in front and to the right of the church. There is so much detail in these ruins – I would come here just to see this tower. Take a moment to observe the tourists passing by. No one seems to notice this tower with its 2000-year-old spolia is even here!

Address: Piazzette Pietrasanta, 17/18
Website: lapismuseum.com
What's nearby: Piazza Bellini, San Lorenzo Maggiore, the Duomo is 2 blocks away, the Sansevero Chapel, the Caravaggio – again, we are on the Via Tribunali in the heart of *everything*.

The Bourbon Gallery

The last of the underground experiences in this chapter began as a 16th century quarry used to extract tufa stone to build the palaces in the area around Piazza Plebiscito. In 1853, King Ferdinand II of Bourbon wanted an underground escape route so nobles could escape uprisings and flee to the safety of the palace. It was also used as an underground passage to secretly move military troops defending the palace. This became known as the Bourbon Tunnel. Two years later, the Bourbons were expelled and the work on the tunnel was never completed.

During World War II, the Bourbon Tunnel became another air raid shelter, and a refuge for citizens whose homes were destroyed in the bombing raids. More than 10,000 people routinely ran down the 90 stairs in Piazza Carolina seeking safety. The Union for Anti-Aircraft Protection provided toilets and an electrical system and brightened the space by covering the walls and vaults with hydraulic mortar.

Here, you can still see WWII-era baby strollers, toys and even hairbrushes left behind. In the 1970s it became a Judicial Depot where old cars and Vespas were stored. Some are still lined up against the walls. In 2005, two geologists founded the Underground Bourbon Cultural Association, cleaned out the trash-filled space and made it into a fantastic tourism experience.

There are four different routes and experiences to choose from, each with its own entrance.

The **Standard Entrance** gives a tremendous tour through the underground area. It costs €10 per person, and is active on Friday, Saturday and Sunday. The entrance is at Via Domenico Morelli, 61

The **Memories Way Tour** is the most recent discovery and takes you through areas where people left their belongings during bombing raids. Open Friday, Saturday, Sunday, the entrance is at Via Monte di Pio, 14

On the **Adventure Tour**, with a hard-hat and torch you make your way through the routes used by the *pozzari* to the water tanks. At one point you even use a raft. This tour also takes you to the underground area where the cars were stored. The tour takes an hour and a half and requires a reservation. Aged 15 and over costs €15, ages 10 to 15 pay €10. No children are permitted under the age of 10. The entrance is at Via Domenico Morelli, 61

The **Speleo Tour** requires a caving helmet with a headlamp as you explore the ancient tunnels of the aqueduct system to the 15th century water tanks, still full of water and decorated with religious symbols. I suggest researching this one online – parts of it would be too claustrophobic for me, but it looks incredibly cool. They do warn you you'll get dusty and dirty too. It also only runs on Friday, Saturday and Sunday and requires a reservation. This tour is adults only.

I recommend always checking ahead. Sometimes the tunnels are also open on other days, like public holidays.

Address: Via Domenico Morelli, 61
Website: galleriaborbonica.com
What's nearby: This is right behind Piazza Plebiscito, the Teatro San Carlo, the Royal Palace and just around the corner from Castel Nuovo.

13.
Ten Unmissable Museums

We spent today in ecstasies over the most astonishing sights. One may write or paint as much as one likes, but this place, this shore, the gulf, Vesuvius, the citadels, the villas, everything defies description.

~ Goethe

Naples is full of fascinating museums. There are museums for all kinds of interests from the most ancient to the super quirky to the modern. Some museums are inside churches, so be sure to read through the **Churches** chapter and *The Veiled Christ* chapter too.

I couldn't pick just one of the following museums to insist you put on your itinerary. In my opinion, you have to see at least these two: the Naples Archaeological Museum (MANN) – block out at least two hours to spend there, if not more – and the Jago Museum. The Jago is very much smaller and doesn't require a huge time commitment, just a drastic emotional one. It is incredible. (And my favorite eatery in Naples is just up the street from the Jago, so you are winning in every direction!)

1. Naples Archaeological Museum

Also known as MANN, the Museo Archeologico Nazionale di Napoli. Straight up, this is the *world's leading archaeological museum for ancient Roman treasures.* It is hard to wrap your head around just how important this museum is. If you have so much as a fleeting interest in Ancient Rome, put this museum at the very top of your **must-see** list. If you find Pompeii interesting, you have even more reason to make this a top priority – the MANN has over 400,000 artifacts from Pompeii alone.

The first two floors are mostly dedicated to the cities of Pompeii and Herculaneum. Expect to see mosaics, frescos and objects from daily life preceding the eruption of Mt Vesuvius in 79 AD. Furniture, papyrus scrolls, statues, glass and ceramics as well as casts of people who died in the eruption. There are also computer animations showing how the destruction of Pompeii and Herculaneum occurred. Honestly, it is absolutely incredible.

Another **must-see** is the famed **Secret Room/***Gabinetto Segreto*. Separated due to their explicit nature, and once part of the private erotica gallery of a Bourbon king, this collection of 250 sexually themed objects from Pompeii and Herculaneum chronicles various aspects of ancient world sexuality. Mythological frescos from ancient Roman homes, menu boards from the *lupanare* brothels, sexual oil lamps, banquet furnishings and wind chimes, phallic symbols galore found around Pompeii and Herculaneum, even elements of beastiality are all here. Perhaps not for the faint of heart or easily embarrassed, this is still a fascinating collection. The Secret Room only reopened to the public in 2000.

My Pompeii guide Pina explains that, back in Ancient Rome, the goddess Venus said making love was a gift and everyone should do it, so sexuality was encouraged and maybe even viewed as a mark of prosperity for the state. There were rules or guidelines but suffice to say it was a very different way of thinking to today. If you think you'd find it offensive, just skip the closed off, raunch-o-rama room of the museum.

The MANN has a plethora of other objects from antiquity. This includes the stupendous Farnese collection, discovered during 16th century excavations of the Baths of Caracalla in Rome. There is a jewelry collection here, a Magna Grecia collection, and even a pre-historic section.

For anyone who has a love of ancient Roman history, this museum is an absolute **must-see**.

Address: Piazza Museo, 19

Hours: Open 9:00 am to 7:30 pm, closed on Tuesdays.
Tickets: Buy tickets online, adults pay €22, 18 to 24 year olds pay €2, and under 18 is free. The Magna Grecia collection has time-specific entry tickets that cost an additional €1,50. Only 20 people are admitted at a time with *no accommodation for late arrival.* You are required to wear flat shoes. Shoe covers are provided at the museum.
Getting there: The museum is 2 city blocks from Piazza Bellini and 2 city blocks from the corner of Via Duomo and Via Foria, so a very easy walk from anywhere in the city center. Or use metro stop Museo.
What's nearby: Piazza Bellini, Spaccanapoli and everything on the Via Tribunali.

2. Capodimonte

This is a tremendous place to spend an afternoon. The museum is in the former Bourbon summer palace in the Reale Bosco di Capodimonte park. This was a 134-hectare hunting ground but is now a gorgeous public park with elegant walking paths and spectacular views out over the Bay of Naples. The park has several historic buildings – lodges, churches, and historic homes, as well as fountains, statues, huge shade trees and plenty of exotic plants. The park alone is worth a visit, but the summer palace, the Museo di Capodimonte, is one of the most popular museums in all of Naples.

Here you'll find significant works by Italian painters representing every important painting school from the 13th to the 20th century – Michelangelo, Botticelli, Titian, Caravaggio, Raphael and Bellini to name a few. The museum also has a rich collection of sculptures, works from foreign painters, as well as some fascinating visiting exhibitions.

The palace interiors are gorgeous too – be sure to visit the **Pulcinella room** while you are here.

The collection is split into two parts: The *Collezione Farnese* was the private collection of Alessandro Farnese, Pope Paul III. The *Galleria Napoletana* collection was collected from churches and palaces in and around Naples.

This is a tremendous and very important museum and is well worth visiting.

Address: Via Miano, 2
Hours: Open Thursday to Tuesday 8:30 am to 7:30 pm, with last entrance at 6:30 pm. Closed on Wednesdays.
Tickets: Buy tickets online. They cost €10 (18 to 25 years old pays €8 and under 18s are free). Admission to the park is free.
Getting there: It's easiest to get here by taxi. Several buses stop near the park including the 606, 680, 650 and the 655a. The bus ride from Piazza Dante takes 10 minutes.

3. The Jago Museum

Quite simply, Jago is the most exciting new artist in my lifetime.

I could just leave it at that, give you the address and tell you to go, but let's dive a little deeper and explore why you not only need to know about Jago, but make sure his museum is on your Naples **must-see** list.

When we think about art in Naples we tend to take massive leaps backwards in history: the Greeks 3000 years ago, the Romans 2000 years ago, the Renaissance 600 years ago. I seldom seek out modern art simply because there is such an extraordinary wealth of ancient art to explore in this incredible city. However, whether you live for art as I do, or you couldn't care less about art, I guarantee you will feel this man's work to the very core of your being. So, let's meet Jago.

Jacopo Cardillo, better known as Jago (*yah-goh*), is a *self-taught* master sculptor. And he is a hip, young, modern guy whose trade is not just a genius working of marble, but also a genius plowing of your emotions.

Pietà

Frequently referred to as a modern-day Michelangelo (to which he counters, 'No, I am a modern-day Jago'), he takes classical, instantly recognizable artistic themes, and reworks them with modern twists and interpretations. For example, the classic *Pietà*. Instead of Mary holding Jesus' body, Jago sculpted a father whose face is twisted in pure agony as he holds the body of his dead son. It is impossible to view this work and not feel the father's tortured emotion. You can attribute this tableau to any major event or conflict happening in the world. This could be a father trapped in any war: Syria, Palestine, Ukraine. He could have lost a child to Covid (it was sculpted during lockdown) or maybe he's outside a child oncology ward. This could be a refugee father whose child drowned making the crossing, or the father from a school shooting in the U.S. Jago leaves it up to your interpretation, but whichever story you connect it to, his Pietà sucks the breath right out of you. It is incredibly powerful.

Aiace and Cassandra

One of my favorite sculptures in Florence is Giambologna's *Rape of the Sabine Women*. In Rome I love Bernini's *Rape of Porserpina*. (Rape comes from the Latin word for abduction. In these sculptures the women are being abducted, not sexually violated.) Jago has a sculpture from this theme called *Aiace and Cassandra*, based on the abduction of the Trojan princess Cassandra after their defeat by the Greeks. Instead of the typical, fate-accepting expression of the woman being abducted, Jago gives us something entirely different. He captures her in the moment, reacting to her abductor, fighting, screaming, pushing his face away as he grips and tries to overpower her. Her backward movement is so fast and severe, her hair whips across her face. Your reaction to it is instantly visceral. There is such beauty in the work, yet you feel her fury and her fear. This is part of his mastery, the ability to capture and communicate human emotions with urgency.

Narcissus

His *Narcissus* reminds us that what we see in the mirror isn't necessarily who we are on the outside. The sculpture features two figures and ponders what Narcissus actually saw when he looked at his reflection in the water. Did he see a stylized version of himself, or an imaginary version? Or maybe he saw another secret world he could escape into?

Circling this work, you come up with multiple ideas about what he is telling us or asking us. It's a work and a message you think about long after you've left the museum.

La David

Each sculpture is a masterpiece, but I want to draw your attention to one more before we leave, this time it's the majestic *La David* – Michelangelo's *David* reinterpreted as a woman. She stands tall and strong, naked but not defenseless, thinking and strategizing. I've read that she is to remind us that all taboos against women must be dropped, but I see something else in her. She reminds me of Charlize Theron (there is a resemblance), with no need to scream or announce her power, instead her demeanor exudes it quietly and efficiently.

On a day when the US media were on full blast about women's reproductive rights, Jago posted a social media video of *La David* moving to an exhibition. Accompanied by menacing music, she looked back at us as she slowly rolled past. Coincidence? Maybe. But Jago harnesses social media like a pro. I recommend following his social media accounts, especially Instagram, not only to get a sense of his work but also to get a sense of him, both the artist and the effective communicator.

THE CHURCH OF SANT' ASPRENO AI CROCIFERI

The Jago Museum is in a formerly abandoned 17th century church at the edge of one of my favorite neighborhoods in Naples, the Sanità. Jago transformed the church of Sant' Aspreno ai Crociferi into his studio and exhibition gallery, utilizing the drama of the high ceilings and the colossal sense of space. The gray and white walls replete with original baroque fittings give a cold simplicity to the museum, infusing even more drama into his sculptures. Compared to the historical museums in town, filled to bursting with statues, this museum is quite spare. There are very few sculptures, spaced far apart. This lets you absorb the majesty of each work, feel the trauma that comes with it, and maybe make your own interpretation of the story being conveyed. The entire experience is fantastic.

All the workers at the Jago Museum belong to La Paranza. (We learned about La Paranza in the **Underground Sites** chapter.) Not only do you fill your soul when you come here, you become part of a bigger solution – 100% of your tourism dollars spent here have a positive impact on the local community. When you combine experiencing the greatest artist of our lifetime with sustainable travel, everybody wins.

Address: The Church of Sant' Aspreno ai Crociferi, Piazza Crociferi, 4, Sanità
Instagram: @Jago. and @Jagomuseum
Hours: Open Monday to Thursday 10:00 am – 1:00 pm, Friday to Sunday 10:00 am – 5:00 pm.
What's nearby: Time your visit for late morning, then walk down to Isabella di Cham for lunch. The famous Poppella pasticceria is next door to Isabella di Cham. The super famous pizzeria Concertina ai Tre Santi is diagonally opposite the two. Also close by and not to be missed is the beautiful Palazzo dello Spagnolo.

4. The Madre Museum

If you're in the mood for something a little more contemporary, check out the Madre Museum. Also known as the Donnaregina Contemporary Art Museum, it takes up three floors of the 19th century Palazzo Donnaregina in the historic center of Naples.

Here you can find some tremendous temporary exhibitions as well as a permanent collection featuring artists such as Mimmo Paladino, Anish Kapoor, Sol LeWitt, Rebecca Horn, Francesco Clemente and Janis Kounellis.

Address: Via Settembrini, 79
Hours: Open Monday to Saturday 10:00 am – 7:30 pm. Open Sunday 10:00 am – 8:00 pm. Closed on Tuesdays.

Tickets: Ticket office onsite.
What's nearby: The Duomo, the Jago Museum.

5. The Museum of the Treasures of San Gennaro

If I told you there's a museum in Italy with treasures more valuable than the British Crown Jewels and the collections of the Czars of Russia, where would you think it was? Rome? The Vatican? The Uffizi in Florence? Heads up: it's right here in Naples. The Museum of the Treasures of San Gennaro is a collection of the world's most valuable treasures and artworks, amassed over seven centuries, displayed in a 700-square-meter haven in the bustling heart of Naples.

Of course there is an interesting story here, starting with the Black Death in 1526.

In 1526, war and pestilence wrecked a massive death toll on Naples. The Neapolitans begged their patron saint, San Gennaro to make it all stop. On January 13, 1527, the city signed a contract between the people of Naples and San Gennaro (who at this point had been dead for 1200 years). It stipulated that he should protect Naples from plagues and from Mount Vesuvius' eruptions and in return they would build a chapel in the Duomo to honor him and fill it with treasures.

In 1601 they established the Deputation of the Real Cappella del Tesoro di San Gennaro. Still going strong today, this 400-year-old lay organization might just be one of the most surprising and interesting institutions in the country. Comprised of ten members of the nobility and two regular folk, the Deputation have guaranteed the inalienability of the treasure for four centuries. (By that, I mean they've kept the pope's sticky fingers off it, and prevented any kings, queens, politicians, Mafia Dons and even Berlusconi from pilfering any pieces, or breaking up the collection.) When you consider the trials and the tribulations, the wars, eruptions and earthquakes Naples has endured since 1601, this alone is just incredible.

Even more incredible, this treasure – one of the largest jewelry collections in the world – doesn't belong to the church, the Italian state or to a noble family. It belongs to the people of Naples.

During World War II the treasures of San Gennaro were hidden in the Vatican but returned to Naples in 1947.

There are so many stunning pieces in this collection and so much history, it's hard to wrap your head around it. Add to this the fact that until recently it was all kept hidden in a vault below the cathedral. This collection, the Treasure of San Gennaro, has only been open to the public since December 2003.

The art collections include statues and busts, fabrics, paintings and jewelry, all of it being immensely valuable. There are many spectacular pieces to see in this vast collection, but be sure to look for the following:

The Bishops' Headgear (Mitre)

Created by Matteo Treglia in 1713 and weighing 18 kilos, this one object is considered *one of the most precious pieces in the world*. It has 3694 precious stones (3,328 diamonds, 198 emeralds, and 168 rubies). Being the strongest stone, diamonds represented faith, emeralds symbolized knowledge, and rubies represent the blood of St Gennaro.

The Necklace of San Gennaro

In 1679 the Deputation decided to make a necklace using jewels from the collection, to drape on a bust of the saint. Over the ensuing centuries pieces were added including a *ciappa* made from emeralds and diamonds. Many of the jewels were donated by members of European royalty.

The Fine Silver Collection

Comprising 70 pieces dating from 1305 to the current age, this collection has never been tampered with nor had items stolen.

The Golden Chalice

Decorated with diamonds, rubies and emeralds, the chalice was made in 1761 and donated by King Ferdinand IV.

Along with many other sacred objects including reliquaries, processional crosses and liturgical vestments, here, you will also find the three sacristies of the *Cappella dei Tesori* where you can see paintings by Luca Giordano, Massimo Stanzione, Giacomo Farelli, and Aniello Falcone, all of which were *never available to the public before.*

Address: Via Duomo, 149
Hours: Open daily 9:30 am – 6:00 pm. Last entrance at 5 pm.
Tickets: www.tesorosangennaro.it
What's nearby: Adjacent to the Duomo. Jago Museum is close, as is Pio Monte della Misericordia (Caravaggio) and everything on the Via Tribunali.

5. The Monumental Complex of Donnaregina

The Diocesan Museum of Naples is inside the church of Santa Maria Donnaregina Nuova. The complex has two churches, the 14th century Santa Maria Donnaregina Vecchia, built for the Poor Clares (an enclosed order of Franciscan nuns), and the 17th century Santa Maria Donnaregina Nuova, intended to replace the old church. This is a unique opportunity to experience medieval Naples and baroque Naples, side by side. This is one of Naples' hidden gems and best kept secrets.

In 2007 the back rooms and side chapels of the new church were converted into the Diocesan Museum. The museum holds more than 300 religious works of art collected from deconsecrated churches nearby. Most of these are phenomenal paintings from Neapolitan artists including Luca Giordano, Massimo Stanzione, Aniello Falcone, and Giuseppe Simonelli.

The church of Santa Maria Donnaregina Vecchia is one of the best remaining examples of Neapolitan medieval art and culture. Be sure to look for Tina Camiano's regal tomb with its collection of pinnacles, turrets and busts, and the wonderful 14th century frescos by Pietro Cavallini and Filippo Rasuti. Meanwhile the church of Santa Maria Donnaregina Nuova is a fine example of gloriously bombastic Neapolitan baroque.

Address: Largo Donnaregina
Hours: Open Monday to Saturday 9:20 am – 4:30 pm. Open Sunday 9:30 am – 2:00 pm.
What's nearby: The Duomo, the Jago Museum, Isabella de Cham.

7. The Certosa of San Martino

If you enjoy a museum with a sensational view, don't miss this one up on the Vomero hill. Considered one of the most beautiful cloisters in Italy, the renovations executed over a half millennia were the work of some of the country's greatest architects, artists and sculptors. The chapter house, treasury, church and sacristy contain an absolute banquet of frescos by some of the best painters of the 17th century, including Guido Reni, Massimo Stanzione and Battista Caracciolo. In the nave, look for Cosimo Fandango's incredible inlaid marble work. Honestly, this place is stunning. Do not miss the chapel – it's breathtaking.

Two cloisters are next to the church, the smaller *Choistro dei Procuratori* and the larger *Choistro Grande.* Originally designed by Dosio, then added to by Fanzago, these Tuscan-Doric porticos are replete with marble statues, and in season, offset by intensely hued camellias. Gorgeous.

Across 70 rooms the Certosa San Martino displays items traversing Neapolitan history from the 13th to the 19th centuries. Beyond the beauty of the frescos, you can also find displays from Naples' naval history, a Vesuvius section, and the most elaborate nativity scene in the world. Covering an entire wall of the former monks' kitchen, the colossal *Presepe Cuciniello* has more than 150 miniature people, angels and animals, and 450+ other miniature pieces. This alone is worth the visit.

You can find most of the monks' historic picture collection in the southern wing's Quarto del Priore, along with a couple of sculptures you need to see. The lovely *Madonna with Child and St John the Baptist* by Pietro Bernini, father of Gian Lorenzo Bernini, and the statue of *St*

Francis by Giuseppe Sanmartino, the same artist who sculpted the staggeringly brilliant *Veiled Christ* in the Sansevero Chapel.

The vaulted *Sotteranei Gothic* (gothic basement) has around 150 marble sculptures and epigraphs, although this area was closed for a while in 2017. Some parts of the museum are only open on certain days, so check ahead online.

While up here be sure to visit Castel Sant' Elmo next door and then wander around the Vomero neighborhood. It's gorgeous. Then, knees and hips willing, take the staircase down into the Spanish Quarter. The 416 stairs take about 30 minutes, but the views are just stunning. Reward yourself with a *pizza fritta* when you reach the bottom. Otherwise, there are two funiculare and a metro stop (Vanvitelli) very close by.

Address: Largo San Martino, 5
Hours: Open Thursday to Tuesday 8:30 am – 4:00 pm. Closed on Wednesdays.
What's nearby: Castel Sant' Elmo is next door, the Pedimentina San Martino staircase is adjacent to the museum. From up here you get the best views across the historic center to Mount Vesuvius, and out across the entire Bay of Naples.

8. The Anatomy Museum of Campania Luigi Vanvitelli

Don't come to the Anatomy Museum unless you have a cast iron stomach. Here you can see human remains preserved in a variety of substances. Some (many) of the exhibits here are the stuff of your worst nightmares and horror movies. It's a bit morbid for my taste, but here we are. Teenage boys *love* it.

The anatomy museum is part of the University Museum of Sciences and Arts. The entire museum is full of interesting historical and cultural pieces, however we are going to focus on the anatomy section. This 18th century anatomy museum only opened to the public recently. Separated into normal and abnormal (my words not theirs) sections, the first has the kind of exhibits you would expect to see. Creepy, because these once were humans, but with scientific merit.

It's the 'abnormal' section that gives me enough content for two lifetimes worth of nightmares. Here you'll find all manner of deformities resulting from birth defects and diseases. On the marginally less traumatic side, you can see faces destroyed by various illnesses, skeletons of conjoined twins, and other skeletal body parts. Then it moves into horrendously malformed fetuses, even cyclops heads, heads with the scalp peeled back revealing the brain, and other items, all preserved in formaldehyde. There are also scary-looking heads from Amazon tribespeople, the long hair eerily still intact.

Med students, scientists and gore-loving teens will find this museum fascinating. (I on the other hand doubt I would ever survive the trauma of accidentally being locked in here overnight.) Usually, there is almost no one here, so you get to have the horrors to yourself.

At the time of writing this, there is no entry fee, but you do need to schedule a reservation online. The website is https://www.unicampania.it You'll find the details under the MUSA Sistema Museale tab.

There are no guides, but you can download the official app to help you understand what you are seeing.

Address: Via Luciano Armanni, 5

Website: https://www.unicampania.it
Hours: Check online when making your reservation.
What's nearby: The Duomo, Pio Monte Misericordia (Caravaggio), Napoli Sotterraneo. The museum is one city block from the Via Tribunali.

9. Palazzo Zevallos Stigliano

This is the place to see Caravaggio's final work, *The Martyrdom of Saint Ursula*. (See the **Caravaggio** chapter.) First, check to make sure the painting is not on tour. Both this one and the *Flagellation* up at the Capodimonte museum are frequently away on tour.

The museum is situated in the heart of the Via Toledo in a palazzo originally home to wealthy merchant Giovanni Zevallos. The building itself is pretty fantastic and over the years became home to a variety of wealthy merchants. At the end of the 1920s, it had significant restoration work done before eventually becoming home to the museum.

Along with the Caravaggio, you can see around 120 works of art from the Neapolitan painting schools. These works are from the 17th through 20th centuries.

Address: Via Toledo, 185
Hours: Open Tuesday to Friday 10:00 am – 7:00 pm. Open Saturday & Sunday 10:00 am – 8:00 pm. Closed Mondays.
What's nearby: The funicular up to the Vomero neighborhood, Piazza Dante, Galleria Umberto, Teatro San Carlo, Piazza Plebiscito.

10. Museo Pignatelli

If you visit Chiaia – and you most definitely should – wander the wide and sunny Riviera di Chiaia and drop in on the Pignatelli house museum. It gives you a window into the opulent homes of the 19th century monied crowd of Naples.

Formerly a noble home with a giant park, the museum is small and doesn't require much time. Along with the main residence, you can also walk up to the carriage house behind and see their historical carriages. I wouldn't cross town to come to Pignatelli, but if I'm walking past it's a nice addition.

What's nearby: Palazzo Mannajuolo, the Aquarium, the Chiaia waterfront and marina, Castel dell' Ovo.

14.

The Veiled Christ (Cristo Velato)

*One cannot blame the Neapolitan
for never wanting to leave this city…*

~ Goethe

Technically this should be in the **Churches** chapter, but if you've maybe heard of it and didn't know that it's inside a church, I've put it here on its own, easy for you to find.

To visit *The Veiled Christ*, we're going just off the Via Tribunali, down a narrow, easy-to-miss road called the Via Francesco de Sanctis. You could easily walk by this chapel without realizing it. If not for the line of people waiting to get in, that is.

In a city filled to bursting with incredible works of art, *this* really needs to be on your **must-see** list (if for no other reason than to ask yourself how on earth Giuseppe Sanmartino was able to create it). I have visited *The Veiled Christ* (Cristo Velato) more times than I care to count, yet still every single time am completely blown away by it.

This backstory takes place in the tiny but magnificent Sansevero Chapel, well worth visiting even without the veiled Jesus. Designed by Raimondo di Sangro, the Prince of Sansevero, the building began life as a mausoleum and a temple for the initiation rites of the

Freemasons. Built in 1613, and remodeled the following century by Raimondo, it is a true baroque masterpiece. Upon entering the chapel, everyone rushes to the centerpiece (*The Veiled Christ*) but make sure you look at everything else as well, from the painted ceiling to the other phenomenal sculptures. Each marble work inside the chapel was part of a greater iconographic design thought up by Raimondo.

Raimondo, The Prince of Sansevero

The chapel and the sculpture become even more fascinating when you have a little background on the enigmatic prince. Raimondo was born to a noble family in 1710. Educated in Rome, he spoke multiple European languages as well as Arabic and Hebrew. Whether true or not, legend says he invented a waterproof cape for his friend Charles Bourbon, King of Naples.

Although a successful military man, Raimondo's great interests were mechanics, alchemy and the sciences. He was quite brilliant, inventing such things as an eternal flame (using chemical compounds he invented), colored fireworks, a hydraulic device to pump water to great heights, and a printing press that could print multiple colors in a single process. He even invented an amphibious carriage with a paddlewheel that could go on both water and land. The prince was also a prolific writer, with some of his work banned by the church.

For a time, he was the Grand Master of the Neapolitan Freemasons, which added to the mystery and intrigue surrounding him, his magical alchemy and scientific experiments. Due to ecclesiastical and political pressure, Raimondo had to give up the position, and they also shut down his printing press, which meant he had to find another method for sharing his masonic message. There are multiple masonic messages inside the chapel, which incidentally, is built on top of a Temple of Isis.

A Masonic Temple

The first clue is the writing on the main portal. Back then the lateral entrance was the main entrance. The headstone above the door tells the traveler how to start the (masonic) path, and in Latin encourages the traveler to read the hidden meaning behind the works inside the chapel.

Inside the chapel look up to the *Glory of Heaven*, the fresco on the ceiling, painted in 1749. Look for the dove with the golden triangle around its head. To masons the triangle represents the Egyptian pyramids and is a reference to their Venerable Master. It also signifies the alchemy of sulphur and fire.

Amongst the statues in the chapel are the ten *Virtues*, each representing steps along the initiate's pathway to knowledge and perfection. You can follow the steps and the secret messages, but there are three sculptures I particularly want to draw your attention to:

Disillusion, Francesco Queirolo, 1753

Francesco Queirolo's masterpiece of a man emerging from a rope net represents a man set free from sin. When you look at this sculpture remember it was carved *from a single block of marble*. It is almost implausible. This piece and *The Veiled Christ* are equally stupendous, yet in my experience fewer people stop to really look at it.

The perfect figure of a man struggles to escape the intricate net that traps him. He is assisted by a little winged figure with a flame on his forehead, symbolizing human intellect. The man has a globe at his feet, representing worldly passions, on which an open book rests – the Bible. This not only represents sacred texts but is one of the 'three great lights' of the Freemasons.

In masonic rituals the initiates entered blindfolded, emerging from darkness into the light of the masonic Truth. Apart from the darkness into light symbology of the man escaping the net, there is a bas relief with the words *Qui non vident videant* those who do not see, will see). This message is emphasized again in another bas relief, this time on the pedestal, telling the story of Jesus restoring sight to the blind. The setting for this is the Temple of Soloman in Jerusalem, important to the masons as the birthplace of Hiram's myth. Hiram, the chief architect of Soloman's temple, was murdered there by three assailants when he refused to give up the Master Masons' secrets. To masons, Soloman's Temple represents the importance of fidelity and the certainty of death.

MODESTY, ANTONIO CORRADINI, 1752

Raimondo dedicated this piece to his mother, who died when he was only a year old (which is really trippy when you consider the statue's pert breasts with erect nipples).

Again, we have a sculpture that would be perfection on its own, but this time instead of a net it is draped in a seemingly weightless marble veil. The draping of the veil is quite incredible, seemingly diaphanous, yet it appears to stick to parts of her body, like her legs, as if trapped against her skin by the Neapolitan humidity. Where it drapes over her face it looks ghostly. Added to this, a garland of roses is strung across her hips.

This sculpture was also carved from a single block of marble. Corradini, a Venetian sculptor, worked on a series of veiled nudes across his career and *Modesty* was the last he completed before his death.

Modesty can be interpreted as an allegory to Wisdom, and to Isis, the Goddess of Magic, Science and Technology. Legend says this statue stands where a Greek statue of Isis stood in ancient Neopolis.

Her gazing away from us, the broken plaque and the tree of life all symbolize Raimondo's mother losing her life too soon. On the pedestal a bas relief tells the story of Christ appearing to Mary Magdalene as a gardener.

It is easy to miss this beautiful statue as everyone hustles to see *The Veiled Christ*, so I suggest googling her first, so you know what to look for, and don't exit the chapel until you have seen her.

THE VEILED CHRIST, GIUSEPPE SAN MARTINO, 1753

This profoundly moving work is one of the most sensational sculptures you will see, anywhere in the world. Smack bang in the middle of the nave, this life-sized marble statue of Christ lying dead, covered in a transparent shroud is quite simply one of the greatest sculptures of all time.

Raimondo de Sangro originally wanted Corradini to create this work, but the artist died after making a terracotta model for it. (The model is now in the Museo San Martino.) Raimondo then awarded the commission to a local Neapolitan artist. San Martino ignored the original model and went in his own direction, adding movement and emotion, and making us feel as though we have stumbled upon the body just moments after the shroud has been placed over it. A swollen vein still pulses in Jesus' forehead. You feel as though this has *just happened*, the immediacy of it still full of emotion.

Somehow the placement of the veil makes Christ seem even more naked. It makes the details of his body seem more real, the very motion of the shroud exaggerating the torment and suffering. Looking at a hundred photos of the sculpture doesn't prepare you for the intensity of the experience when you stand before it. The sculpture is so lifelike that people thought Raimondo had killed someone and put a marble veil over him. Other myths suggested Raimondo had used his skills with alchemy to create a fabric that marbleized when placed over the statue. The truth however, as proven by scientists, is that this was created by a genius from a single block of marble.

THE ANATOMICAL MACHINES

Downstairs in the underground chamber two huge glass cases hold life-sized skeletons of a man and a woman. Also called anatomical studies, the two bodies each have their arteriovenous systems perfectly intact.

It's actually pretty creepy, yet brilliant at the same time. A Sicilian doctor, Giuseppe Salerno created the male skeleton which was purchased by Raimondo in 1756. He then brought the doctor from Palermo to Naples and had him create the female. Originally the female had been pregnant, but at some point in the 1960s the 'fetus' was stolen.

Legend said Raimondo killed his servants and injected one of his potions into their veins, creating the macabre anatomical machines.

In reality, Salerno created them using wire wrapped in silk then dipped in beeswax and varnish.

The anatomical machines are equal parts ghastly and fascinating.

I sincerely recommend having an extensive look through the chapel's tremendous website before coming here. There is so much to see in this tiny space, each item accompanied with stories and intrigue. You can also find endless blog posts and articles about everything here. I normally do extra research in preparation for each time I come here and write myself notes so I know which new things to look for. Just tracking all the masonic symbology alone is fascinating.

You need to book tickets well ahead, and all entries are time specific. You only get a short amount of time inside, which is why I always arrive with a list of things to seek out. Even if you're only planning on looking at *The Veiled Christ* you'll still want to know what else is around you.

Address: via Francesco de Sanctis 19/21
Website: museosansevero.it
Hours: Open Wednesday to Monday 9:30 am – 6:00 pm. Closed on Tuesdays.
What's nearby: The Sansevero Chapel is just off the Via Tribunali, right in the heart of everything. San Domenico Maggiore, Pio Monte della Misericordia (Caravaggio), Napoli Sotteraneo, Santa Maria delle Anime del Purgatorio ad Arco.

15.
Eight Incredible Churches in Naples

The story is here. The magic and the superstitions are here.

If you skip the churches in Naples, you miss the majesty and the madness.

Before you run away screaming, telling me you're all churched out and don't want to see inside another one, I have to stop you. Churches in Italy are incredible and, depending on where you are, they tell you much more than just Bible stories. Here in Naples many of the churches are full-on museums. Some take you downstairs into ancient Roman ruins. Some have crypts where they hung dead monks to drain their fluids. There are spectacular cloisters and spooktacular crypts full of skulls and bones.

There is So. Much. Here. And so much of it is absolutely *wild*! Historically, Neapolitans have had a very different attitude toward death and an intriguing relationship with superstition and magic, and the best place to see this is inside (some of) the churches and church-museums.

Naples has an insane number of churches. If I spent the rest of my life trying to get inside them all (some are locked up and only open periodically), I still wouldn't get it done. So, the following is just the list of churches that I particularly love in Naples.

Even if you're not overly churchy, make sure you read through this chapter, regardless of your personal religious beliefs or lack thereof, and please visit at least one of the churches on this list. There's a very good chance you'll find several that you'd like to pop into or would be disappointed to get home and discover you'd missed.

There are also some churches in other places in this book (for example, the **Museums** chapter), and the Sansevero Chapel has its own chapter because many of you will be looking for *The Veiled Christ*, and I wanted you to be able to find it quickly.

Sunday 9:00 am – 12:45 pm, then 4:30 pm – 8:00 pm.
Tickets: Tickets to the cloisters cost around €6.
What's nearby: The Dante Metro stop is 200 meters away. Gesù Nuovo is across the street, the Sansevero Chapel and Sant'Anna dei Lombardi are all within about 5 minutes' walk.

2. The Church of Gesù Nuovo

The Church of Gesù Nuovo is considered the most beautiful church in all of Naples. Along with its astounding beauty it also has some interesting history and a hidden secret on the facade. Once you've spotted it, your eyes can't un-see it.

HISTORICALLY

Originally this was a palace, built in 1470 for Roberto Sansevino, the Prince of Salerno. The palace was renowned for its beauty, the plethora of frescos inside, and its gorgeous interior garden. It was a prime example of the Renaissance in Naples, and a couple of centuries later, Neapolitan Baroque.

One of the interesting aspects of the original palace is the external facade, which remains the facade of the church today. The front wall is covered in pyramid shaped stones. This was a style used in Venice but not seen in the south until now.

Political skullduggery and intrigue led to the palace being confiscated from the Sansevino family in around 1547. In 1580 it was sold to the Jesuits who between 1584 and 1601 turned it into a church, incorporating the garden of the next-door neighbor, Isabella Feltria, Princess of Bisignano. The was already a Church of Jesus in Naples, so this one became the New Church of Jesus, or Gesù Nuovo.

In 1767 the Jesuits were expelled from Naples and the church was given to the Franciscans. The Jesuits returned in 1821 but were expelled again in 1848. Over the centuries the church interior went through some facelifts, its final resting place being what I consider *extreme* Baroque.

THE INTERIOR

The opulence and beauty of Gesù Nuovo will take your breath away. Frankly it is gloriously excessive. Every surface inside this massive church is triumphantly adorned. You might feel as though you have sudden onset ADD, but just breathe for a moment. It won't reduce the sense of overstimulation, but the church is huge, so an extra couple of breaths as you arrive surely has to in some way be beneficial.

Gesù Nuovo is in the shape of the Greek Cross, with a great dome in the center and four minor lateral domes. Neapolitan sunshine streams through the high windows around the domes and in the barrel vaults, giving you a different sense of things at different times of day.

The original great dome, decorated by Giovanni Lanfranco, was the largest in the city. Sadly, only the corner arches survived the earthquake of 1688 and the allied bombing in World War II. (An unexploded bomb that blew through the ceiling can still be seen inside the church today.) Lanfranco also painted the frescos of the four evangelists, decorating the four pillars of the dome.

The church is lavishly decorated with marble everywhere you look, from the magnificent floors to every vertical surface, columns, pilasters, bas reliefs and statues. Colored marble, white marble, illusions of vases of flowers, masks, festoons of garlands and flowers

– it's magnificent. Then, good lord, there are frescos! Painted by Neapolitan masters including Francesco Solimena, Massimo Stanzione (known as the Neapolitan Guido Reni) and Luca Giordano, and Spanish Jusepe de Ribera. For art lovers, Gesù Nuovo is an absolute feast for the eyes.

QUIRKY BUT COOL

It's easy to get overwhelmed by the art and color and majesty of a church like this one and in the process miss some of the quirky/smaller points of interest. Gesù Nuovo has five chapels on each side of the aisle, each of them full of fantastic art. The last chapel on the left as you exit the church is the Chapel of San Francesco de Geronimo. Inside this chapel is a random treasure I find interesting.

Look for two large wooden structures called *lipsanothecae*. These are containers to hold reliquaries. Each of the two units hold dead bits of 35 saints and martyrs. The units are divided into five rows, each with seven cubbyholes holding a relic of a martyr from the early Christian age. The front of each cubbyhole has its own small, intricately carved bust to tell you whose body part is inside. (These can be pieces of bone, a tooth, an ear – who knows?)

I always think the business of selling relics must have been a scream back in the day. You could dig up any old grave, pull out some finger bones, and sell them, saying this knuckle belonged to Saint X and this fingertip belonged to Saint Y. Even today no one is checking.

Anyway, these *lipsanothecae* are quite remarkable. They were thought to have been made in around 1617 by Neapolitan wood carver Giovan Battista Gallone. The carved busts are each quite beautiful. Be sure to check them out before leaving the church.

THE FACADE

Let's talk about the secret hidden on the facade of the church. I know many of you won't go inside Gesù Nuovo, but you are likely to at least walk past. This is the original palace wall, so doesn't look particularly church-y. In fact, it looks like a fortress.

Look for mysterious symbols etched into the lower side of the pyramid shaped ashlar stones covering the wall. Legend said these were symbols designed to draw good luck and good energy into the building. The error of placing them on the underside of the stones instead drew bad luck. The building suffered fires, earthquakes and the massive dome collapsed *twice*.

However, this legend has recently been proven wrong. These are in fact letters from the Aramaic language – the language Jesus spoke. Each letter corresponds to a musical note, and when read from right to left, from bottom to top, the secret code forms a 45-minute-long concert. There are videos of the Renaissance piece on YouTube – it's quite fantastic. A secret code musical score has also been found on another of the Sanseverino palaces.

One last thing on the facade, look for the original marble door from the 15th century. Built for the palace, it was later modified by the Jesuits, who altered the bas reliefs, frieze and cornice in the 17th century.

Address: Piazza Gesù Nuovo.
What's nearby: The Monumental Complex of Santa Chiara, Sant' Anna dei Lombardi, Spaccanapoli begins here and leads you across the historic center of Napoli.

3. Saint Mary of the Souls of Purgatory (*Santa Maria Delle Anime in Purgatorio ad Arco*)

Before entering the church hang about outside for a few minutes. You'll notice local Neapolitans reaching out and touching the bronze skulls mounted on the pedestrian columns outside the church as they walk past. This is your first sign that something's up.

Remember me telling you there was so much more to the churches in Naples and you never know what you'll discover? Well here again, I want to tell you about the cult of the *anime pezzentelle* (I talked about this in the **Underground Sites** chapter), a fascinating practice involving abandoned skulls of the long dead, souls trapped in Purgatory and regular folk who care for them.

Surrounded by 3000+ years of identifiable, touchable history, a volcano that could blow at any moment and a super-volcano under the bay that could take out much of Europe, it's fair to say some Neapolitans have a very different relationship with death.

The very fascinating church of **Santa Maria delle Anime in Purgatorio** was consecrated in 1638, and takes place on two levels. The upper level represents life, the lower level represents death. The upper church is interesting enough, with some tremendous artwork including Luca Giordano's *Death of St Alessio* and Massimo Stanzione's *Virgin with the Souls of Purgatory*. But look at the pilasters behind the altar and you'll see skulls sculpted into frames you'd otherwise expect cherubs to be peeping from. Behind the altar itself, another skull and crossbones glares out at you.

But I think the most intriguing part of this church happens on the lower floor. From the 17th to the late 19th centuries, a large, nameless mass gravesite was down here. It was a burial place for countless impoverished locals who couldn't afford a proper burial. A Potter's Field of sorts, loaded up with anonymous bones and skulls, it was made worse no doubt in 1656 when the Black Death was thought to have killed at least 150,000 local people.

This hypogeum became the epicenter of the cult of the *anime pezzentelle*. Think of this as a Neapolitan cult of skulls, where people adopt a skull and take care of it as if it were a family member. They pray to the soul once attached to said skull in the hope their prayers will help the soul escape Purgatory and ascend to Heaven. Once through the pearly gates the soul hopefully will offer blessings (and maybe some lottery numbers) back as a form of gratitude.

As many as 60 masses took place down here each day and on All Souls Day the line to get in here can stretch 500 meters along the road.

The Hypogeum

Now it's time to discover something rich in mystery and ghoulishly fascinating: the hypogeum, also known as the Crypt of the Abbots. Your access to this otherworldly space is via one of the church guides. The guide we had while I was writing this book was tremendous and added a whole new level of intrigue to the experience. He was a walking, talking encyclopedia with a glorious sense of theater, which in a place like this was just priceless.

Behind the altar of the church, a grand imperial staircase leads you down to a magnificently fresco'd elliptical space, a crypt from the 1400s. You descend into a dusky space that feels a little gloomy. As you acclimate to this weird space, you'll notice a curving wall of what looks like a series of conjoined stone cupboards with no doors. The openings are part of a process called *scolatura* – the draining of bodily fluids used to mummify a corpse.

Dead abbots were hung in these *scolatoi* to drain their fluids. I'm not kidding. The naked dead abbot was inserted into his space, held upright by hooks in the wall. Below him, a vase or bowl collected the drained fluids. (By the Middle Ages, it was already understood that contagions spread via the fluids from dead bodies.)

There are various theories about how long the draining of a dead abbot took, from weeks to months. Some of this depended on how rainy or humid the weather was at the time. Workers assisted the process by beating the bodies or cutting extra draining holes in them. (In the upstairs world, these fellows had to squish entire families into a single coffin when the family couldn't afford individual burials.)

Once mummified, the living abbots gently lowered the body through a hole in the floor to a room 6 meters below. Here, mummified corpses were layered across the floor, covered with a layer of dirt, then a layer of cement. At any given time, there could be as many as 200 monks at Monteoliveto. In the Middle Ages the average life span was much shorter, so those 200 would have cycled through at a faster pace. This burial space was in use for nearly 400 years from around 1411 to 1799, so who even knows how many bodies are down there doing the dust to dust, ashes to ashes thing?

Along with the abbots, various noblemen paid to go through this process when they died. They believed if their sins were drained away, they could fast track their way to the pearly gates.

This draining process was gaseous and stinky, so air tunnels (perhaps from prior millennia or maybe created by the monks) allowed the air to flow. Below the church are multiple tunnels, with most of their entrances cemented over. There are even tunnels connecting to the tombs in the two Renaissance chapels above, which can still be used to escape down here to the hypogeum. Others lead all the way to what is now the post office, as well as one that leads to the building next door, which is now the headquarters of the Carabinieri. When in Naples never forget there is an entire world below your feet!

Immediately above the draining cupboards and below the fresco of Christ on Calvary, a row of 24 glass boxes hold the skulls of the notable. It's hard to tell if they're grimacing, menacing, or laughing like lunatics, but there they are. Be sure to have an extra look at the one in the middle, directly below Jesus' feet. He has a hat on and looks like he's shrieking at us. Or laughing.

Now let's talk about the metaphoric frescoes. As the naked, dead abbot was carried down the imperial staircase, he passed through the Garden of Eden as a reminder that we have all sinned. Look closely inside the garden and you'll see what appears to be a Greek temple. This may be a nod to Naples' past, or maybe it's symbology I'm not aware of, but I find it interesting.

Moving on, the frescos become a forest of sacred funerary trees – the kind you would see around cemeteries. Perhaps this symbolized new life, or life reaching up to the heavens? Then in the middle, Christ on the cross centers us.

Consider all of this alongside the draining chambers and the bodies buried below and perhaps we can infer that the draining of the fluids represents the sins draining down into the earth. From there the soul can leave the weight of the body that has been holding it down and float up to Heaven as light as helium.

Address: Piazza Monteoliveto, 4
Hours: Open Monday to Saturday 9:30 am – 6:30 pm, and Sunday 9:30 am – 5:30 pm.

Getting there: Everything around here is in walking distance, but for reference it is quite close to the Dante metro station and less than 10 minutes' walk from Via Tribunali. It is less than a 5 minute walk from our next two **must-see** churches in Naples.

5. San Domenico Maggiore

You will be close to this church anyway, so you might as well pop in for a look. I hope you come through this neighborhood with a private/small group guide. There are so many tiny and intriguing details around every corner that you'd otherwise miss. Even an explanation of the street art in this immediate area, and on the Vico San Domenico Maggiore, is just *fascinating*. It completely changes how you otherwise view graffiti and wall art in Naples. You can get a list of the private guides I work with and recommend at www.GlamItaliaBooks.com/Naples–Private–Guides.

Strolling the Vico San Domenico Maggiore just a few meters from Via Tribunali, you'll find this wonderful church on your right, in a piazza of the same name. Don't be put off by the deceptively austere gothic facade – this is one of Naples' most beautiful churches.

Before entering the church, check out the huge, sculpted obelisk in the piazza. This is one of the three spires of Naples, built to celebrate the end of the plague. Commissioned by Charles I Anjou and built between 1283 and 1324, San Domenico Maggiore became the royal church of the Angevins. The church and adjacent Dominican monastery are among the most historically important religious complexes in Naples.

Inside, bright creamy walls with golden edges emphasize huge gothic arches. These flank twin rows of grey columns topped with golden

Corinthian capitals, drawing your eye to the dramatic altar at the end. It really is stunning. The grey and golden organ rising above the altar is a baroque masterpiece.

Cosimo Fanzaga, the greatest architect and sculptor of Naples' Baroque period, created the sculptures and marble work. Take a moment to enjoy his perfect *putti* sculptures on the altar. Also be sure to look up at the spectacular paneled ceiling, installed in around 1670.

Of course, this church is filled with sensational paintings and sculptures, including some beautiful paintings by Francesco Solimeno. In the Brancaccio chapel you can still see some of the original, staggeringly beautiful frescos painted by Pietro Cavallini in 1309.

In the first chapel on the left look for a replica of Caravaggio's *Flagellation*. (The original is now at the Capodimonte Museum.)

While here, also look for a wooden work called the *Madonna of Zi' Andrea*, the monk for whom the chapel was named. He ordered the work for a lady who rejected it because the face wasn't good enough, so decided to keep it for himself. Overnight a miracle happened and when he woke the Madonna had a new, beautiful visage.

There are 24 chapels in the church, each of them tremendous and deserving of your attention, but I want to draw you to one at the end of the right nave. This is the Chapel of San Michele Arcangelo a Morfisa. It was the original 10th century church on this site and was incorporated into the new church back in 1283.

There is lots to see in the sacristy too. First there is Francesco Solimeno's frescoed ceiling, *The Triumph of Faith Over Heresy By The*

Domenicans. Then check out the three sided two-tiered gallery, where 38 coffins hold the remains of members of the Aragon's royal family, including King Ferdinand I.

THE MUMMIES OF SAN DOMENICO

This is actually fascinating. These mummies are unique both for their excellent state of preservation, and for the fame of those mummified. A wealth of information has been extracted from them.

The sarcophagi are stacked in two rows. The upper row has names and family crests telling us who is inside, while the inhabitants of the lower row mostly remain anonymous. Eight of the coffins were empty and one had a pair of bodies inside. Before being entombed the bodies were drained in a sand-floored room below the church. The air then created a natural mummification.

Paleo-pathologists tested the bodies and learned some intriguing details about life and death in 15th and 16th century Naples. They found smallpox, bubonic plague and hepatitis, gallstones, signs of atherosclerosis and pubic lice. One of the bodies had blackened teeth, a sign of mercury used at the time to treat syphilis. There was evidence of tumors – we now know King Ferrante probably died from colorectal cancer. In Maria of Aragon, they found multiple HPV tumors. This was the first time HPV has been discovered in a mummy and provides a wealth of knowledge for oncologists. They also found signs of malaria and obesity.

The clothing they were wearing was studied, cleaned and is now on display behind the basilica.

St Thomas Aquinas

The monastery was the original university of Naples. Saint Thomas Aquinas lived and taught here between 1272 and 1274. You can visit his cell, see the crucifix that spoke to him, and see the remains of his left arm in the Sacred Relics Chamber. Apparently Thomas would levitate while meditating and chatting to Christ. However, his levitation skills didn't help him when he fell from a donkey. The injuries from the fall ended up killing him. He left behind a very important body of work on Christian philosophy and theology, and a piece of his left arm. The reliquary is worth a look – a black hand reaches heavenward, the piece of bone visible through a little window in the arm's golden sleeve. Next to the hand there's a preserved heart, but no one knows who it belonged to. Which depending on how you look at it, is quite funny. Safe to say it probably wasn't the janitor's heart.

Three other famous hearts were kept here for centuries: those of Charles II of Naples. Alfonso V of Aragon and Ferdinand II of Naples. During the Napoleonic occupation of Naples in the early 1800s someone stole them. (You have to wonder what on earth would possess you to steal the preserved hearts of dead kings?? It's not like you could sell them.)

Another famous Dominican friar who lived here for a while was Giordano Bruno, who appears in both my Venice and Rome books. Bruno was a philosopher and cosmology theorist who posited that stars were actually distant suns, surrounded by their own planets. He also thought the Earth orbited the sun rather than the church's theory that the sun orbited the Earth. On February 17, 1600, the church had him burned at the stake in Rome's Campo di Fiori for his heresy.

THE 40 HOUR MACHINE

While you're here, look for the only remaining 40 Hour Machine in Naples. In 1537 the church introduced a prayer marathon during the 40 hours that Christ was in his tomb pre-resurrection.

Churches were plunged into darkness other than the light radiating from a special altar called *la machine della quarant'ore* (the machine of the 40 hours). In the wild 1600s, the population was out partying and getting crazy, so a spectacular sideshow was needed to draw them in. The various religious orders all tried to out-Liberace each other with 40-hour altars each more bombastic and Vegas-y than the next.

The one here was found in pieces. It took enormous research to figure out where all the parts went, and to find the missing ones. This is one of those seeing-is-believing deals. It is mad baroque gold with a centerpiece and a cluster of sun rays firing out from the back. Made of multiple individual parts, around 200 candles will have bounced light off all the sun rays. It must have looked like a cross between fireworks and the Las Vegas strip at night.

To make things even funnier (to me anyway), during Lent the performance of music on a stage was forbidden. So the church hired baroque composers and musicians to write and play music inside their churches, giving rise to the musical form known as *oratorio*. I absolutely love the madness of churches vying to get prayer customers by having musicians and sparkly lights!

On the bottom of the 40-hour machine, look for a dog with a torch in its mouth. This is the symbol of the Dominican Order.

6. Sant' Angelo a Nilo

It's easy to be completely bamboozled by all the ancient Greek and ancient Roman history, and the over-the-top baroque architecture and art in Naples. But don't forget, Naples was a very important renaissance city too. And right here, in this little church off the Spaccanapoli we can see one of the first major artworks of the Neapolitan Renaissance. Not only that, but this story involves some of my favorite characters from my Florence book, including my all-time favorite pope – Baldassare Cossa, the pirate pope from Procida.

At the end of the Via San Biagio dei Librai section of Spaccanapoli you can't miss the eye-catching red and grey 18th century facade of Sant'Angelo al Nilo. The original gothic church was built in 1385 by Cardinal Rainaldo Brancaccio. Brancaccio's tomb is our Tuscan Renaissance treasure. Brancaccio was friends with Cosimo de' Medici and both were friends with the Antipope John XXIII (real name Baldassare Cossa).

Baldassare and his brothers kept their noble family financially fluid by raiding ships off the coast of Procida. After earning doctorates in civil and canon law in Bologna, the totally immoral Baldassare got into the religion business. He became a cardinal and then convinced Giovanni di Bicci de' Medici (father of Cosimo) to finance him into the big prize – the papacy. I go into the full debauched (and, in my opinion, hilarious) story in my book *Glam Italia! 101 Fabulous Things To Do In Florence.* (Note: he actually staged raids on convents, availing himself and his cohorts of an endless supply of young nuns.)

On Baldassare's death, Cosimo de' Medici had the job of commissioning his tomb in the baptistry in Florence. This was another wildly entertaining story, well worth reading, but the final result was the first truly Renaissance tomb. An absolute masterpiece, crafted between 1422–1428 by Cosimo's friend Donatello and his architect Michelozzo.

And now the story comes back to Naples. Rainaldo Brancaccio died in 1427, but before passing, he commissioned his friend Cosimo de' Medici to organize his tomb. Cosimo hired Donatello, Michelozzo and Pagno di Lapo to work on the piece. They created the tomb in Pisa then transported it by boat down to Naples.

Michelozzo designed the very Renaissance-looking sepulcher with its canopy, Corinthian columns and matching pairs of pilasters. One interesting feature is the marble curtain, typical to gothic tombs but reimagined here in a minimized fashion. It frames statues of the Madonna and Child flanked by Saints John the Baptist and Michael. Two angels hold up the bottoms of the curtain on either side above the tomb, while three beautiful virtues (women) stand in front of it. Look above the head of the middle virtue and you'll see a relief of Donatello's *Assumption of the Virgin*.

If you enjoy Donatello, Michelozzo, pirate popes and Cosimo de' Medici, this is a wonderful church to drop in on, just to see this piece. This is Donatello's only work in Naples.

The church gets its name from an ancient statue of the Egyptian god Nile, standing in the piazzetta. The statue was carved by merchants from Alexandria but was lost for centuries, only showing up again in the 1400s. The current head was added in the 17th century.

Address: Piazzetta Nilo.
What's nearby: The Sansevero Chapel, San Domenico Maggiore, Santa Maria in Purgatorio, San Gregorio al Armeno.

7. Girolamini

This largely unvisited treasure is at the top end of the Via Tribunali. On your left immediately before the Via Duomo, a marble clad church anchors the piazza Girolamini. This is part of a massive complex with cloisters, a convent and paintings by some of the Renaissance's greatest artists. The church was closed for more than 30 years after suffering severe damage in World War II.

Before we walk around the corner to enter the complex there are a couple of things here to look for. Work began on the church around 1592 and was completed in 1619. The facade is a 1780 renovation by architect Ferdinando Fugo.

Up high, next to each belfry look for statues of St Peter and St Paul. These were sculpted by Giuseppe Sanmartino, the artist who created *The Veiled Christ*.

On the wall at the corner of the piazza, Banksy's *Madonna with a Pistol* is protected under glass. We talk about Banksy in the **Street Art** chapter, but while you're in the piazza be sure to check it out.

Entrance to the complex is around the corner on the Via Duomo.

As you enter the complex there are two cloisters. The first is the *choistro maiolicato,* named for its majolica tiles. The second, larger cloister with the orange garden in the center has the entrance to the Quadreria or Pintoteca (art museum) and the Biblioteca.

The Pinoteca, on the right-hand side of the courtyard, is not to be missed. It is one of Naples' lesser-known attractions and is full of works by Neapolitan masters. Look for my favorite mustachio'd Mary in Niccolo de Simone's *Madonna and Child*.

Between the pinoteca and the church you can see incredible art from major renaissance artists including Guido Reni, Francesco Solimena (*Stories of St Philip Neri*) Pietro Corton (*St Alexius Dying*, 1638) multiple by Josè de Ribera, and sculptures by Pietro Bernini.

The church is enormous and is filled with artwork and baroque treasures. The gilt ceiling is fantastic, most of it ruined during bombings in WWII, but much of it now restored. Above the entrance look for Luca Giordano's incredible *Christ Expelling the Merchants from the Temple* (1684).

The art here is astounding, yet no one seems to know about it. Even on days when the Via Tribunali is packed with tourists, hardly anyone is here.

The Looting of the Library

This is the site of one of the biggest international scandals to hit the world of rare books. You can't make this stuff up …

Dating back to 1586, the **Girolamini Library** is the oldest library in Naples and *the second oldest library in all of Italy.* Below spectacularly decorated walls and ceilings, for nearly 500 years its wooden shelves held centuries-old editions of books by luminaries including Descartes, Aristotle and Machiavelli. There was a 1518 edition of Thomas Moore's *Utopia*, a 1610 edition of Galileo's *Sidereus Nuncius* with 70 plus drawings of the moon and the stars, and Johannes Kepler's *Astronomia Nova*. Published in 1609, this book was the result of Kepler's 10-year study of the movement of Mars and is recognized as being *one of the most important books in the history of astronomy.*

With centuries worth of books and no complete cataloguing system, there is no way of knowing exactly how many priceless works belong to the library. And so, here is the site of the most dramatic book theft in our lifetime. It turns out the guy running the library, Marino Massimo De Caro, was also plundering its riches until, in 2012, art historian Professor Tomaso Montanari visited it with a student. The library had been closed to the public for years and Montanari found it in a state of complete chaos – trash and papers scattered everywhere, precious books thrown on the floor, some 17th century books were even pulled from their bindings. One member of the staff took the professor aside and told him the director was looting the library.

Investigators discovered more than a thousand books in a storage unit owned by the director. Thousands more, stripped of their Girolamani Library seals and impossible to trace back to Naples, had been sold through the international rare book markets. In one instance a German auction house gave the thieves $1.4 million for a batch of 500 books. Some books sold for hundreds of thousands, others for tens of thousands. Investigators believe the accumulated sales raked in tens of millions of euros.

They estimate 80% of the lost books have now been recovered, as book lovers and associations of antique booksellers around the world keep an eye out for books that could potentially come from this library. The rare book market, however, is full of dastardly collectors who, like the more nefarious art collectors, squirrel away high-priced pieces they know to be stolen. The problem with trying to trace stolen art and artifacts is that the trail typically runs cold at the Swiss border.

You have to wonder how someone like De Caro, with no relevant qualifications, could have been put in charge of such an important historical collection in the first place. It was definitely a case of the fox guarding the henhouse. De Caro moved in the orbit of Italy's corrupt former Prime Minister Silvio Burlesconi. This gave him political cover, allowing him to reach various coveted positions in institutions run by the Ministry of Culture. And as a result, he pulled off one of the greatest heists of all time.

Address: Piazza Girolamini. Entrance is around the corner at Via Duomo, 142
What's nearby: The Duomo, Pio Monte della Misericordia, San Lorenzo Maggiore (Underground).
Hours: Open Monday to Friday 8:30 am – 7:00 pm. Open Saturday and Sunday 8:30 am – 2:00 pm.

8. The Duomo

When we imagine Italy's duomos we picture colossal structures exploding skyward, festooned with intricate and expensive decoration, grabbing God's attention with lavish displays of money and power. From Basilica San Marco in Venice to the duomos of Florence and Milan, Siena and Orvieto, the Cathedral in Amalfi and St Peter's in Rome (although the actual cathedral of Rome is San Giovanni in Laterano), they're all selling the deal from the outside.

It's easy to walk right past Naples' cathedral without realizing it. There's no giant piazza out front and no giant space to herald the arrival of popes and bishops. Instead, it sits shoulder to shoulder with other buildings on a somewhat narrow street. The gothic facade is simple and clean. But don't be deceived. What this duomo lacks in curb appeal, it more than makes up for inside.

Santa Maria Assunta, the cathedral of Naples, was commissioned by Charles II d' Anjou in the 13th century and consecrated in 1314 under King Roberto the Wise. The 4th century Church of Santa Restituta and the old Baptistery of San Giovanni in Fonte were incorporated into the new duomo serving as side chapels, but another old basilica on the site, Santa Stefania, was destroyed. (This is Naples, so like a majestic layer cake, of course they discovered remnants of Ancient Rome and Ancient Greece below that.)

The hub of Neapolitan religious life, the Duomo is also home to the twice-yearly liquefaction of San Gennaro's blood. (See the **Unusual and Interesting Things** chapter.)

Across 1000 years of complex history, multiple renovations happened here, in a variety of architectural styles. The interiors started out gothic, later became baroque and are currently a neo–gothic. Few traces of the original Angevin cathedral remain.

Looking to the back left of the church you'll spot a section from millennia ago. You can imagine the original cathedral, paired down and stark, the light from the heavens pouring through the stained-glass windows while the structure soared skyward. It must have been astounding. The decorative layers of the next 10 centuries each added more splendor.

The Duomo survived earthquakes, collapses, wars and bombings, each time coming back even better than before. Throughout history the greatest artists of their time worked here – Francesco Solimena, Giorgio Vasari, Perugino, Marco Pino, Pietro Bernini. The gothic arches and wooden ceiling were painted by Luca Giordano.

The Basilica of Santa Restituta

Along the left aisle, past the third chapel, you'll find the oldest early Christian basilica in Naples. Santa Restituta was built in the 4th century, *a thousand years before* this nearly thousand-year-old cathedral. Standing here, you'll need a moment to wrap your mind around the amount of time we're talking about. The artwork is from the 14th century, executed by Luca Giordano. Santa Restituta leads to the Baptistery of San Giovanni in Fonte, built by Emperor Constantine at the very cusp of Christianity.

The Minutolo Chapel

Meanwhile, on the right corner of the presbytery, the Gothic-Angevin Minutolo Chapel is one of the most important in the cathedral. It dates back to at least 1301. On its left wall look for the sarcophagus of Oso Minutolo, built in the mid 1300s. It wasn't until 1402 that Archbishop Enrico Minutolo entrusted the chapel to the Minutolo family (*his* family!) who incredibly still hold the patronage today. Can you imagine having a chapel in your family for 700 years?

The frescos in this chapel date back to 1288 and are attributed to Montano d'Arezzo. It is the first example of a new artistic language, created by Cimabue in the Basilica of St Francis of Assisi, making its way to Italy's south.

The Treasure of San Gennaro

Possibly the most important part of the cathedral is the Chapel of The Treasure of San Gennaro, the patron saint of Naples. Frescoed by Domenichino, with sculptures by Cosimo Fanzago and painting by the magnificent José de Ribera, it really is tremendous.

Twice each year the ceremony for the liquefaction of San Gennaro's blood happens right here. (See the **Unusual and Interesting Things** chapter.) Next door to the Duomo, the Museum of the Treasure of San Gennaro is home to the largest and oldest collection of treasures *in the world*. (See the **Museums** chapter for more.)

Even if you didn't look at the chapels or didn't bother with the history here, this cathedral is astounding. Your eye will immediately be drawn upward – the ceilings and the cupola, the mosaics and the frescos all are mesmerizing.

It has been argued (by me) that no trip to Naples is complete without a stop at this spectacular cathedral.

Address: Via Duomo, 147
What's nearby: The Jago Museum, Pio Monte di Misericordia (Caravaggio) and the Via Tribunali which has half the things in this book!

16.
Remarkable Castles and Palaces in Naples

Never fear Rome, the serpent lies coiled in Naples.

~ Sicilian proverb

In Naples, castles and palaces are entirely different structures. While the castles are solid, heavy, medieval defense structures, the palaces of Naples are a sumptuous reflection of the city's crushing beauty.

At one time Naples was known as *la città dei sette castelli,* the city of seven castles. It is possibly the city with the most castles in the world. This important port city needed a strategic defense system, so over the centuries the following castles were built: Castel Capuano, Castel dell'Ovo, Castel Nuovo (Maschio Angioino), Castel Sant'Elmo, Castel del Carmine, Castello di Nisida and Forte Vigliena.

Naples is also home to multiple beautiful palaces. Caserta, just outside the city, is the largest palace *in all of Europe*.

Find a way to get at least one of the following locations onto your **must-see** list and into your Naples itinerary.

1. Castel Nuovo/ Maschio Angioino

Known by Neapolitans as *Maschio Angioino*, in 1279 this somewhat forbidding castle on the bay was built by Charles I of Anjou. It is still one of Naples' most iconic architectural landmarks 800 years on. From 1279 until 1815, this was the royal seat of the Kings of Naples. The castle looks medieval with its five imposing round towers but look a little closer and you'll see a magnificent Renaissance marble arch that was added in the 15th century.

In 1309 King Robert renovated and expanded the castle, turning it into a center of culture. His passion for the arts and literature had him host important personalities of the time, like Petrarch and Boccaccio (writer of the *Decameron*). The most important painters of the time were called to Naples to adorn the castle walls, including

Pietro Cavallini, Montano d' Arezzo, and the greatest painter of the time, Giotto, who painted the Palatine Chapel in 1332.

In 1343 Castel Nuovo became the official residence of one of the 14th century's most intriguing women, Queen Joanna I. I recommend listening to a couple of podcasts about Joanna. I enjoyed both *The Rest Is History* podcast episode about Naples, which tells her story, and Noble Blood's episode on *The Trials of Joanna of Naples*. (I also have a book recommendation about Joanna in the **Reading List** chapter.) Her life reads like *Game of Thrones*, without the dragons. Knowing about the intrigue, deception, subterfuge and murder that was going on inside these walls during Joanna's reign makes both this castle and Naples itself even more compelling.

To be honest though, it was the tales of mad King Ferrante that had me racing to Castel Nuovo. When I heard the crazy stories about his *museum of mummies* and murder in the *Salon of the Barons*, I had to come see it for myself. So, let me tell you about King Ferrante.

Who Was King Ferrante?

In 1443 Ferrante's father King Alphonso V of Aragon conquered the throne of Naples. He rebuilt Castel Nuovo in its current Catalan-Gothic style with the five round towers, adding the beautiful Renaissance marble arch in the entryway. Alphonso's court of artists and great minds rivaled that of the Medici in Florence.

Alphonso had no children with his wife, but did manage to father a few with his mistresses, one of which was the endlessly interesting (and completely crazy) Ferdinand I, known as Ferrante. Wanting Ferrante to be his heir, Alphonso moved the illegitimate son into the castle to live with him. When his father died, Ferrante became King at age 35.

Under his reign (1458–1494) Naples did well. Ferrante was a prominent character in the Italian Renaissance, surrounding himself with artists and humanists. He built a strong military and a formidable navy and was recognized as one of the most powerful political minds of the time. He was also utterly ruthless.

And here's where things get a little quirky. Although his father had legitimized him, there were still plenty of contenders wanting to steal his throne. Ferrante knew that to be seen as a powerful and respected leader he needed to utterly defeat his enemies. In the process he became more and more ruthless, and crazier.

Ferrante devised a special punishment for nobles who rose up against him. In a wicked twist on *keep your enemies close*, he not only killed them, but had them embalmed and mummified. Then he dressed them in everyday clothes and posed them in what he called his 'black museum'.

He routinely took potentially treasonous guests on tours of this macabre museum, giving them insight into what lay ahead should they betray him. Whether just the license of TV writers or whether it actually happened (I've heard both), in the TV series *The Borgias,* Ferrante staged a madcap last supper with 18 of his mummified enemies sitting around the table. The shock value of these nutty antics must have been sensational. I have no idea whether it is fact or legend. I asked the guide on my most recent foray into the exploits of King Ferrante if that dinner party actually happened. She thought for a moment, then told me, 'The atmosphere of the castle seems more intense when we believe this to be true'. So, let's believe it to be true.' I wouldn't put it past him.

Ferrante and the Conspiracy of the Barons

Between 1485 and 1486, the Neapolitan aristocracy staged a mini revolution against mad king Ferrante. The short version of the story says he defeated them pretty quickly. He awarded some of the traitorous barons amnesty, which turned out to be yet another of his wacky tricks.

Ferrante cooked up an elaborate plan to lure the enemy barons to the castle. He staged a fake royal wedding to which they were all invited guests. Decked out in their royal wedding-appropriate finery, they entered the throne room, spectacular with its frescos and high vaulted ceilings. The doors were locked, trapping the unsuspecting barons inside. Ferrante's archers (until this point hidden on the circular balcony high above) stood up and rained arrows down on them, killing the barons like fish in a barrel. Ferrante had said the barons would never leave the castle, which proved to be true. They were in fact, never seen again.

Skeltons that are potentially theirs were found below the castle, some with fragments of clothing that match a baron's clothes from that time. The bones have been tested and proven to be from that era. You can see them when you visit the castle.

Ferrante, the Prisons and the Crocodile

This one may only be legend as archaeologists have yet to find crocodile bones, but the story is part of Castel Nuovo's lore, so let's run with it.

During Ferrante's time, prisoners held in the dungeons below the castle kept disappearing. They soon discovered a crocodile had been slipping through an opening in the basement. He would quickly grab a prisoner by the leg and drag him back out into the moat to eat him. Supposedly Ferrante used this as a convenient, no fuss death sentence. Throw a convict down there and let the crocodile in the moat get him. Eventually the crocodile was fed a poisoned horse leg, captured, taxidermied and hung on the entrance door of Castel Nuovo.

I recommend taking the tour of Castel Nuovo. It really is fantastic. As part of the guided tour of the castle you ascend the stone exterior staircase into the tremendous Sala dei Baroni, an absolute masterpiece of French-Gothic architecture. Even without the story of the barons, I think this former throne room is cool to see. (You can only access this part of the castle with the castle's private tour.) The tour not only lays the story out for you, pointing out where everything went down, but it also takes you downstairs into the castle basement to see the bones of the barons, patches of clothing intact. They'll show you archeological ruins, and also take you to the top of the castle to look out over Naples. The castle's guides are walking talking encyclopedias of knowledge about the building and all of its principal occupants. They are also wonderful storytellers.

While all the cruise ship people are shoulder to shoulder squished into Via San Gregorio Armeno, make your way over here. Each time I've come, there has been hardly anyone else here.

Tickets: The tour ticket office is on the right-hand side of the courtyard.
What's nearby: Be sure to check out the archaeological ruins in Piazza Municipio and, depending on when you're reading this, the underground museum at the Municipio metro station if it has opened. Teatro San Carlo, Galleria Umberto I, Piazza Plebiscito, the Palazzo Royale and Gran Gaffe Gambrinus are all right here too.

2. Castel dell'Ovo

A gorgeous little walk along the coastline from Castel Nuovo, this 12th century Norman castle is probably the most famous of Naples' castles. It owes its name, the *Castle of the Egg*, to the Roman scribe Virgil. Virgil wrote that he hid a magical egg in the foundations of the fortress and, were that egg to break, Naples and the castle would fall. Luckily for us, both are still standing.

Another legend is attached to this castle. This is the place from which the heartbroken siren Parthenope failed to seduce Ulysses with her song. One story says from here her tears created the Gulf of Naples, others say it was here that she washed ashore. Regardless, this is where it all began, where the ancient Greeks first settled, naming the island *Megaride*. Then the Roman general Lucullus built a villa here, taking advantage of the stupendous views. Roughly 1100 years later the Normans built the current castle, home to Naples' rulers until King Charles I of Anjou built Castel Nuovo.

When the new castle became home to the kings, this one was briefly the seat of the Royal Chamber and the State Treasury, before becoming a prison. Empress Constance of the Holy Roman Empire was imprisoned here as was my favorite, Queen Joanna I of Naples. Today the castle is mostly used for exhibitions and special events, and is a super popular spot for weddings. The castle itself is mostly empty, but you can (sometimes) get a booking to go inside and see the Byzantine frescoed rooms, the towers, the loggia and the prison of Queen Joanna. You can walk around the outside for free, and the views are sensational.

Personally, I think a walk to this castle is a must. In the old days Mr. Mode and his friends would bring my little tour groups here to have pizza in one of the restaurants along the Via Partenope, after which we would walk over to the castle. It is lit up beautifully at night and is quite magical to walk around.

More recently I have liked walking here from Castel Nuovo, stopping for warm taralli from the food trucks along the way. You'll see locals sitting at the wall with a cold beer and a warm taralli, looking out over the water. I'm not a beer drinker, but even beer–free, the experience is *lovely*. Warm taralli are pretty fantastic too.

The 17th century Fontana del Gigante is just before you arrive at the castle and makes for fabulous photos both day and night. I also love nights spent dining al fresco at one of the restaurants on the little island. It's a gorgeous way to spend an equally gorgeous Neapolitan evening.

3. Castel Sant' Elmo

This is the medieval castle majestically watching over Naples and the bay from the Vomero hill. Adjacent to the beautiful Certosa di San Martino and the Pedamentina, its name pops up a few times inside this book. Sant' Elmo is the largest medieval castle in Naples.

The name comes from a 10th century church of Sant' Erasmo which became shortened to Sant' Ermo then eventually St' Elmo. The castle structure dates to the 1200s, but underwent major rebuilds over the next two centuries. In 1537 it took on its current hexagonal star-shape.

The castle was a prison from the 19th century until the 1970s. Now it is known for the Museo Novacento, a museum of 20th century Neapolitan art museum, and home to the Campania Museum complex.

I come up here partly because the calories expended walking to the top counteract every gastronomic sin you plan to commit for the rest of the day, and partly because, good Lord – the views! These have to be the most jaw dropping views in all of Naples. From here you can see most of the city, all of Vesuvius, the islands (Capri, Ischia and Procida), the Phlegraean Fields and the Matese mountains. Add in the azure Neapolitan skies and lemon-hued sunshine and you just know you are about as close to Heaven as a human can get.

There is lots to walk see up here, along with a coffee shop/eatery where you can enjoy the most average cup of coffee available in a city bursting with the world's best coffee (but take in the view from the giant semicircular window and all coffee sins are forgiven).

Check out the **City of Staircases** chapter and then, from the castle take the Pedamentina staircase down the hill to the Spanish Quarter (about 30 minutes).

What's nearby: Certosa di San Martino, the Pedamentina, the beautiful Vomero neighborhood.

4. The Royal Palace of Naples

A two-minute walk from the Castel Nuovo brings you to the 17th century Royal Palace of Naples. For 150 years this was the home of the Spanish Viceroys. Designed by Domenico Fontana, the most prestigious architect in the Western World, the palace has a high Renaissance design rather than a fortified castle look.

In 1743, when Charles of Bourbon became king, he decided this beautiful palace would be the royal residence. He enlarged it and gave it a new baroque facelift courtesy of Francesco De Mira and Antonio

Vaccaro. This was Naples' heyday, the time when the two most important and most cultural cities in Europe were Paris and Naples, as such the palace reflects the fabulous opulence of the time. It is now a museum full of art, frescos, tapestries and decor from the greatest artists of the Spanish and Bourbon eras. After the unification of Italy, it became the residence of the Savoy royal family.

The palace lets you experience the glorious wealth of 18th century Naples. Take the majestic Staircase of Honor, considered the most beautiful staircase in all of Europe, up to the Historical Apartment. The apartment is splendorous and contains masterpieces from the Bourbon period's most prestigious artists. These rooms were originally used for hosting royal parties.

The palace is also home to the two million books of the National Library, not only the most important library in all Southern Italy, but one of the first libraries in the world.

The palace offers several outdoor spaces including the Courtyard of Honor, with its access to the park-like royal gardens with their secret paths, avenues and statues. There are also the Courtyard of the Coaches, the Belvedere Courtyard and the Hanging Gardens with their fantastic view of Vesuvius and the Gulf of Naples

When Charles of Bourbon moved in, he built Europe's oldest opera house next door, the Teatro San Carlo.

There is so much to see right here. Along with the palace and the Teatro San Carlo, there's the Galleria Umberto I shopping center. (Put it on your **must-see** list – the building is sensational.) The palace looks out over the Piazza Plebiscito and the Gran Caffe Gambrinus. Cross the piazza to via Toledo and you are moments away from the

Spanish Quarter. From the piazza you are also just a few minutes' sunshiney walk from the Chiaia neighborhood

The Royal Palace is so central and close to so many incredible sites in Naples, it makes an ideal place to build a day of nonstop entertainment around.

What's nearby: Piazza Plebiscito, Teatro San Carlo, Galleria Umberto I, Gran Caffe Gambrinus, Castel Nuovo.

5. Palazzo dello Spagnolo

Our next adventure takes us to one of my favorite neighborhoods in Naples, the Sanità. Imagine if Rome and Cairo had a baby, but it turned out to be twins. One would be the chaotic, crowded Spanish Quarter, while the other less manageable twin would be the Sanità. Exciting, loud and incredibly cool, the Sanità reminds me a bit of Berlin twenty years ago – artsy and vibey.

THE SANITÀ

During the Greek and Roman times this area was a burial site, just outside the city walls. We looked at some of the subterranean attractions of the Sanità in the **Underground** chapter, but today we fast-forward to the late 16th century.

Located immediately north of the historic center and just below the Capodimonte Palace (museum), this neighborhood became a new home for the rich and noble families of Naples. While the plague and cholera ridden streets of the historic center were perilous to the health of those who had options, this new woodsy neighborhood with its fresh streams was considered healthy – *sanità*. Wealthy folk moved here and filled its streets with beautiful baroque architecture, palazzi, and churches suited to the monied class. For a time, this was the place to be.

Now let's visit one of the most magnificent palazzi in all of Naples:

Palazzo dello Spagnolo

In the heart of the Sanità you will find two breathtakingly beautiful baroque palaces, the Palazzo San Felice and the one I want to show you, the Palazzo Spagnolo. Both were built by 18th century architect Fernando Sanfelice, one in 1724 for himself and the other in 1738 for Nicola Moscati, the Marchese di Poppano. Just around the corner from one another, they look like twins, except one of them (Spagnolo) is in better shape than the other. Sanfelice worked on many other Neapolitan buildings, but these two were his greatest pride.

From the street you could easily walk past the Spagnolo palace. An archway with giant old wooden doors keeps the palace secret from prying eyes. For a couple of centuries these same doors kept the wealthy inhabitants of the palazzo safe at night. Inhale deeply before walking through the arch, because even when you've done it a hundred times, you are only one second away from having the breath sucked right out of you.

The archway opens into a small courtyard from which this architectural work of art erupts skyward. Four floors of fairytale magic burst up to the heavens, the energy of the building made more dynamic and forceful by the small space surrounding it. It would still be pretty if set in large grounds with trees and grass and pathways, but there is something about the immediacy of this environment that makes your heart pound.

What you are seeing here is a double open staircase, crisscrossing its way upward, manifested in a series of arches. The central spine is made of four tall arches stacked atop one another, with gorgeous stucco'd ceilings that draw the eye up. On either side of each center arch, two more arches spread out like wings. The facade is made with shifting planes on each level, causing a hawk wing effect. Moving up the helix staircases, the stucco'd transoms of these wings hold sculpted busts above the doorways on each level. Standing in front of the palace, the architecture looks like the wings of a hawk as it takes flight. Except this optical illusion happens in calming shades of cream and a soft pastel green. I am completely biased, but in my opinion, this is the most beautiful building in Naples.

The central staircase building connects the rest of the palazzo which takes up the remaining three sides of the courtyard. Although part of the complex is now offices, the bulk of it is private apartments and I think possibly an Airbnb, although that could be wishful thinking on my part. Because it is private homes, you can't explore the staircases. Really you can only spend a few minutes here, taking it all in and imagining yourself living in one of the apartments with their 8-foot-tall windows and Juliet balconies.

The palazzo was originally known as Palazzo Moscati. When Tommaso Atienza, nicknamed *Lo Spagnolo* (the Spaniard), purchased the lower floor apartments, it became known as Palazzo dello Spagnolo.

Although somewhat gentrified, the palace still looks a little dilapidated, reminding you that in the very recent past this was part of an impoverished neighborhood. Just up the street it's worthwhile looking in on Palazzo Sanfelice, the once gorgeous home of the architect. You can see the bones of how fabulous this palazzo must once have been, but unlike Spagnolo it hasn't been prettied up, and looks very run down.

Getting there: Stroll two blocks from the Duomo, cross via Floria and you're in the Sanità. I would pair visiting this palazzo with a visit to the Jago Museum, a wander up the outdoor market street, lunch at Isabella de Cham or Ai Tre Santi (super famous pizzeria diagonally across the street from Isabella) and an afternoon visit to the catacombs.
Address: Via Virgini, 19
What's nearby: The Jago Museum, Isabella de Cham, Ai Tre Santi, Poppella, San Gaudioso catacombs.

From here we go to a palace that needs its own chapter, the largest palace in all of Europe, let's visit the Palace of Caserta.

17.
The Royal Palace of Caserta

Pale death beats equally at the poor man's gate and at the palace of kings.

~ Horace

Did you know the largest royal palace in all of Europe is just outside of Naples? The Royal Palace of Caserta was designed to rival both Versailles and the Royal Palace in Madrid. When construction began in 1751, this massive palace was intended to be the primary residence of the King of Naples.

Although built for Charles VII of Naples (Charles III of Spain), he never actually spent a single night here. In 1759 he abdicated the Neapolitan throne to become King of Spain. His son Ferdinand IV of Naples and Sicily became his successor. (Confusingly he is also known as Ferdinand I of The Two Sicilies.)

A UNESCO World Heritage Site

To give you an idea of how huge this UNESCO World Heritage site is, the total volume is 2 million square meters, it covers an area of 47,000 square meters, and the floor space across the five stories takes up 138,000 square meters. Did I mention it is *huge*?

Part of what makes Caserta so exceptional is the way it marries the palace with its spectacular park and gardens, the natural woodland, hunting lodges, and believe it or not, a silk factory. It all feels integrated into the natural setting, instead of being imposed upon it, which is part of why it became a UNESCO site.

Versailles was the model for this project, and you can definitely see the similarities. The greatest aligning factor however, was the way both provided not only a home for the King, but also for the court and the government, all under one gigantic roof. Essentially both Versailles and the Royal Palace at Caserta took on the social structure of small cities. In fact, the original proposal contemplated a virtual city, housing not just the court and King, but all the main political and cultural elites of the kingdoms of Naples and Sicily. Architect Mario Gioffredo envisaged it containing a university, a museum, a library, cabinet bureaus, even the military high command.

Along with governmental logistics, Caserta provided the King and the administrative center of the kingdom a safe base. Far from a potential sea front attack, they could also maintain a safe distance from the revolt-predisposed and overcrowded city of Naples.

The Palace

The Royal Palace of Caserta has a long, balustraded facade overlooking long, beautiful gardens. As with Versailles, the intention was to showcase power and wealth, but this time it was of the Bourbon dynasty. The palace has five floors, 1200 rooms, 24 state apartments, 34 staircases, and 1,026 fireplaces.

Above the opulent *piano reale* (the King's floor), there is another equally magnificent floor. The palace also has a big library and a theater in the design of the beautiful Teatro San Carlo in Naples.

Forty monumental rooms in the palace are completely decorated with frescos, almost double that of Versailles, which has a mere 22 monumental rooms.

The Park

The park and gardens of Caserta are a sight to behold. Starting at the back facade of the palace they run more than 3 km/2 miles, swooping up the hill at the end. The park has two gardens, an Italian–style garden with an artificial lake and an English garden, considered one of the most important and most picturesque in all of Europe. Covering 120 hectares (300 acres), the gardens are bordered with woods and have statues scattered throughout. Fed by their own aqueduct, the gardens are replete with cascading fountains. The original plans included a monumental 20 km avenue connecting the palace to Naples, but it was never built.

You can walk the length of the gardens, take a horse and carriage, or rent a bike. Expect to encounter locals from the town of Caserta, walking, jogging or even stretching out in the sun on the grass.

Maria Carolina

Ferdinand was actually pretty hopeless and rather disinterested in running the kingdom, so that job fell to his fascinating wife Maria Carolina, born an Archduchess of Austria. When they married in 1768, she became Queen of Naples and Sicily.

Maria Carolina's mother, Empress Maria Teresa, had already made two unsuccessful attempts to marry off her daughters to Spanish royalty – unsuccessful because each of the prior brides died of smallpox before the nuptials could be arranged. Maria Carolina wasn't at all thrilled about the proposed wedding. It felt like a bad omen with two previous sisters dying after becoming betrothed to Spain. Also, she thought Ferdinand was ugly. Nonetheless something was working, as she bore him 18 babies over the next 21 years (only seven of which survived into adulthood).

Basically, she ran the show. Maria Carolina ruled the Kingdom of Naples and Sicily brilliantly and successfully for 40 years. During her tenure she implemented reform and modernization of Naples.

Between you and me, I had never heard of her until my first trip to Caserta. However, she was vastly more interesting and more consequential than her beloved and famous younger sister, Marie Antoinette.

More Recently

From 1923 to 1943 Caserta was home to the Italian Air Force Academy. Unfortunately, it was bombed by the US in 1943 and subsequently looted, losing almost all the furnishings. (After the war, the Italian government took care of the palace, returning and restoring everything as best as possible.) During the 1943 allied invasion it became headquarters to the Allied Supreme Commander. In 1945, the signing of the surrender of Germany's forces in Italy took place the Palace of Caserta. The first war crimes trial took place here too. German general Anton Dostler was sentenced to death here, although the execution took place in nearby Aversa.

In 1998 the Palace of Caserta was one of the filming locations for *Star Wars: The Phantom Menace*. All the scenes involving explosions were shot on a replica set in Leavesden Studios.

Visiting Caserta

I recommend making an afternoon out of visiting the palace at Caserta. There is tons to see and do here. Plan on having lunch, or at least coffee and a pastry at the cafe overlooking the gardens, then rent a bike or walk the entire length of the gardens. The views from both directions are magnificent. After the outdoor experience, head inside and make your way up the grand staircase to visit the royal apartments.

A Comedy of Errors

My first trip to the palace was equal parts a comedy of errors and proof of my travel philosophy that if Plan A doesn't work out, Plan B invariably turns out better anyway.

I had planned out the entire day to fit in a long list of things I wanted to see and do at Caserta. Yet as I ran onto the train platform in Salerno everything went sideways – the train was already pulling out of the station. It was a Monday in December, the days were short, and the next train wasn't for a couple of precious hours.

Of course, I didn't have any spare days on that trip to swap out, so I had to shift to Plan B. I took the next train and arrived at the palace somewhat late in the afternoon. The lady in the ticket office took pity on my dashed plans and told me to do the gardens first as they would close in an hour or so. Then she showed me a specific gate, which would be the only one still unlocked, and told me to slip through that into the palace.

I went straight to the cafe so I could enjoy a coffee with the view, but they had already closed. Then I went to the bike rental guy, who told me he wouldn't rent me a bike as there was only an hour before closing time. So, I walked through the gardens. And what a joy that was! Statues hidden in the trees and bushes – I would surely have missed them had I been on a bike. Walking the gardens I got a much better look at everything, was able to take loads of photos, and could really appreciate the long views in each direction.

Then, like a thief in the night, I slipped through the only unlocked gate and into the palace proper. The ticket lady's directions helped me find the reverse way to the bookshop to trade my driver's license for an audio guide, and I was off to explore the royal apartments.

At first, I thought I must have made a wrong turn, because when I got to the grand staircase, a *monumental* staircase packed with tourists in every photo and video I'd ever seen, there was not another human in sight. Of course I swanned around taking photos, draping myself over the balustrades, not quite able to believe my luck.

But it got even better. It turns out I was the only person left in the palace! Other than a scattering of employees sitting in the corner of random rooms, I had the entire palace to myself. And it was *incredible*. I took photos down long hallways with not a soul in sight. I ducked under the velvet rope in the throne room and lay on the floor to look up at the frescoed ceiling, figuring at worst I would get kicked out. But no one came by. I learned all about my new friend Maria Carolina as I wandered around her former home. It was one of the most wonderful experiences ever.

When I returned to the bookshop to swap back the audio guide for my license, I asked the guy behind the counter where everybody was and if Mondays were normally quiet. He told me there had been 10,000 people over the weekend and also mentioned the palace was pretty full all day until about 3pm, when I'd arrived.

I had an hour before my train home and it was already dark out, so asked him where to get a glass of wine nearby. He not only told me about a gorgeous wine bar in the circular piazza a few blocks from the palace, but while I was enroute he called the bar and had them send a waiter to meet me along the way.

I sat outside in the square that was a circle and enjoyed a glass of local wine and some snacks while looking at one of the prettiest Christmas trees I've ever seen. When it was time to head to the station, the bar owner had one of the waiters walk with me, not because it was dangerous (it wasn't) but just because it was a nice thing to do.

My Plan A could never have been as magical as my default Plan B turned out to be!

Getting there: Take the train from Naples then cross the street to Reggia Caserta, the Palace of Caserta.

18.
The Teatro San Carlo

Nothing contributes more to a man's fame than to have written operas, and especially for Naples.

~ Wolfgang Amadeus Mozart

Across from Piazza Plebiscito, right in the middle of everything, stands the oldest opera house in all of Europe. Built 41 years before the Scala in Milan and 55 years before La Fenice in Venice, Naples quite literally set the stage for what was to come.

In 1737 King Charles of Bourbon built the magnificent Teatro San Carlo, cementing Naples' position as one of the greatest culture capitals in all of Europe. No detail was spared in its construction and decoration. From the frescoed ceiling to the horseshoe-shaped six tiers of elaborate opera boxes, from the royal box to the velvet draped stage, this opera house was and still is *stupendous*.

Each of the 184 opera boxes has a mirror on the wall angled to the royal box. Ostensibly so that you could display the same reaction as the king, it also became a perfect way to spy on everyone else. Who was sleeping, who was smooching, who was getting up to no good. To this day, you can still keep an eye on the goings on during a performance at the San Carlo.

Performing at the San Carlo instantly became a prestigious event and across four centuries the greatest artists of all time have performed here. Opera, orchestra, ballet – the San Carlo has always been home to a broad range of performing arts. In fact, the San Carlo's dance company is the oldest in all of Italy.

From the beginning, the four conservatories of Naples (the Neapolitan School) put the city at the cutting edge of the musical world. Remember, in the 1700s the two most sophisticated cities in all of Europe were Paris and Naples. The San Carlo drew the attention of the greatest composers of the time including Haydn, Händel and even Mozart, who in 1778 set the first act of *Così Fan Tutte* in one of Naples historical coffee houses.

Over nearly 300 years, the San Carlo has survived wars, a great fire and a revolution. However, it wasn't until March 2020's coronavirus pandemic that the doors were shuttered for the longest time in the theater's history. Before long, the San Carlo adapted to Covid 19's restrictions by providing virtual performances online. In order to make opera accessible to all, the theater offered tickets for a mere 99 cents. For an art form that can feel as though it's the exclusive playground of the monied classes, this gave everyone a sense of equality.

It wasn't, however, the first time the theater had made the opera accessible to all. We know about Naples' suspended coffee/ *caffè sospeso* (see the **Coffee** chapter), where you pay for a second cup so someone less fortunate can have a quality coffee. The same thing has been happening at the San Carlo over the past few years. Members leave a *suspended ticket*, money to provide an opera ticket for someone who cannot otherwise afford to attend. The suspended ticket concept has opened the world of opera to an audience who would otherwise have been excluded. I *love* this.

While writing this book I went to a performance of *Turandot* at the Teatro San Carlo. One of the things that blew me away was the cross section of the community in attendance. All ages were represented – not just wealthy old folks. Kids with blue hair and multiple facial piercings, college students, hippie dudes, working class folks and fashionably dressed hoi-polloi. Watching from my opera box (and spying in the mirror), I was surprised at the number of young people in the audience – teens and twenty-somethings, as fully engaged and mesmerized by the show as I was.

The couple sitting next to me (season ticket holders in their late 50s) told me that it's always like this. The thirty-somethings sharing our box concurred. There's always a full house for each performance and an audience comprised of all types and all ages. Both couples 'suspend' their tickets to any performance they can't attend.

Maybe it's about Neapolitans pride in their city, their culture and their heritage. If you live somewhere with all this magic available to you, why not make it part of your life's experiences?

Which brings me to my next point. Seeing Turandot in this sensational, historical venue, with some of the world's finest acoustics, was one of the great moments in my life. To witness Calaf sing 'Nessun Dorma' in this setting gave me goosebumps and definitely brought tears to my eyes. I'm not entirely sure I breathed during the aria.

If staying a few nights in Naples, and I really hope you will, try to take in a performance of *anything* at the San Carlo. My plan had been to go see whatever was playing, regardless of whether it interested me or not, just for the experience of being at the San Carlo. How I lucked my way into *Turandot* I will never know.

If you can't get to an evening performance, take a tour of the theater during the day. It really gives you a sense of the opulence of 18th century Naples, and a window into how the other half lived. Until you're inside the Teatro San Carlo, it's hard to get a concept of how awe-inspiring the six floors of opera boxes really are. The decoration, the majesty, the beauty – all of it. Put this one on your Naples **must-see** list!

Address: Via San Carlo, 98F
Website: https://www.teatrosancarlo.it/en/
What's nearby: Piazza Plebiscito, The Palazzo Reale, Gran Gambrinus Caffe, Galleria Umberto.

19.
Interesting & Unusual Things to See in Naples

Naples is a city of contrasts, where chaos and charm dance together.

~ Unknown

Naples is filled to bursting with completely fascinating things. Whatever gets you excited in life, Naples has it in spades. I could have written a book called *1001 Fascinating and Unusual Things To See in Naples* – there is so much intrigue here. Instead, I'll try to narrow it down to just a few.

The following items are random things I find fascinating in Naples.

1. San Gennaro's Magic Blood

Naples can rest easy tonight, for its saint still bleeds.

Naples is a glorious mix of superstition, religion and magic, and I cannot get enough of it. One of the city's big superstitions revolves around the blood of their patron saint, San Gennaro. Before you blow it off as a load of hooey, wait until you find out what happened historically when Gennaro's blood didn't do its magic trick. But first let's get acquainted with San Gennaro.

Back in the late 3rd and very early 4th centuries Gennaro was the Bishop of Benevento. At the time Diocletian was the emperor of Rome. He was one of the greatest emperors, unless you happened to be a Christian. Christianity was a new religion at that time. The empire welcomed and hosted loads of different religions, and Diocletian didn't really have a problem with Christianity, except that this brand spanking new religion stipulated there could only be *one* God. So Christians couldn't revere both their God *and* the emperor. This was problematic because emperors were semi-deified, so having Christians around weakened the power of the emperor. They had to go. Persecutions ran rampant and for the next hundred years or so Christians had to practice this new faith on the super down-low.

Gennaro was given the chance to recant but refused, so he was sentenced to death. Supposedly he was meant to be mauled by beasts in the amphitheater, but when they bowed down at his feet and refused to eat him, the Romans opted for beheading instead. On September 19, 305 AD in Misenium, Gennaro's head was chopped off. Legend says the stone where his blood fell turns red on September 19 each year, to this day.

Meanwhile, back in Misenium someone scooped up some of Gennaro's blood. This blood is kept in a sealed glass ampoule under lock and key. And here's where the magic comes in. Three times per year: the Saturday before the first Sunday in May, September 19 and again on December 16, the faithful gather, Gennaro's blood ampoule is brought out, and (if luck is on our side) it liquifies.

If San Gennaro's blood liquifies, it's a good omen, which is lucky because it does in fact liquify most of the time. On the other hand, on most of the rare occasions the dried blood hasn't become liquid, really bad juju has hit. For example, some of the years it didn't liquify: 1939 World War II began; 1940 World War II; 1943 the Nazi's occupied Naples, also a few months later Vesuvius erupted again; 1973 Cholera epidemic; 1980 Earthquake in nearby Irpinia (50 km east of Naples) killed 3000; 2016 (December) some think this played into American politics the following year; 2020 Covid (this was the December 16 round – the other two that year were fine).

The superstitious believe the worst of the bad omens occur if the blood doesn't liquify on the Saint's Day – September 19.

When disasters occur, Neapolitans turn to their patron saint to save them. Famously, when Vesuvius erupted in 1631 and Naples looked to be in danger, on December 16 Gennaro's blood was brought out and, wouldn't you know it, the eruption stopped. (Hence the December 16 celebrations.)

If you are in Naples on September 19, there will be massive festivities to celebrate Saint's Day. All three of the days see huge events in Naples.

2. An Archaeological Secret in the Middle of Town

Technically it's not a secret, but since even my friends who've been to Naples a million times have never heard of this, I thought you might enjoy it too.

I was super excited while exploring the streets and alleys around the Duomo to stumble upon a complex of Roman ruins. The **Carminello ai Mannesi Archeological Complex** dates back to the 1st century BC. The oldest parts of the complex are from a house or *domus* of some unknown person. Then, roughly a hundred years later, a thermal complex was built on top of it. This complex was built on two levels – the lower level probably had the cistern, worker areas, storage etc, while the upper area had the thermal rooms (think day spa) and socializing areas.

In the 2nd century AD two rooms on the bottom floor were made into a Mithraeum. This is the equivalent of a church or temple, but for the 4000-year-old Indo-Persian religion of Mithras. When slaves were brought to the Roman Empire they brought their religions with them, which is probably how Mithraism arrived on these shores. When you see pagan temples in scary movies, they are normally based on Mithraea. If you are not familiar with Mithraism, I suggest doing a little research – it's fascinating.

After an earthquake in the 5th century, the complex was abandoned and fell into decay. Twelve hundred years later the church of Carmine ai Mannesi was built on top of their buried ruins. They were only rediscovered when the church was destroyed by a bomb in 1943. The ruins then languished for 30 years before excavations began in 1973, revealing just how important this discovery was. Madness followed, however, when in the 1980s the area became an illegal parking lot and (apparently) the stable for a Mafia family. In 1993 the court took charge and evacuated the area.

When it's open (it's often closed) you can still see several rooms that were part of the thermal baths, a big rectangular room covered in mosaics and also walls with frescos from the original domus. In the rooms used for the Mithraeum, a white stucco relief represents Mithras sacrificing a bull. There is a central fountain and a staircase that would have originally been covered in marble.

Although it is frequently closed, you can see much of the complex from the street. It is only a 3-minute walk from the Duomo, so it is definitely worthwhile popping by when you're in the area.

Address: Vico Primo Carminiello ai Mannesi
What's nearby: The Duomo, the Girolamani Complex.

3. The Pappacoda Chapel

This is one of those quirky things that I get a kick out of but wouldn't necessarily make a special trip across town to see. However, you'll be in the area anyway, so you might as well stop by for a quick look.

The Pappacoda Chapel is now owned by the Oriental Institute of the University of Naples. Remember, Naples has literally hundreds of churches, many of which were deconsecrated during Napoleon's time, others were abandoned and plenty are still locked up. If you keep your eyes peeled as you explore Naples, you'll spot churches with chains and padlocks on their front doors. Plenty of them haven't been unlocked in decades. (So, it's not so unusual to find a church that has been repurposed – like the Jago Museum.)

This small, single nave church with a tremendous marble facade was built in 1415, commissioned by King Ladislaus of Durazzo, Artusio Pappacoda. The church was named for the tombs of two Pappacoda brothers buried here, one a bishop, the other a cardinal. The original frescos inside were destroyed during a restoration in 1772, but we're not here to see what's inside – this time it's what's *outside* the church that counts.

Outside, surrounding the door, you can see a huge, gothic portal made of marble. It would be so easy to walk past, but once you know it's there you can't help but be wowed by how elaborate it is. Sculpted by Abbot Antonio Baboccia da Piperno (1351–1435), it is incredibly intricate and completely magnificent.

Facing the church, look to the campanile down the left-hand side of the building. It would be lovely on its own, layered with different colors and textures, but look upwards and see the two hidden faces in the front facade next to the window. You have to wonder A) who are they and B) why are they up there? It's one of those oddball mysteries where no one seems to know the answer, and you can't find two people to tell you the same story. If I were doing a treasure hunt with kiddos, this would for sure be on it.

Address: Largo San Giovanni Maggiore, 118
What's nearby: The complex of Santa Chiara with the majolica cloister, the church of Gesù Nuovo, the Basilica of San Giovanni Maggiore.

4. Pizza Margherita Plaque

This is another one to keep an eye out for if you're walking past (but I wouldn't make a special trip specifically to see it).

Naples is the home of pizza. We always thought the history of Neapolitan pizza went back centuries, but it turns out it actually goes back millennia. At least two of them in fact.

Recently, a fresco was excavated in Pompeii depicting a tray of finger foods and what looks to be a pizza. Tomatoes didn't arrive to Italy until the 1500s, so our Pompeii pizza lacks *pomodori* and instead it appears to have pomegranate seeds on top.

The most iconic pizza to order in Naples is the Margherita. Like pretty much everything else here, this type of pizza is steeped in legend (although the truth of said legend may be a little bit wiggly). *Supposedly* this pizza was invented in 1889 by Rafael Esposito at Pizziera Brandi, when King Umberto I and Queen Margherita of Savoy were visiting the capital of the former southern kingdom. Legend says the queen was bored with the rich, French food popular with the European royal and noble classes, so asked Esposito, the most famous pizzaiolo at the time, to make her three different flavors of pizza. She didn't care for the first two, a garlicky marinara and a pizza Napoli with anchovies, but loved the third one. This one had three simple toppings – mozzarella, basil and crushed tomato, representing the red, white and green of the new Italian flag. (Italy unified and became one country in 1861.) Esposito immediately named the pizza for the queen and asked for her Royal Seal. Again *supposedly*, her chamberlain Camillo Galli then sent a handwritten note which still hangs on the wall in **Pizzeria Brandi** today.

And here is where it all gets a bit wiggly. Historians dispute the veracity of the note. They question the difference between the royal stamp used and the other royal stamps of the time, as well as the placement of said stamp. The stationery used to write the note is apparently not right either and the handwriting isn't a proper match for the chamberlain's. Added to that, this type of pizza was already widespread in Naples and is even mentioned in a book from 1866. Some folks say it could have been named for the placement of the mozzarella like the petals of a daisy, which is *margherita* in Italian.

Regardless, in 1989 on the 100th anniversary of the event, Pizzeria Brandi unveiled a plaque marking the location as the birthplace of the Margherita Piazza. If you're walking by, be sure to check it out. And maybe stop for a pizza.

Address: Salita Santa Anna di Palazzo, 1/2
What's nearby: Galleria Umberto I, Piazza del Plebiscito, Teatro San Carlo and the Bourbon Tunnel.

5. The Fountain of Spinacorona

Also known as *Fontana delle Zizze*, or the fountain of the boobs. This fountain is another oddball spot to have on your radar if you're wandering around the area, but I wouldn't necessarily make a trip specifically to see it.

Against the wall of the **Santa Caterina della Spina Corona** church, once again we meet our Greek siren friend Parthenope. It all likelihood there will have been a fountain here long before this one, but documents tells us this one was rebuilt in 1498, then again into its current form in the mid-16th century.

If you're wondering what they were thinking about in Naples in the mid-1500s, here is the answer for you. Parthenope with the legs of a centaur and the wings of an angel stands a little awkwardly atop Mount Vesuvius. From there, she heroically extinguishes the volcano's flames by firing water out of her clutched boobs. Like an Austin Powers Fembot.

An inscription reads: *Dum Vesevi Syrena Incendiary Mulcet* (While the Mermaid Softens the Fire Of Vesuvius).

To make it even more non-sensical, a violin is carved awkwardly into Vesuvius' left flank. (On our right.) The fountain also has the heraldic symbol of the Holy Roman Emperor, Charles I, because again, why not?

I often think the heads of the women who live in my neighborhood in the US would blow right off if they saw the water firing boobie fountains scattered around Italy (or the condom vending machines on public walls around every city).

This is a replica fountain, the original is kept safe inside the Museo San Martino.

Address: Santa Caterina della Spina Corona Church, Via Giuseppina Guacci Nobile, 9/13
What's nearby: Close to the port, two city blocks from Spaccanapoli and the San Severo church.

6. The Fontana del Gigante

This enormous 17th century work of art makes for a fabulous photo spot next to the **Castel dell' Ovo**. The Fountain of the Giant is three huge, gleaming white arches decorated with marine creatures and heraldic symbols.

In the 1600s, the fountain stood in the Piazza del Plebiscito near the Royal Palace. It was named for a neighboring statue of Jupiter known as *Il Gigante* – the Giant. Multiple paintings created in the 17th and 18th centuries show the two works in the piazza together.

In 1807, restoration works in the area required *Il Gigante* to be moved into storage, followed six years later by the fountain. The two remained out of sight for 70 years. An entire generation of Neapolitans never laid eyes on them. In 1882, the fountain was moved to the beautiful red and white Palazzo dell' Immacolatella at the Port of Naples. This stop was short lived though, as the expansion of the port required it to be moved again. Next the fountain went to the Villa del Popolo park, also near the port. It was 1889 now and the neighborhood was soon surrounded by warehouses and became super sketchy. Definitely not a good location for such a magnificent work of art. So, in 1906 the *Fontana del Gigante* moved to its final and suitably majestic location, overlooking the sea near the Castel dell'Ovo.

I love coming by here on bright sunny days, or at blue hour. The gleaming white marble becomes even more luminous by the intense blue of Naples' sea and sky during the day, or the potency of a Neapolitan evening blue hour. It's fantastic. The fountain is enormous, unusual looking, and is a tremendous backdrop for photos.

Address: The corner of Via Nazario Sauro and Via Parthenope. **What's nearby:** Castel dell'Ovo, the hot taralli stands along the waterfront. This is a 9-minute, gorgeous walk from Piazza del Plebiscito, The Palazzo Royale and Gran Caffe Gambrinus.

7. La Santerella

Now we move into the realm of a nun with magic powers. Most people know of San Gennaro, the patron saint of Naples. But outside of Neapolitans very few seem to have heard of the city's second co-patron saint, the only female saint of Naples, Mary Frances.

She was born Anna Maria Gallo to a middle-class family in the Spanish Quarter, in the early 1700s. Anna Maria's father was excessively violent, severely beating his family members on a regular basis. When she was 16, he tried to force her to marry, but she refused, instead asking permission to enter the Franciscan Third Order and become a nun, allowing her to stay in the family home.

She was accepted into the order in 1731 and became known as Maria Francesca (Mary Frances). She spent the next years doing charitable work in the neighborhood. Maria Francesca remained in the family home until 1753 when she and another nun moved into the small house of a priest. The two women lived on the second floor, sleeping on the floor, while the priest occupied the rooms above. While living there she received the stigmata and had many physical ailments, hardly surprising when you sleep on a hard floor in Naples. During this time, she wore gloves to hide the cuts on her hands while she was out and about doing her good works.

Pope Pius IX canonized her in 1867, making her the patron saint of pregnant women and women having trouble conceiving. In 1856, Ferdinand II, King of the Two Sicilies, turned the little house she had lived in until her death into a small church named Santa Maria Francesca della Cinque Piaghe – Saint Mary Frances of the Five Wounds.

Devotion to her has remained strong in the Spanish quarter, and she is credited with protecting her neighborhood during World War II. Her immediate neighborhood suffered only a little damage even though over 100 bombs were dropped on it.

At 7 am, expect to see a line of people waiting to enter **Santa Maria Francesca delle Cinque Piaghe**. Known by Neapolitans as *La Santarella,* it was (and still is) believed that by sitting in the saint's wooden chair your infertility will be cured. The ground floor of the apartment is now a little chapel. First you attend mass, then the nun opens a door behind the altar and those in need of help file upstairs. The room is a mini museum to Santa Maria Francesca with relics, paintings and some of her personal items hanging in frames on the walls. There is even a fantastically frightening wax figure of her, which would be funny if not for the seriousness of the scene.

The nun takes each man and woman one by one to sit in an old chair by the window. Here she quietly asks a question, says a benediction in a low voice and then holds a fereter or reliquary to the person's forehead and then their breast. Hopefully the fertility of the recipient is then restored or, if she is already pregnant, she will have an easy birth and a healthy baby.

La Santerella certainly seems to have been successful judging by the baby toys, pillows and baby acknowledgments in the room next door, sent from all over the world. Who knows – maybe the chapel was built over a temple to the fertility goddess? Regardless, something seems to be working here.

Quirky as it might seem, it's also quite beautiful. When you have hope, you can take on the world.

INTERESTING & UNUSUAL THINGS TO SEE IN NAPLES

Address: Santa Maria delle Cinque Piaghe, Vico Tre Re, 13
What's nearby: This is in the heart of the Spanish Quarter, just below the Vomero Hill. Take the staircase down the hill from the Castel Sant' Elmo and the Certosa San Martino, or meander down the street from the Toledo metro stop. Everything is within easy walking distance from here. The Maradona mural is close, as is the Vico dell' Amore.

8. The Skull with Ears

A unique and quirky skull holds court below the majolica tiled floor of the tiny 14th century church of **Santa Luciella ai Librai**. Dozens of skulls line the shelves of the hypogeum, but one in particular needs your attention: the skull with ears.

For centuries this skull was extra popular with the Cult of the Souls in Purgatory (Neapolitans who adopted and prayed for the skulls of abandoned souls from the mass graves). The hope was that if you prayed these souls out of Purgatory and up into Heaven, they would do you a favor in return. Who better to hear your entreaties than a skull with ears? Surely, he could hear you praying and be more likely to extend you grace.

The church was heavily damaged in the earthquake of 1980 and was closed. Before long, the skull with ears was relegated to local legend, a mythical oddity in a city full of the unexplainable. But when the church was restored and reopened in 2019, our skull friend was rediscovered, hanging out on his shelf. He neither moved during the earthquake nor sustained any damage.

Forensics determined the skull was indeed male. He had a condition called Portico Hyperostosis, which caused the cranial tissue to become spongey and porous, likely due to chronic malnutrition. Radiocarbon testing dates him to sometime between 1631 and 1668. A plague struck Naples in 1656, and he was discovered in a mass grave, so chances are he died during the outbreak.

Regardless, he is fascinating and definitely unusual.

Address: Vico Santa Luciella 5/6
Hours: Open daily 10:15 am – 6:00 pm.
What's nearby: *The Veiled Christ*, San Domenico Maggiore, the precept street of San Gregorio Armeno.

9. The Vico dell'Amore: Vico Santa Maria Alle Grazie

As you explore the winding streets of the Spanish Quarter, you'll likely stumble upon the Vico dell Amore, the Alley of Love. Definitely Instagram famous, the alley is festooned with messages of love. Here, instead of Grandpa's underpants, the traditional clothes lines strung from one side of the street to the other have love hearts and love quotes clipped to them.

On posters and banners, you'll see everything from little *I love you* phrases to Pino Daniele lyrics. It's a little kitchy, yet also quite endearing. At the end of the day, love wins.

Address: Vico Santa Maria Alle Grazie.

10. The Cornicello

The twisted, horn shaped *cornicello* fights bad luck, repels the evil eye and has to be the most famous good luck charm in Naples. You see them everywhere as key rings, ornaments, necklace pendants – you name it. Apparently, the tradition goes back as far as 3500 BC when hunters hung the bloodstained horns of big prey on their doorways to ward off enemies. In ancient Greek and Roman mythology the *cornucopia*, a goat's horn filled with fruit and flowers, was a symbol of fertility. Today the cornicello is a symbol of protection and good juju. It does however come with some rules.

The first rule is that you must only ever give one as a gift to another person. You can't buy yourself a lucky horn. The good juju comes from the other person's well wishes to you.

Next, although you will see them in silver and gold, and made from different materials, the real cornicello must be blood red. In the past they were made from red coral, a precious stone thought to protect pregnant women. Red coral was sacred to Venus, the goddess of love, fertility, virility, sex and prosperity.

Traditionally the horn must be handmade (now you see them everywhere, made in plastic factories, so this is an old superstition). In the past, craftsmen would made the horn hollow inside. This was part of a Neapolitan superstition to do with salt. A salt-filled horn was thought to be more effective. Mine is plastic and I've never cracked it open to see if it's hollow inside.

If you wear your cornicello as a pendant around your neck, it will protect your person. On a keychain it guards and protects the object (car/house/safety deposit box etc) to which the keys belong. A cornicello hanging from your rearview mirror protects your car and all who drive in it. Put one in your wallet or purse and your money will be protected.

As you meander the streets and alleyways of Naples, you'll also notice garlands of red chili peppers hanging everywhere, from doorways to shops to street corners. Similar to the cornicello, these chili peppers not only look cool but are thought to protect you from envy, hurtful gossip and the harmful intent of others, as well as bringing you good luck.

I've been told this superstition started in Naples, before spreading across southern Italy and then to other western cultures. During the Middle Ages red symbolized both victory over the devil and good luck.

11. Via San Gregorio Armeno Presepi

This is one that I often skip because it just gets so packed. However, it is something Naples is incredibly famous for so I would be remiss not to include it. And it for sure is interesting and unusual.

Via San Gregorio Armeno is also known as the Via dei Presepi. This short, narrow street is lined with shops selling Neapolitan *presepi* (nativity scenes). Traditionally every piece here would be made by hand, by specialty artisans. You can see everything here, from giant nativity scenes to individual pieces, from the characters to the animals to watermills, bridges, houses and mangers – everything you can think of. They're pretty fantastic.

The history of this dates back to 1223, when St Francis of Assisi supposedly made the first one, depicting baby Jesus in the manger. By the 16th century, Neapolitans were placing nativity scenes in churches and homes during the lead up to Christmas. By the 17th century these nativity scenes became increasingly elaborate, with multiple figurines joining the religious figures, acting out local life. You can see many of these works of art from the 17th and 18th centuries in churches, museums and palaces. The *presepe* at the palace of Caserta are tremendous.

If you can catch Via San Gregorio Armeno when it is not packed with tourists, it is well worth seeing.

The first time I came here was well over a decade ago. The street was wall to wall artisans making incredible nativity scene characters. It was beyond fantastic. Mr. Mode knew a bunch of them so every shop we walked into came with introductions and explanations of what they were making and why. I was beyond enamored of this street and thought it was incredibly cool and quirky. To me it became an enduring symbol of Naples. On this particular trip one of the artisans put a small *cornicello* into my open palm, folded my fingers over it, and told me it would bring me good luck. To this day it has remained in my travel wallet, protecting me from pickpockets and thieves.

Fast forward to the most recent time I came here, again in December. This time it was shoulder to shoulder packed with tourists moving at the speed of double-thick molasses. However, I have never seen pieces like this in America, and they make a great souvenir from Naples. Just keep your hand firmly on your handbag – crowds like this tend to be full of slippery fingers.

What's nearby: This is right in the heart of it all, so if it looks too busy maybe swing back a little later. The amazing church and cloisters of San Gregorio Armeno are right here, via Tribunali is at the end of the street, the mural of San Gennaro is a 5-minute walk from here, the Sansevero Chapel and Napoli Sotteraneo are both less than 5 minutes.

12. The Port'Alba

Built in 1625, Port'Alba (The Dawn Gate) is Naples' oldest surviving city gate. It connects Piazza Dante to Piazza Bellini via a short but cool passage. The alley is a bibliophile's paradise. From the secondhand book shops occupying the 18th century buildings that line the passageway, to the book carts and stands along the sidewalk, here you can find everything from historical texts to comic books.

Festooned with street art and serenaded by street musicians, this tiny passageway is also a great little street food block. It is home to the oldest pizzeria in the world, **Antica Pizzeria Port' Alba**, which opened in 1738. Although it's open until midnight, you'll find the place popping in the mid-afternoons as students from the nearby university collide with other hungry folk in-the-know for €2.50 pizzas to go (€6-ish to dine in) and to browse the books.

Port'Alba is atmospheric at night and well worth strolling through after the sun goes down. It is also home to the **Libreria Berisio**, one of the coolest bars in Naples. Opened in 1956, the bookstore bar offers a selection of 200 cocktails. The book lined shelves give the bar a cozy but intellectual ambience, perfect for literary chats or just a low key evening with a little jazz in the background.

Address: Via Porta Alba, 28
What's nearby: Piazza Bellini, the MANN (2 blocks away), Via Tribunali.

13. The Doll Hospital/Ospedale delle Bambole

Since 1895, the *Ospedale delle Bambole* has been repairing dolls and teddy bears.

Set designer Luigi Grassi was laboring in his workshop on Via San Biagio Librai when a woman came in carrying a broken doll. The mustachio'd artisan, who was wearing a white lab coat at the time, promised her he would bring the doll back to life. Before long other mothers were lining up at his door with dolls to be fixed, and one of them said, 'This looks like a doll hospital!' Thus inspired, Grassi hung an official-looking *Doll Hospital* sign and created an infirmary for children's toys, replete with beds and 'nurses'.

Still a family-run business (now run by Luigi's great-granddaughter), the **Ospedale delle Bambole** repairs every type of doll you can imagine, from all over the world. Part museum and part repair shop, drawers and shelves throughout the building overflow with body parts, eyes and doll clothes. Children watch mini movies from overstuffed chairs in the main room, before being escorted to the laboratory where they can assist in doll surgeries or just observe the doll doctors and nurses at work. It's delightful.

Address: Palazzo Marigliono, Via San Biagio Librai, 39
Email: ospedaledellebambole@gmail.com
Hours: Open Monday to Saturday 10:00 am – 6:00 pm.
Tickets: Entrance fee is €3.
What's nearby: Via San Gregorio Armeno, Naples Underground (San Lorenzo Maggiore and Lapis Museum), *The Veiled Christ*.

14. Walk Between the Horses in Piazza del Plebiscito

Two Canova equestrian statues grace the Piazza del Plebiscito. One is Charles III of Bourbon, the other Ferdinand I of the Two Sicilies. Starting at the gate of the **Palazzo Reale**, close your eyes (or wear a blindfold) and walk a straight line up the piazza between the two horses. Don't be surprised to find, once you open your eyes, you not only didn't walk between the horses, but veered off somewhere else entirely!

Legend says this is due to a curse from Queen Margherita. She offered a pardon to any prisoners of the Kingdom who could pass this test but cursed the piazza so they couldn't be successful. In reality, it's more about the conformation of the piazza. The cobblestones are not perfectly linear which makes walking a straight line with your eyes closed almost impossible.

Address: Piazza Plebiscito
What's nearby: Palazzo Reale, Gran Caffe Gambrinus, Galleria Umberto, Teatro San Carlo.

20.
Pompeii

You could hear the crying of women, the wailing of infants, and the shouting of men. Some prayed for help. Others wished for death. But still more imagined that there were no gods left, and that the universe was plunged into eternal darkness.

~ Pliny the Younger

Pompei is the single most important archaeological site in the world.

Take a moment with that.

There are endless incredible archaeological sites across the former Roman Empire, but what sets this one apart is the very act of its destruction. The other ruins around the empire all wear the effects of 2000+ years of exposure to the elements, many of their stories and secrets eroding away with them. Some were buried after hundreds of years, their unearthing bringing exciting new discoveries. Pompeii, on the other hand, is like a photograph – a snapshot of a moment in time, of a city that was here one day, gone the next, buried under roughly 23 feet (6 meters-ish) of ash and pumice, for upward of 1700 years. As I am writing this book, a third of Pompeii is still buried.

The ruins at Pompeii (and its neighbors) give us otherwise unprecedented access into the daily life of an ancient Roman city. We can observe lives at every stop along the socio-economic strata, from the poorest slave to the wealthiest merchant. We can see the ingredients they cooked with and the plants growing in their gardens. We get insight into the mind of a former slave, now a freeman, from the plaque he kept at his bedside proudly announcing he is now a Roman. In the new museum, we can see the body of a young slave who died with his master. Sadly, we can see damaged vertebrae in his teenage spine and his remarkably perfect teeth.

In Pompeii we can walk ancient Roman roadways and see with our own eyes the things we might have assumed were innovations from *our* centuries. For example, traffic controls – from what we now call zebra crossings or crosswalks to one-way streets, pedestrian streets and the management of two-way traffic; reflectors in the ground to help traffic at night – all of it was invented by ancient Romans. Also, underfloor heating, the concept of health through water – day spas with hot, tepid and cold pools, fast food stands and Beware of the Dog signs. Did you know the ancient Romans standardized the length of wagon axels across the entire empire? In Pompeii you can see the grooves created in the roads by centuries of wagons and carriages passing along their thoroughfares. This same axel length became the standard width of train tracks across most of the world.

Being able to see these vast numbers of Roman innovations all in one place, and in the environment for which they were intended, is quite breathtaking. And alarming. All this incredible technology was lost when the Roman Empire fell. Much of it would not reappear for another 1400–1500 years. (Even indoor plumbing with running water inside a home was lost!)

A Little History

Although Pompeii is best known as an ancient Roman city, it was actually founded by the Greeks in around the 8th century BC. When the Romans took over in the 2nd century BC, Naples and the Vesuvian Coast became a summer retreat for wealthy Romans. They built elaborate villas along the waterfront, some of which are still visible. The second Roman emperor, Tiberius, ran the entire empire from his luxury homes across the bay on Capri. This was absolutely *the place to be*.

Pompeii was an important port town. The forum was a place of business with extensive shopping options in the buildings fanning out from it, as well as market stands in the center. Merchandise arrived on ships, was transported up the main street during the night, and made ready for sale in the central forum and shopping streets surrounding it by morning. Interestingly, the eruption moved the coastline out as far as 2 km. As you enter Pompeii, look for the rings on the city walls where boats were once tied up.

The forum of Pompeii was also a fashion center, with more than 60 toga shops, some of which can still be seen today. There were also ancillary fashion businesses – for example, there were businesses that could bleach your togas and other items whiter. The clothing/ship sails/whatever needed whitening were placed in pools filled with urine and stomped on by the lowest tier of slaves (the ones with a shortened life expectancy). Some storefronts advertised their superior bleach – elephant urine. (I wonder if after washing to get rid of the smell, did they give the togas a final lemon-scented rinse?)

It is thought that around 20,000 people lived in this fabulously innovative city. With elegant, frescoed homes, shops, a magnificent forum and a vast basilica built in the 2nd century BC, there is so much to see here.

Basilica

The word *basilica* was later co-opted by the church, but its original purpose was as a site for court hearings and other legal and city business matters. It was also used to hold both official and public functions

Walking the streets of Pompeii, you'll see public water fountains placed strategically around town providing everyone with access to fresh, cool aqueduct water. Pompeii provided each person with a loaf of bread per day, endless fresh, clean water, and access to free entertainment. Be sure to visit the amphitheater where gladiator games were played (long before the Colosseum was built) and the Greek theater where poetry readings, plays and concerts were held. (The cruise ship/mass tourism crowds don't go there.)

There wasn't much need to go criming if your belly was filled, you had limitless fresh, cool water, and there was free entertainment. It was brilliant propaganda, buying the loyalty not only of the locals, but also the slaves – as a slave, you knew this wonderful life could be yours too if you chose to become Roman at the end of your slavery. (There were a couple of main ways to end your slavery. One was to age out of it, after something like 15 years as a slave you could become free. The other main way was to earn your way out. As you achieved different things, your owner would reward you with a coin called a *talent*. Once you earned enough talents you were awarded your freedom and the chance to become a Roman citizen. This is where our word *talented* comes from.) This was the most advanced society on Earth, so why would your average slave want to return to a dusty shack in their homeland? Why give up running water, modern city infrastructure, fast food stands, public baths and the opportunity to become upwardly mobile? Why cause trouble and lead uprisings if all this could be yours too? Not only that, but you would also be welcomed to your new life as a Roman with open arms.

Romans knew this propaganda wouldn't work if the streets were filled with *homeless* ex-slaves. Slaves came from every country conquered by the empire, so there was a dense cultural mix. Propaganda doesn't work if there's *othering* – rejecting people because of race or religion. It only works if you have inclusion. So as a slave you would see former slaves of all skin colors and religious beliefs who arrived the same way you did, but now were living the high life.

Depending on your skillset, your owner would set you up in a business and get you started in your new life. Some took on major wins – my favorite home in Pompeii belonged to two former slaves, the Vetti brothers. The **Casa dei Vettii** is one of the grandest villas in all of Pompeii. A massive, opulent home with absolutely breathtaking frescos, it reopened in 2023 after a 20-year renovation. These brothers are a great example of ex-slaves opting to become Roman and making a huge success of it. They may have been blood brothers, or simply two slaves released from the same master. Either way, they were brilliant and incredibly successful. (Put the Casa dei Vettii on your **must-see** list. I've been here about 10 times now, and each time Pina tells me new stories about the artwork, the architecture, the gardens, and as much as is known about the Vettii themselves. Each visit becomes even more astounding.)

But back to our story. At the time, no one knew Vesuvius was a volcano – in fact, there wasn't even a word yet for volcano – and Vesuvius was a particularly fertile mountain that was heavily farmed. The area did suffer from earthquakes, which we now know may have been precursors to the big eruption. A massive earthquake occurred in 62 AD, just 17 years prior to the eruption. Many buildings suffered major damage, and were newly renovated and repaired shortly before Vesuvius blew.

One new build was the thermal baths and brothel on the outer wall of the city. This one had a gorgeous view over the bay and an outdoor gym, where slaves would advise clients which muscles to work and how to do it. The changing rooms, fountains, sauna and the baths themselves are beautiful. Some of the 2000-year-old frescos remain and are in incredible condition. As with the other brothels in the city, there was a frescoed menu board, so time wasn't wasted trying to communicate sex positions in other languages. You could point to a 'number 3, with a side of number 7', and be led upstairs to go about your business.

The thermal baths and brothel were recently opened to the public (around 2022/2023) and is a **must-see** while you are there.

Researchers think only around 2000 people perished in the eruption, with most of the population escaping prior to Vesuvius blowing. Having survived the terrible earthquake of 62 AD, it makes sense that people would have fled in the days prior when the earth began to rumble again. Many of them relocated to Naples, and it appears that most settled within a few streets in the historic center.

There has been some controversy surrounding the exact date the eruption happened. I was always told it was August 24 and most history books still reflect that date, but more recently, autumnal fruits were discovered along with an inscription unearthed in 2018, which all indicates it was more likely to have been October 24.

Eruption Day

Another reason we know so much about the events that began at 1pm on October 24, 79 AD, is thanks to the journaling of an 18 year old eyewitness named Pliny the Younger. Young Pliny was staying with his mother and his uncle at a villa across the bay in Misenum. Mom was the first to notice something going on over at Mount Vesuvius. She saw a cloud that looked like a massive umbrella pine spreading its branches out wide, rising up high on an extremely tall trunk. She alerted her brother, Pliny the Elder, an Admiral in the Roman Navy, whose ships were docked at Misenum.

The 55-year-old Pliny the Elder was more than just a military man, he was perhaps the greatest naturalist of the ancient world. His 37-volume series *Natural History* compiled not only his own research but also information learned from 2000 volumes by Greek and Roman philosophers, botanists, geographers, artists and physicians. Effectively he created the first ever encyclopedia. He was an important and well-respected figure. Seeing the strange cloud – like a mushroom cloud we would see from an atomic explosion – he launched several of his ships to not only see what was going on, but also to rescue as many people as possible. Ultimately, he died trying.

Meanwhile, Pliny the Younger stayed behind to document this never-seen-before phenomenon and we still have these writings today. Along with blow-by-blow details about the eruption, he also wrote of their escape. He and his mother tried to escape by carriage, but the roads were blocked by the fleeing masses. They ended up abandoning the carriage and running, eventually finding safety. He wrote of being shrouded in complete darkness: 'Not so much a moonless or cloudy night, but as if the lamp had gone out in a locked room'. In other words, everything turned pitch black.

We now know the volcano erupted with the force of 100,000 atomic bombs, ejecting 1.5 million tons of molten rock, pumice and ash per second. Columns of hot gases and ash blew 21 miles/33 km high into the stratosphere where they cooled and then rained pumice and ash, blanketing the towns below. We know the eruption lasted two days. The eruption also included pyroclastic flows – fast moving currents of gases as hot as 1000 degrees Celsius (1800 Fahrenheit) – sweeping along the ground at speeds as fast as 700 miles per hour, effectively microwaving all living beings in its path. The force of the eruption blew the top third of Mount Vesuvius off. (We can see the shape of the original, pre-eruption mountain in frescos recently opened to the public in the Pompeii forum.)

Every aspect of life was effectively frozen in that moment. Loaves of bread have been discovered in bakery ovens along with foods awaiting customers in the terracotta urns of the *thermopolium*. Bodies of humans and their animals were caught in situ at the moment of death. Families, masters and slaves who died hiding or trapped in their homes – they're all still here.

Pompeii and the neighboring towns disappeared overnight, not to be rediscovered for 1700 years. Much was lost in the first two centuries of excavations, but now the most advanced archeological technology and the most brilliant minds are helming the recovery.

The Plaster Casts

Most of the deaths in Pompeii were caused by the poisonous gases emitted in the eruption. The bodies were buried in ash which formed and hardened perfectly around them. As the bodies and organic matter decomposed, they left perfect cavities in the ash, now hardened to stone. In 1870, archaeologist Giuseppe Fiorelli created the technique of filling the cavities with liquid plaster through a straw/pipette. When the plaster hardened, the surrounding stone was removed, leaving a perfect cast of the person or being within. Details including clothing, sandals, teeth and jewelry were perfectly replicated. Many of these casts are still viewable both in Pompeii and inside the new museum.

Another detail I am fascinated by is the *dentition*. The people of Pompeii had astoundingly good teeth. Dental specialists have been able to use state of the art tomography and CAT scans to examine their teeth. They found remarkably low incidences of cavities, possibly due to the healthy, low sugar diet combined with genetics and fluorine in the water thanks to Mount Vesuvius. I am stunned at the perfect alignment of teeth, including those of the slave boy in the museum – perfect sized, perfectly aligned teeth, seemingly only attainable to most of us now via orthodonture.

The Men Who Changed Modern Pompeii

Not all heroes wear capes. You cannot talk about Modern Pompeii (the one you and I get to visit) without telling the story of two visionaries who transformed the previously poorly managed archaeological site into the genius experience it is today.

The first is Massimo Osanna, known as the Man Who Saved Pompeii. An archeologist and former professor of archaeology at the University of Naples, Osanna became the Director of the Archaeological Park of Pompeii in 2014. He immediately executed massive restoration and maintenance work to make the buildings safe again, then embarked on new research and excavations, completely changing the face of Pompeii. In the process, he turned the previously mismanaged site into an international management model. After seven years, he was promoted to Director General of all Italian Museums and is now renewing the entire museum system.

Since Osanna's arrival to Pompeii, excavations have taken on hypermodern technologies including geo-radars and drones. He created interdisciplinary teams from vulcanologists to paleo-botanists, archaezoologists to anthropologists, computer engineers, radiologists, orthodontists – all manner of specialists. The expertise is unparalleled and keeps bringing us incredible new information. The forensics employed to examine the 2000-year-old plant-life alone are fascinating as they recreate the exact gardens of homeowners when the eruption happened.

When Osanna left for his new job, a young German archaeologist by the name of Gabriel Zuchtriegel moved from his directorship at the nearby archaeological site of Paestum to run Pompeii. My guide friends told me one of the first things he did was call all the private guides into a meeting and asked them what they needed. The guides talked about bottlenecks at the main attractions within the archaeological park, and how time was wasted waiting to get inside the various brothels and houses. They said they needed more things open to show clients, so Zuchtriegel got to work on it immediately.

Consequently, between the brilliance of these two men, the entire Pompeii experience has been elevated and is vastly more user friendly. Actually, it is incredible.

I visit Pompeii around six times per year – I can't get enough of the place. I really noticed the fruits of Osanna's labor when Pompeii reopened after Covid. At that time, a huge number of new sites opened to the public, from ancient homes to the fantastic new museum inside the park. Since then, my good friend and private guide Pina, who has worked with me and my Glam Italia Tours for around a decade, has been able to show me new things in Pompei *every time I go.* It is astounding just how rapidly they are opening new excavations and formerly shuttered ones. As you make your way through the archaeological park, you'll see archaeologists and restorers hard at work. This is an ongoing excavation, so like me you can keep coming back over and over and keep seeing new treasures.

Initially I had planned on giving you a list of my favorite things to visit at Pompeii, but during the year I've been writing this book so many new things have opened, some of which jettisoned to the top of my list and by the time you read this book there will be loads more. Most people won't have the same level of obsession as I do and won't want to give up entire days to visit Pompeii, but I hope this chapter will give you the desire to come here for a morning and spend a few hours with a guide exploring and learning about this most important archaeological site in the world. I also hope you will leave the experience as astounded and excited as I do every time I come here!

Tips For Visiting Pompeii

1. HIRE A PRIVATE GUIDE

My first tip is to hire a private guide to take you through the park. There is far too much detail here that you will miss if you're visiting on your own. Download my pdf of private guides at www.GlamItaliaBooks.com/Naples-Private-Guides for a list of people I work with and can recommend. These guides are brilliant and they're not expensive. The stories they tell elevate the entire experience and really bring Pompeii to life. Even after coming here all these years, I'm still learning new things every time. Pina not only explains the building I'm looking at, but also takes me inside the lives of the people who lived and worked here.

With so much open now in the archaeological park, a good guide will anticipate where the mass tourism crowds are causing log jams and will get you around them or ahead of them. This means you get to see so much more!

2. Do Pompeii First

I like to have the same guide take us first to Pompeii, then to Herculaneum. If you see Pompeii first you will have a much broader understanding of life in 79 AD, how everything worked, and what happened throughout the days of the eruption. Herculaneum then adds more texture to the experience. Both sites are incredible and need to be on your **must-see** list.

3. Timing is Everything

There are several things to consider regarding when to visit the park. If you will be there June through September, you need to know it will be *really* hot. As such, I get my Glam Italia Tour groups through the gates the moment they open at 9:00 am. This lets us get ahead of the dreaded cruise ship and bus tour crowds who tend to block all the views and cause delays in getting inside the various houses and attractions within the park.

Alternately, if you can handle the heat, they're all back on their buses by mid-afternoon, so the crowds are greatly diminished from about 3:00 pm onwards. The summer afternoons are too hot for me, so June–September I come here in the mornings.

If you are blessed enough to be here in the off-season, you'll find vastly fewer people. I sometimes come in December and spend the entire day here (even though I've already been four or five times that year) and it is just fantastic. It feels as though Pina and I almost have the whole place to ourselves.

4. Go to the Back of the Park

Most visitors don't realize just how far back the park goes. It is enormous! The crowds tend to stay in the front third of the archaeological site and miss some of the really cool things. There's a

20,000-seat amphitheater built around 70 BC (roughly 100 years before the Colosseum). This is one of the oldest surviving amphitheaters in the world. There is also a small theater called the Odeon at the back end of the park. The Odeon was used for plays and musical performances and was built in 79 BC.

You'll also find a small vineyard, which is really cool to see, and loads of ancient homes. If you find yourself stuck in crowds of cruise/bus folks, go to the forum then take the main street all the way back. There is honestly so much to see here – like me, you can come multiple times per year and still not see it all!

5. Wear the Right Shoes

I can't stress this one enough. Pompeii requires a lot of walking and it's all ancient Roman roads, which are quite unforgiving. As you enter Pompeii, you walk up a steep road that is not particularly sandal-friendly. Plan on wearing sneakers or something similar that is flat and supports your feet and ankles.

6. There's No Shade

If coming during the hot summer months, be aware there's not really any shade here other than what you can find against buildings. You won't find trees to shelter under, so make sure you're wearing a hat and a ton of SPF.

7. You'll Need Water

Again, if you're coming during the hot months, make sure you have a water bottle with you and fill it up at the various water fountains as you move through the archaeological site.

Getting There

Pompeii is 14 miles south of Naples. Some guided tours will provide transport, but I don't recommend driving yourself in or around Naples unless you are Neapolitan. (After all, who needs that kind of stress?)

By train: The easiest way to get to Pompeii is by train. The cheaper Circumvesuviana takes you to the Pompei Scavi station for €3, while the slightly nicer Trenitalia train costs €15. The train ride takes about 30 minutes. (I normally take the Circumvesuviana.)

By bus: The bus costs €2,80 and takes 45 minutes. There is also a shuttle bus that charges around €20 roundtrip.

21.
Other Stupendous Archaeological Sites

I saw Baiae and I do not recall a happier day in my life.

~ Petrarch (in a letter dated November 23, 1345)

Everyone has hopefully heard of Pompeii, but most people have *no idea* of all the other incredible archaeological sites scattered around the Naples area. Consequently, hardly anyone visits them, so they make fantastic additions to your Naples itinerary.

I have selected seven sites to tell you about. Each is sensational and, except for the first one, you'll hardly find anyone else there. This means you'll not only wander through ancient Roman life with almost no one getting in your way, but you also can take gorgeous photos of historical sites with no fanny-packers mucking up your shot.

So, let's talk about some of the other archaeological sites around Naples.

1. Herculaneum

This is a **must-see** archaeological site that I like to pair with a visit to Pompeii. Do Pompeii first, then backtrack to Ercolano ~ Herculaneum. Both of these cities fell on the same day due to the eruption of Mount

Vesuvius, but to a degree that is where the similarities end. Pre-eruption, the cities were quite different and, although the cause of their destruction was the same, the manner was completely different.

Nestled on the bay between Pompeii and Naples, Herculaneum was a small seaside resort for the Roman elite. Smaller than Pompeii, Herculaneum had a population of around only 5000 and was the wealthier of the two towns. You can see this by the sheer volume of lavishly appointed, marble clad, heavily frescoed homes, miraculously still in incredible condition. The most famous of these is the **Villa dei Papyri**, named for its unique and priceless library of 1800 papyrus scrolls, this is the *only surviving library from the Greco-Roman world.*

This was possibly at one time the home of Julius Caesar's father-in-law, Lucius Calpurnius Piso Caesoninus. From its beautiful architecture to the extraordinary number of frescos, statues, bronzes, and its unfettered view across the bay, Villa dei Papyri is considered one of the most luxurious homes in all of the Roman world. It also had the largest collection of ancient Greek and ancient Roman sculptures ever discovered in a single home.

The first thing you'll notice about Herculaneum is that it was preserved in even better condition than Pompeii. This is because the eruption of Mount Vesuvius happened in two principal phases. The first phase saw the huge column of rock, ash and gas shoot up into the stratosphere, then drop back down from the sky. A south easterly wind was blowing at the time, causing the pumice and ash to fall on Pompeii, trapping people in their homes and causing buildings (and primarily the upper floors) to collapse. Pompeii had a higher death count because once it started there was no chance to escape. Meanwhile most of the people of Herculaneum saw what was happening and had time to flee.

The second phase of the eruption happened around 1:00 am on October 25. With fewer gases firing up through the eruption column, the column collapsed, causing massive pyroclastic flows (fast moving currents of gases and volcanic detritus). These raced down the mountain at speeds greater than 100km/h, reaching Herculaneum in less than 4 minutes. With temperatures of between 500 and 1000 degrees Celsius, forensics have established that those who remained in Herculaneum were killed in less than one second. Excavations of the boat houses found skeletal remains of around 300 women and children who had huddled under the stone arches waiting for help. The men were probably on the beach waiting for the rescue boats.

Following this, Herculaneum was buried, largely intact, under an 18-meter-thick wave of mud. This mud compacted and became rock, which made excavation much more difficult, but prevented looting and other tampering with the treasures within. These special conditions and the ground humidity created a unique environment which preserved the wooden frames of the houses, wooden furniture, textiles, food, books, and even the hull of a wooden boat. The mud flow allowed the upper levels of buildings to survive. This lets us see how these seaside towns actually looked, how tall the buildings were and how completely magnificent they must have been. Vibrant frescos and mosaics survived along with other organic matter including wooden bed frames and furniture. You can walk through intact 2000-year-old homes and buildings and really see how private lives played out here, in living color.

You can also see the boat (inside the museum) and walk along ramps to see where the skeletal remains were discovered. The modern town built on the rock above has meant (for now at least) Herculaneum cannot be fully excavated. So this grandiose, cultured town has many more secrets and treasures still hidden in its depths.

Herculaneum is *astounding*. It is also quite small and very manageable. I recommend coming here with a licensed local guide because once again you glean so much more from their stories and the details they provide.

You can very easily visit Pompeii and Herculaneum back-to-back, with the same local guide, then have a late lunch or a spritz with a sea view. Don't miss this one.

Getting there: Herculaneum is roughly 7 miles from Naples. You can either take the train directly here or, if combining the two archaeological sites, it is only 20 minutes by train from Pompeii heading toward Naples.

2. Oplontis

Just along the coast heading toward Sorrento you'll find the somewhat unappealing town of Torre Annunziata. Although it is inland now, before Vesuvius blew this was a madly chic beachfront suburb called Oplontis.

Ten meters below the streets of Torre Annunziata, two of Oplontis' homes have been excavated. Of these only one is open to the public: the spectacular **Villa Poppaea**. Named for Nero's second wife, Poppaea Sabina, this villa is also referred to as **Villa Oplontis**. It is massive and absolutely sensational.

At the time of the eruption the villa, which originally belonged to Poppaea's family, is thought to have been about 100 years old. No one was living in the villa at the time. The discovery of workmen's tools, disassembled columns and the removal of some of the sculptures indicate repair work from the earthquake of 62 AD was still in progress.

This is one of the best examples of an *otium* villa, a home designed for summer vacations, and in this case one fit for an emperor. Thought to be one of the most luxurious, extravagant villas along the entire Gulf of Naples, this is where Poppaea lived *the dolce far niente* in style.

POPPAEA SABINA (THE YOUNGER)

Poppaea Sabina was born in Pompeii in 30 AD. It is thought her family owned the enormous **Casa del Menandro** in Pompeii. This 19,000 square foot/1800 square meter home is one of the most luxurious homes in all of Pompeii, named for a 4th century BC painting of the playwright Menander.

She was married off at the age of 14 and gave birth to a son, Rufrius Crispinus (the younger), who supposedly was drowned by Nero after Poppaea's death. Her second marriage was to a friend of Nero's. This was part of a scheme to get close to Nero, who then met and fell in love with her. She became his mistress, and then his second wife. Nero was madly in love with Poppaea Sabina and they spent quality time together, luxuriating at her magnificent Villa Poppaea. They married in 62 AD and she bore him a baby girl, Claudia, on January 21, 63 AD. Nero honored both mother and baby with the title Augusta, but little Claudia died at 4 months. In the summer of 65 AD, the heavily pregnant Poppaea died. Nero's enemies said he kicked her belly until she and the baby died, however that is probably not true. (All my guides tell me to question everything we are told about Nero.) Pregnancy complications and childbirth were the main killers of women at the time, so perhaps that's what happened to her too. Papyrus has been discovered with a Greek poem lamenting a deified Poppaea ascending to Heaven on a goddess-driven chariot after giving Nero a loving farewell speech, which implies she didn't die a violent death at Nero's hands.

Nero went into deep mourning. By all accounts, he truly loved her. She was given a state funeral at which Nero burned an entire year's worth of Arabian incense. So I think we can assume the seaside villa in Oplontis – her main residence outside of Rome – was quite the love shack.

Nero

If you've read my book about Rome, you might remember an archaeologist at *Domus Aurea*, Nero's golden house, emphatically telling me that everything we know about Nero is *wrong*. She proffered that she was underground with him all day every day and *knew* him.

All my Roman and Pompeiian tour guides have felt the same way, explaining to me that everything we've been told about Nero was written by senators who hated him. One of them said to me "imagine if the only surviving information the world had about Obama was written by Mitch McConnell and Ted Cruz. Then add more venom." Interestingly, not long after that fateful trip to *Domus Aurea*, when I became completely fascinated with all things Nero, archaeologists discovered ancient graffiti praising him. So maybe the people of Rome didn't hate him after all.

The Villa

Villa Poppaea has 99 rooms and is sumptuously decorated with Second Style frescos. This was as an architectural style that introduced three-dimensional reality and the use of perspective. It was huge in the 1st century BC. (Interestingly, the concept of perspective was lost after the fall of Rome, not to be rediscovered until the Renaissance.) Frequently the Second Style created illusions of imaginary scenes. An enclosed wall would be painted as if you were looking out a window into a wonder-world beyond. Vases and bowls of fruit appeared to be sticking out from the wall, making you believe you were inside the scene, and all of this was happening around you.

The oldest part of the villa wraps around a Tuscan atrium, with luxurious living rooms, dining rooms and rooms for resting, beautifully lit by windows onto the gardens and the sea. The villa had its own private thermal baths, beautiful gardens and even a huge swimming pool measuring 61 meters x 17 meters. Alongside the pool were more dining rooms and living rooms, as well as apartments for guests. Bio-archaeologists identified and recreated the original plants, with oleanders, roses, and climbing ivy complimenting the architecture, offset by lemon trees, cypress, plane trees and box hedges. The quality of the artwork and architecture, along with the use of marble columns and capitals instead of the usual stucco'd columns, indicates this was a home suitable for the emperor.

The slave quarters were on the east side of the villa. Built around a peristyle with storage rooms, the servants' bedrooms faced a central fountain.

Parts of the villa trapped underneath the apartment buildings of Torre Annunziata are still unexcavated.

The massive walls of volcanic ash and the apartment building on top of them dwarf the villa. In its day it would have been towering structure, with expansive views out across the Sorrento peninsula and to the islands. Archaeologists discovered evidence of man-made structures below the cliffs, indicating retaining walls and ramps providing access between the villa and the seafront.

This is one of my absolute favorite archaeological sites and I recommend coming here if at all possible. If you can come with a guide, even better.

Don't be surprised to only find 20 other people here while you're visiting. It is well off the tour bus/cruise ship radar, which puts it high on my list of things to see and do in Naples.

Getting there: Villa Poppea is 300 meters walk from the Torre Annunziata train station.
Hours: Open Wednesday to Monday 9:00 am – 6:00 pm. Closed Tuesday.
What's nearby: Technically you're not far from Villa Regina, Pompeii and Stabiae.

3. Stabiae

For I doubt not that in that study of yours, from which you have opened a window into the Stabian waters of the bay and obtained a view of Misenum, you have spent the morning hours of those days in light reading.

~ Cicero, in a letter to Marcus Marius Gratidianus

Stabiae was another ancient city along the bay, now the modern township of Castellammare di Stabia on the road to Sorrento. Only 4.5 km/2.8 miles from Pompeii it too was buried during the eruption of Mount Vesuvius, but at a much shallower depth of only 5 meters. Its history dates back to at least the 7th century BC, but it really came to the forefront between 89 BC, when Roman general Sulla destroyed the old town, and 79 AD, when Vesuvius destroyed it again.

Pliny the Elder wrote that after the Social Wars ended in 88 BC, the town, perched high on the hill overlooking the Gulf of Naples, was rebuilt as a resort area for wealthy Romans. Miles of luxury villas were built along this stunning stretch of coastline, with breathtaking views across the bay. These villas are some of the most exquisite architectural and artistic remains from the Roman world. They are the most substantial concentration of massive, wonderfully preserved seaside villas from this time in history.

These luxurious, beautifully decorated residential villas were only used for part of the year, as summer retreats. The villas had thermal baths, long stretches of shaded porticos, and elaborate nymphaea – water monuments of varying sizes dedicated to the nymphs.

Two of these villas can be visited, each of them sensational, although only partially excavated. (Before we go any further, I recommend you check out Stabiae on the pompeiisites.org website for a little preview, just to see why you 100% should make the effort to come here. Not only will the villas blow your mind, chances are you'll be amongst only a handful of visitors here. If in fact, there is anyone else here at all.)

In a letter to Tacitus, Pliny the Younger says that during the eruption his uncle, Pliny the Elder, sought refuge in one of these two villas. In all likelihood, the historian spent the last hours and minutes of his life here in Stabiae at the Villa San Marco.

Villa San Marco

Covering around 11,000 square meters (118,403 square feet) and named for a church built here in the 18th century, Villa San Marco is one of the largest Roman villas to have been used as a private home. It was huge. The original structure was built in the Augustian age. During the Claudian period the property added a panoramic garden, swimming pool and a beautiful three-sided portico.

The villa is incredibly well preserved. Walking through the rooms, decorated with 2000-year-old mosaics and frescos, is just breathtaking. Many of the objects discovered here are now in the MANN, along with some of the frescos lifted from the walls.

The villa's thermal baths are accessed through a small atrium festooned with frescos of cupids and wrestlers and boxers. These are in the Fourth Style, from the Claudian period.

Remains of a travertine stairway and winding ramps show the path they took from the baths to the pool area. You can imagine 1st century Romans luxuriating here, strolling along the shaded porticos on hot sunny days.

Villa Arianna

Crossing a narrow lane, you reach the older of the two villas, Villa Arianna, named for a huge mythological fresco of Ariadne abandoned by Theseus, on the back wall in the villa's triclinium (dining room). The oldest parts of the villa including the atrium and surrounding rooms are from the 2nd century BC.

In the 1st century AD, thermal baths, winter and summer dining rooms, and more rooms were added. At the west end of the villa a palestra, or gym was added sometime between 60 AD and 70 AD. The villa's mythological frescos here are gorgeous and vivid.

The approximately 2500 square meter (26,909 square feet) villa is full of arcades, rooms and staterooms decorated with beautiful frescos. You can even enter the kitchens and visit the thermal baths.

Just as important as the frescos found in Pompeii, these ones are practically a secret, gloriously unknown to the masses. This means, for the most part, you get them to yourself. It almost seems indecent. You'll find yourself questioning how you can possibly be so lucky to have all this history and majesty to yourself.

From the meticulously intricate details in the artwork, panoramic views over the sea, and the relative silence from the hill behind you, Villa Arianna oozes power and prestige. It is magnificent.

The parts of the villa closest to the sea collapsed down the cliff, and other parts of the property are still waiting for excavation, but the areas open to the public are astounding.

Getting there: Stabiae is a little over 1 km/25 minutes' walk from the Via Nocera Circumvesuviana train station, though I've not walked it myself. You can get a taxi from the Castellammare station.

I usually come here by car with my friend Pina. We end our adventures with a spritz (and fantastic snacks) on the waterfront in Castellammare, from where I take the train back to Naples and she heads home to the peninsula.

4. The Amphitheater of Capua

If you have time up your sleeve and you love ancient Roman history like I do, you'll enjoy this next one.

The largest Roman amphitheater ever built was the Flavian amphitheater, better known as the Colosseum. The *oldest* existing amphitheater is the one in Pompeii. The *second largest* amphitheater is 30 minutes outside Naples, near Caserta, in a town called Capua (Santa Maria Capua Vetere).

The current structure was built by Augustus in the 1st century BC. The amphitheater was enormous. It was four stories tall, reaching a height of 46 meters, and could hold 60,000 spectators. The Colosseum in Rome was modeled on this very amphitheater. Not only was Capua a really important city in the ancient Roman epoch, it was also home to the first gladiator school. This is thought to be where gladiator games were created, beginning a tradition that became a symbol of Roman culture for more than 500 years.

Some historians argue that the current amphitheater is a rebuild of an older one. This makes sense when you consider this is where Spartacus fought in 73 BC, before escaping the gladiator school and fleeing to Mount Vesuvius with his band of 70 slave-gladiators.

Suffice to say, the Amphitheater of Capua is really old.

After the fall of Rome in 456 AD, the Vandals and then the Saracens, destroyed the amphitheater as well as most of the city of Capua. Later, the ruins of the amphitheater were used as a marble quarry to build the new Duomo, the Lombard Castle and other buildings in the city, much like the Vatican pilfered most of the remaining marble from the ancient buildings in Rome.

While visiting the site be sure to also check out the Gladiator Museum and the ancient *mithraeum*. Mithraism is a 4000-year-old Indo-Persian religion, brought to Ancient Rome by slaves. Many of the key aspects of Christianity were lifted from Mithraism – it's quite freaky if you look into it. The mithraic version of a church or a temple was called a mithraeum. They are fascinating to visit, even more so if you've read up on the similarities between the two religions or if you have a guide explain them to you.

Getting there: The easiest way to get to Capua is by train (or private driver). I recommend pairing a visit here with a visit to Caserta, which is just up the road. (See the **Caserta** chapter.)

5. The Roman Villa at Positano

Did you know that an ancient Roman villa, full of 1st century frescos and mosaic floors, is hiding out smack bang in the middle of Positano?

Formerly one of my favorite hangouts along the coast, Positano has now devolved into a cruise ship nightmare. Throughout the season this town, which was once just glorious to meander through at leisure, is now wall to wall, shoulder to shoulder, cruise ship passengers. Fannypacked and sweating, they stomp down the steep walkways en-masse, desperately watching the paddle or umbrella of their tour guide, missing all the beauty and character along the way. They trudge past, oblivious to (and probably with no interest in) this sensational archaeological site – which is fantastic for you and me, my friend, as it increases the chances of us procuring tickets and getting inside!

In the 1920s, long before Positano became the most over-touristed destination along the Amalfi Coast, a local butcher was digging extra space for cold storage in the back of his shop. Surprise of surprises, he discovered part of a 1st century Roman villa. Proper excavations didn't begin until 2004. They took place in two phases, the first being 2004–2006 and the second phase in 2015–2016. This extraordinary archaeological site only opened to the public in August 2018. (Allowing for two years closure during Covid, and factoring in the small numbers that can visit the site each day, know that very few people have ever been down here. It's fantastic!)

Eleven meters below the church of Santa Maria dell' Assunta, a guide leads you down a staircase into a *triclinium*, or dining room of a 1st century villa. It takes a moment for your brain to compute just what you are seeing here – the colors of the frescos are so intense and dynamic! The frescos are in four main colors: a very bold Pompeii Red, intense green, a luscious ochre and a vibrant blue. The volume of blue alone indicates this was an incredibly wealthy family. Blue was made from lapis lazuli and was the most expensive shade of paint to make. The triclinium is approximately 30 square meters and also features a beautiful white mosaic floor. Most of the villa has been lost, but this section is in amazing condition.

At the time of the eruption no one was living here while the villa was undergoing significant renovations after the earthquake of 62 AD.

Archaeologists found workmen's tools, a carpenter's saw, buckets, a spade and even scaffolding. They also found domestic items, including two frypans that melted together from the heat of the eruption. All these items are on display.

We also know renovations were in progress because the frescos are in the most fashionable style of the time, the Pompeiian Fourth Style. This style happened between 60 AD and 79 AD and was much more complex than its predecessors. Paintings were more intricate and much busier. They took up entire walls with framed scenes from mythology and panoramic landscapes, showing the newer artistic concepts of space and light. This artistic style was not seen again until the 17th/18th century. Once again, it is astounding how much Roman ingenuity and innovation was lost to the world for 1700–1800 years.

THE CRYPT

To access the Roman villa, you traverse two crypts from the church above. In the larger crypt you will recognize the 69 *sedili funebri*, the funeral seats where dead monks sat as their bodies drained and decomposed, similar to the ones we talked about at Sant' Anna dei Lombardi in Naples.

Only 10 people can be in the Roman Villa of the Museo Archeologico Romano at one time, and you do need to book a timed entrance. The mini tours are done by language group, so be aware when booking. The tour takes 30 minutes and, as with most underground sites, it does get quite cold, so I recommend at least having a sweater, jacket or scarf with you. If all the English language tours are sold out for your day, still drop by around that time. Sometimes people don't get there on time, over-schedule their day, or decide to go to the beach instead.

Although a mountain range separates Positano from Vesuvius, the two are only 20 km apart as the crow flies. Archaeologists believe there are more villas with ocean views buried below the volcanic ash along the coast. Most of which can probably never be excavated.

Getting there: You can reach Positano from Naples via train to Sorrento, then a SITA bus to Positano. Or hire an NCC driver to take you to the coast and make Positano a (brief) part of your day trip.
Address: Museo Archeologico Romano Santa Maria Assunta, Piazza Flavio Gioia, 7
Website: marpositano.it Email info@marpositano.it
Hours: Open April 1 to October 31 9:00 am – 9:00 pm. Open November 1 to March 31 10:00 am – 4:00 pm.

6. Villa Pausilypon

Perched on the promontory of the Posillipo hillside, with views across Procida and Ischia, the stupendous Villa Pausilypon is one of the most incredible ancient sites you've never heard of.

Built in the 1st century BC, this was the summer home of an exceedingly wealthy Roman, Publius Vedius Pollio. Pollio, a wine merchant and politician, was the son of a freeman.

Known for his overwhelming cruelty to slaves, Pollio kept a pool of lampreys (horrifying, jawless sharp toothed carnivorous eel-like creatures) to throw slaves to. On one occasion when Emperor Augustus was dining at Pausilypon, a slave broke a crystal glass. Pollio ordered him fed to the lampreys, but Augustus stepped in and not only saved the slave but ordered the pool to be filled in and all of Pollio's crystal to be smashed.

When Pollio died in 15 BC he willed the property to Augustus with the stipulation a monument to himself was to be built. Instead, as a *damnatio memoriae* or condemnation of Pollio's memory, Augustus instead built a colonnade, *The Porticus of Livia*, and dedicated it to his wife Livia. The property became an imperial villa and was passed down to every emperor until Hadrian.

The property has an odeon and a 2000 seat Greek-style amphitheater nestled into the hillside overlooking the bay. You can't walk inside the amphitheater, but you can still get a very clear view of it.

Although open to the public, the site is still a live archaeological dig. Throughout the years of the Roman Empire the villa underwent several renovations and expansions, but in 2022 an ancient mosaic was unearthed and has been dated to the villa's first construction phase. Based on the style, the mosaics are deemed to be from the late Republican era or the early Augustan era.

You reach the villa via the **Grotta di Seiano**, a 770 meter/2300 feet long tunnel with 120 internal arches. This 2000+ year old tunnel was used as an air raid shelter during World War II. At the far western end of the tunnel, look for a headstone with ancient Roman engravings, marking the grave of a freed slave. Exiting the tunnel, a path lined with lush mediterranean trees and shrubs leads you to the remains of the villa and the amphitheater.

You can only visit the site on a 90-minute guided tour. The once daily tours are in Italian, but if you call ahead, they can arrange an English-speaking guide. The tour takes you through some of the ancient rooms and you see frescos, tiled floors and a small geometric garden. You also get to take in the views from the gallery over the bay. Much of the estate is still off-limits due to the ongoing excavations.

Address: Discesa Coroglio, 36

Getting there: The archaeological site is easily reached by car, but there is no off-street parking. You can also get here by bus. The F9 bus stops right outside, but you can also take the C21, C27, C31. 44 or 11 buses. Frome the Campo Flegrei Metro station (metro line 2) take the C1 bus to Grotta di Seiano.

Email: info@gaiola.org

7. Baiae

Just when you think you've seen it all, be prepared to have your socks knocked off. I've saved this one for last because it really is one of the most stupendous travel experiences you could possibly dream up. (Especially if, like me, you love ancient Roman ruins.) Baiae is one of Italy's most fascinating (and overlooked) ancient sites.

AN UNDERWATER ARCHAEOLOGICAL PARK

Can you imagine visiting an ancient Roman city submerged underwater like Atlantis? One replete with buildings, statues, marble columns and mosaic floors? If you enjoy scuba diving, snorkeling, or taking in the view from glass bottom boats, read on.

THE ULTIMATE RESORT TOWN

Ten miles west of Naples (16 km), almost directly opposite Pozzuoli on the edge of the bay, sits the Roman Empire's most exclusive zip code, the town of Baiae. In 178 BC it was already known as *Aqua Cumanae* due to its famously healing sulfur springs and its proximity to Cumae. By the last century of the Roman Republic (the Republic was from 509 BC – 27 BC), Baiae was already a fashionable, luxury resort town. Rome's rich and powerful were building themselves lavish villas along this stretch of the coast from at least as far back as 100 BC.

Julius Caesar had a magnificent villa here. Pompeo liked to come here. When Octavian became the first emperor of Rome he made a large chunk of the town imperial property. Nero built a home here, and in 138 AD Hadrian died here.

Not only was it the ultimate destination for the elite, but it was also known for its hedonistic lifestyle, scandalous behavior and overall raunchy depravity. Supposedly in his 1st century AD *Moral Epistles*, Seneca wrote of Baia as being a *vortex of luxury* and a *harbor of vice* (though I haven't been able to find the citation). Far from the prying eyes of the capital, Roman senators, consuls, emperors and businessmen journeyed south to the Bay of Naples to let their hair down and indulge their pleasures. Unsurprisingly, Nero spent much of his Imperial reign here.

THEN AND NOW

An enormous amount of the ancient city still remains and is now a stunningly beautiful archaeological park *that hardly anyone comes to.*

In the upper level (on dry land) there are ruins from multiple huge buildings and villas. A multi-level bath complex is built into the hillside. The original mosaic floors are in situ, their aquatic themes still visible. Although 2000+ years of exposure to the elements has left them in disrepair, they are nonetheless magnificent. Baiae had three large bath complexes similar to the thermal baths in Pompeii and around Rome – huge complexes with hot, tepid and cold pools, enormous swimming pools, workout areas and rooms for meetings and philosophical discussions.

The massive **Temple of Mercury**, erroneously named in the 18th century, is actually a frigidarium (cold pool). It has an oculus-punctured concrete dome that predates the Pantheon.

The even larger **Temple of Venus** comes from Hadrian's era in the 2nd century AD and was also part of the swimming pool complex – not a temple.

Meanwhile, the **Temple of Diana** with its gigantic dome may have been built in the 3rd century by Emperor Alexander Severus. He was known to have built a sumptuous palace here for his mother, Jukia Avita Mamea.

You can also see a theater and the **Villa dell' Ambulatio**.

The hydrothermal volcanic activity of the Campi Flegrei made this area perfect for thermal baths. (The Campi Flegrei are 24 volcanic craters bubbling away below the Gulf of Naples. ancient Romans believed this to be the home of Vulcan, the fire God.) Both the private and the public baths at Baiae were fed warm mineral water directly from underground hot springs. In Ancient Rome, hot springs were thought to have great medicinal value. Doctors would send patients to them for various illnesses and even treat their patients at the bath complexes.

A surprising amount of the buildings' original plaster has survived, along with fragments of frescos. Their styles seem to date to the middle of the 1st century AD and also to the 2nd century AD. Look for evidence of the Third Pompeiian Style where faces and characteristically Egyptian animals are present.

Honestly there is so much to see in the upper part of Baiae that were this all there was to see, it would be well worth the trip. But now let's get aquatic.

Other Stupendous Archaeological Sites

The City Under the Sea

While a portion of Baiae's ruins remain on land, more than half of this ancient city is submerged beneath the sea, forgotten for a thousand years. For reference we are talking about an area three times the size of Pompeii. And this, my friend, is one of the least explored yet most fascinating places on Earth. Which makes it perfect for you and me to explore.

Down here below the sea, archaeologists found miles of brick walls, and a network of ancient Roman roads, yet puzzlingly, no public buildings. No forums or temples or signs of local businesses. Instead, they found around 177 hectares/437 acres of palatial ruins and architectural structures. One luxury villa after another. For a long time, no one knew specifically who these luxurious homes belonged to. Then, while mapping every inch of the city below the sea, archaeologists discovered a room full of perfectly preserved marble statues. This room could only belong to a private villa of unparalleled wealth. Who could possibly have owned it? The statues were brought to land to the safety of the museums, after all, this volcanic region could disappear at any time. In the process they discovered one of the statues was of Antonia Minor, niece of Augustus, mother of Emperor Claudius, at the time the wealthiest man on Earth. They now believe this must have been the imperial villa, owned and lived in by Claudius and later by Nero.

Not only did they discover elaborate statues and water features, they also discovered fish ponds on what would have been *terra firma* – land. Not decorative fish ponds, but actual fish farms. It turns out some of these super wealthy villas guaranteed their own supply of fresh fish. In another example of the genius of Roman engineering, fresh water was piped into these farms as needed. Under the hot

Neapolitan sun, seawater would have evaporated, leaving these pools too salty for fish to survive, so fresh water flowed in as needed. In the bay they found signs of oyster farms based around the same principals used today in oyster and mussel farming.

So What Actually Happened?

Hedonism didn't sink Baiae, Bradyseism did.

Baiae sits in one of the most seismically active areas on Earth. In the 4th century, built up pressure from gases and lava caused underwater chambers of hot molten rock and gases to empty, which in turn caused the land above to sink 60 feet. Bradyseism is the gradual rise or fall of the Earth's crust. In this case it caused half of the seaside town to sink. More than a thousand years later, the chambers have slowly refilled, raising the lost city of Baiae closer to the surface. Volcanic forces are now reversing the sinking that took place in the 4th century. Isn't that *wild*?

None of this happened overnight. Realistically it happened over centuries, some say as long as 300 years. In the 8th century, Muslim raiders destroyed what was left of the city on land, which later became completely abandoned after outbreaks of malaria.

Archaeologists are still making new discoveries in the underwater city. In 2023 they discovered another new Roman villa. This one has gorgeous Portasanta inlay marble floors. Exclusive to the Greek island of Chios, this type of marble was considered one of the most expensive and desirable marbles in the ancient world. Chances are, by the time you go there they will have discovered even more.

Baiae Today

What really makes Baiae a unique experience is the opportunity to dive beneath the waves and explore the world hidden below. This is one of the few underwater archaeological parks in the entire world.

For visitors like you and me it provides another exciting way to interact with Ancient Rome. You can take a glass bottom boat, a snorkeling excursion or even a scuba diving excursion to explore the sunken city. Can you imagine clipping on a Go-Pro and scuba diving across 2000 year old mosaics and multi-colored marble floors? Weaving your way around statues (replicas – the originals are safely in museums) and through villas in a massive archaeological site?

There are multiple companies working a variety of experiences for travelers, depending on the level of water exposure you are looking for. They even offer classes and scuba experiences for people who have never dived before. I recommend plotting out your aquatic excursion first, be it in a boat or with a snorkel or dive tank, and then build the rest of your day around that.

Getting there: By car, if you hire a driver it takes about 30 minutes. The number 9 train leaves every 20 minutes or so from the Montesanto station at a cost of €3–5. It takes 40 minutes to get to the Fusaro stop, followed by an 11-minute walk.

22.
The Greek Temples at Paestum

A society grows great when old men plant trees whose shade they know they shall never sit in.

~ Greek Proverb

Did you know the eight best preserved Greek Temples in the world are all in southern Italy? Five are in Sicily, the other three are right here, just a quick train ride from Naples. The train brings you to Paestum, a seaside town just below Salerno, famed for its crisp white wines and fresh bufala mozzarella – and a jaw-dropping archaeological park that few people know about and even fewer take the time to visit.

Poseidonia (now Paestum) was founded by the Greeks in around 600 BC. Part of *Magna Grecia* or Greater Greece, the town was named for Poseidon, the Greek God of the sea. This Greek settlement thrived for three centuries before becoming part of the Roman Republic. During this time the Greeks built themselves a series of temples. Three of these temples are still standing, in excellent condition. They erupt up out of the ground like a force of nature, majestic in their simplicity, and breathtakingly enormous. Older than the Parthenon, they are a testament to the strength and ingenuity of the ancient Greeks. Their scale and beauty is just awe inspiring.

They first built the **Temple of Hera**, in 550 BC. In 500 BC they built the **Temple of Athena** at the highest point in town. In 450 BC they built the third surviving temple, the **Temple of Hera II**. It is hard to reconcile just how huge these temples are.

Other than in Sicily, there is nowhere in the world to experience anything like this or see Greek buildings of this magnitude.

The Temples

It's interesting to compare the three temples and see how the Greeks kept adjusting the dimension and style across a one-hundred-year period. From the width of the columns to the number of columns, the degree of entasis to the shape of the capitals, they were constantly evolving in their search for perfection, harmony and beauty.

THE TEMPLE OF HERA

The Temple of Hera I was built in 550 BC. It is a peripteral style, with 18 columns along the long sides and 9 columns across front and back. Terracotta statues found here, along with inscriptions identify this temple as being to the goddess Hera, known as Juno to the Romans. Hera was both sister and wife to Zeus, with whom she ruled Mount Olympus.

An altar was set up outside the temple so the faithful could take part in sacrifices and rites without entering the inner sanctuary or *cella*. We know this was wider than most Greek temples by the two doors and by the seven columns running through the center of the *cella*. The external columns are huge and have a strong *entasis*, or convexity in the body. Apparently, the Greeks believed this created an optical illusion that made the columns look straight. You can still see traces of the original paint on the capitals.

Things to look for here include how horizontal and heavy this place feels. The capitals look almost squashed by the weight of the roof, while the columns with their swollen mid-sections almost feel like they're bulging under its weight. They're not – it was just the style at the time. Also notable, the columns don't have feet, instead they stand directly on the platform. Although heavy, it still is in perfect balance and proportion with its 9:18 ratio.

18th century archaeologists erroneously called it the *basilica*, mistaking it for a Roman construction. The basilica was a familiar structure in Roman city centers, used as the seat of justice. Centuries later the church copied the structure and pilfered the name.

At one point this was part of a *heraion*, or larger sanctuary dedicated to Hera. That also included the Temple of Hera II.

The Temple of Hera II

Just north of Hera I you'll see the 'modern' temple, also dedicated to Hera. Built in 460–450 BC, it resembles the Temple of Zeus in Olympia, which was built around the same time. This temple is 60 meters long and 24.5 meters wide. The columns are 8.88 meters (29 feet) tall, with an entasis that measures 7 feet wide at the bottom and 5 feet wide at the top. They're wider than usual with a narrower gap between each. Normal doric columns had 20 vertical flutes. The external columns of this beautiful temple each have 24 flutes, the smaller columns in the *cella* have 20 and the even smaller ones up in the architraves have 16. This temple feels distinctly more vertical than its neighbor. The capitals flare more and don't look flattened, while the columns seem more slender. The triangular pediment is still intact, and immediately under it you can see the frieze.

Hera II is from the classical period, also known as Greece's Golden Age, perhaps the apex of Greek architectural beauty. From the front it feels more harmonious and balanced, the 6 columns allowing for a natural gap for the entrance. Meanwhile 14 columns along the sides add to the sense of balance. It is beautiful.

The Temple of Athena

On the north side of the ancient Greek town center, the Temple of Athena was built in 500 BC. The style is partly doric and partly ionic. This may be the first example of the two styles co-existing in a single temple. It has a high pediment under which you can see a doric frieze with metopes, a type of ancient Greek bas relief. This temple has 6 columns across the front and back and 13 along the sides. Each column is 6.12 meters/20 feet tall.

We know this temple was used by the Romans thanks to an inscription written to Minerva, the Roman name for Athena.

In around the 8th century the temple was used as a church. The walls of the *cella* were torn down, new walls were erected between the columns (they were taken down during excavations in the 1940s and three Christian tombs were found in the floor).

The Greeks also built paved roads, sewer and drainage systems that ran out to the sea, new houses, and the public structures needed to run a successful town. This included the (still intact) **ekklesiasterion**, a 35 meter wide, 9 meter deep, tiered, circular structure that looks like a theater. From here politicians and officials could speak to the citizens. As one of the first democracies, in public meetings the citizens made their voices heard too. Public assemblies were held here to elect magistrates and vote for laws. Massively dwarfed by the temples, it's still definitely worth checking out.

Also in the *agora*, or public meeting section of town, you can see a **heroon**. This was a structure built to celebrate the cult of a specific hero. This odd-looking building would traditionally contain the mortal remains of the founder of the city.

The Tomb of the Diver

In the 1968 a small cemetery containing an ancient Greek tomb was discovered just outside of Paestum. The walls and ceiling of the tomb were plastered and painted, creating a private world for the deceased fellow inside to enjoy for all eternity. Painted in around 480 BC and now safely ensconced in the wonderful Paestum Museum, these are the oldest surviving wall paintings from Ancient Greece, which also makes them *the oldest wall paintings in all western art*. Their discovery changed our knowledge of ancient Greek culture and art.

So, what did a wealthy man from ancient Poseidonia want to take with him into the afterlife? It could be argued that Ancient Greece (or some measure of it) was a homo-erotic world. It was for this chap anyway. Women were for making babies, but if you were going to be in love, be in love with a man. So, our tombsman went to eternity with a symposium of naked men. Well-muscled and six-packed, lounging around in pairs, some with musical instruments, others embracing, and all of them just oozing intimacy. None of them were portrayed as feminine or as boys in drag, instead their very manliness is celebrated.

Most interesting is the ceiling painting, effectively what he would spend eternity looking up at. Here, another naked fellow dives from a great height into the immense unknown of the sea. As he is diving down with his junk flying free, to the left a tree is thrusting upward. Perhaps this was portraying a circle of life where we come back in another form? Or maybe it's a message that something dies and something else is born? Either way it's intriguing and compelling, and you must go to the museum before leaving Paestum to see this and all the other treasures kept safe there.

The Greek City Walls

The remains of Paestum's original Greek city wall is one of the best-preserved defensive walls in all of Magna Grecia. Walking the trapezoidal perimeter, you see remnants of what would have been 28 towers, 2 of which were restored in the 19th century. Modifications and restorations took place from the 6th century BC to the 1st century BC. It is still astounding to me, after all these years, that I can walk up to this 2600-year-old wall, study it and even *touch* it. (For reference, this wall was erected around the same time as the old city wall we talked about in the **Piazza Bellini** chapter. But now instead of looking down into the ruins, you stand face to face with them.)

The original walls were around 7 meters high. There were four city gates within. Porta Giustizia (the Justice Gate) to the south, the Porta della Marina on the west side is the best preserved. On the East side the Porta Sirena (the Siren's gate), look to the keystone for a small relief of a siren (mermaid).

The Porta dell' Aurea (Golden Gate) to the north was destroyed when the city was cut in half to build the Road of the Calabrias / SS18. (Would it have been so hard to route the stupid road *around* this absolute treasure from antiquity??)

The Roman Era

After the Pyrrhic War in 273 BC, Posiedonia came under Roman rule. Romans loved Greek architecture, so instead of knocking down the Greek temples and the remains of the city, they built their own city *around* it. All of it is still here, wide open for you to walk through.

In Pompeii you learnt how Roman houses were laid out and how a successful Roman city was built and functioned. That knowledge is a massive advantage here because this huge archeological park gives complete access to both the Greek city and the Roman one that followed it.

I love walking through all the public buildings of the town, but also the entire residential area. You learn to identify the front door of each home and the back door, and which views they had from each. You know where the living took place and where they slept. You walk across their mosaic floors, still intact and beautiful after 2000 years of exposure to the elements. There are huge homes with swimming pools in their central courtyards and smaller homes with cat eyes lighting up their entrances (made from white marble chips that reflected the moonlight).

You can walk down endless Roman roads, following a path from the city buildings to homes. This Roman town is vast and you can explore as much of it as you want. I'm somewhat obsessive (this is, after all, what I live for), so when I come here I tend to be one of the first arrivals of the day and one of the last to leave.

THE AMPHITHEATER

In the 1st century the Romans built a tremendous amphitheater here, used both for gladiatorial games and circus spectaculars. Still only partially excavated and cut in half by the stupid road mentioned above, the amphitheater sits adjacent to the ekkliasterion. Entering the grand archway, you can walk along the tunnel the animals and stage sets came in through, sit in the tiered seats and walk around the now grassed floor. It's pretty fantastic. From here it's a short walk along the ancient Roman road to our next stop, the forum.

THE FORUM

The heart of every Roman town was the forum. This one, measuring 200 meters by 60 meters, is from the Augustan era. The colonnade lined floor level was lowered, then surrounded with buildings used for commerce. A trained eye can point out the various public buildings, temples and shrines that made up a typical Roman city center.

The Pool Dedicated to Virilis

I find this fascinating. This time we're looking at a pool measuring 47 meters x 21 meters, just shy of the dimensions of an Olympic pool.

Constructed in the 3rd century BC, this pool was dedicated to fertility. Women without rank or social status sat in the pool, praying to Venus to bless them with fertility, while pregnant women prayed for a safe birth. In the ancient world more than 30% of mothers died from complications during childbirth.

A ritual called *Veneralia* was celebrated on April 1. A procession led through town ended at the sides of the pool, where a statue of *Venus Verticordia* was lowered into the water to bless it with her godly powers.

There is of course, much more to see here. You can come with a guide or explore on your own, though I do recommend downloading the audio guide before coming here (Google the Capaccio Paestum audio guide).

Apart from being completely overwhelmed by the temples – even though I come here regularly I still am – there is something else here that will shock you. **There is no one here.** While just up the coast, Amalfi and Positano are overcrowded with tourists, you'd be lucky to spot 100 people here. The first time I came to Paestum the only day I could come was free Sunday. I worried it would be exploding with tourists and that I wouldn't even be able to get a clean photo of a temple, but I doubt I saw 80 people across all the hours I was there. And they were Italian families and a handful of British tourists.

On one of my more recent trips here, a group of college boys from Naples were taking turns explaining to each other what the various ruins were. They spotted me eavesdropping and folded me into their group, switching to English when I couldn't understand things. I learned so much and it was such fun!

A trip to Paestum is one of the most incredible experiences you can have in all of Italy. If you are interested in Ancient Rome or Ancient Greece, you need to come here. It is sensational.

Getting there: Either come here with a driver, or by train. The train from Naples takes a little over an hour and costs about €8 each way. Salerno is at the bottom of the Amalfi Coast, and this is 30km below Salerno, so is also very doable if you are staying on the coast. You can take a ferry to Salerno, walk 5 minutes to the train station and be in Paestum 30 minutes later.

What's nearby: Pair your trip to the archaeological park with a visit to a bufala mozzarella farm and/or a local winery. The museum across the street from the park is definitely worth visiting too.

Smell the Sunshine

Before we leave Paestum, I want to tell you a story.

One day I came back to my vacation rental apartment in Vomero and found a shopping bag hanging on my door with fresh Caseficio Rivabianca bufala mozzarella inside. I figured some delivery guy had made a mistake, so called my landlady Veronique. She told me she had been on a field trip to Paestum with her 7-year-old son's class. 'Of course,' she said, 'I had to stop for mozzarella on the way home, so of course I got you some too.'

She went on to tell me that I needed to eat it with a very specific type of tomato. 'Don't go to the supermarket,' she said. 'You must go to *my* fruit and vegetable shop.' And proceeded to give me directions: head to the end of the long driveway to the villa (now a road lined with apartments), turn left under the ancient arch, pass the first vegetable shop and go to the second one on the left. 'I've told Nunzio you're coming and which tomatoes you need. You can smell the sunshine on them.'

So, I wandered through Vomero to Nunzio's tiny shop, the shelves laden with piles of the most intensely colored fruits and vegetables you've ever seen. He was expecting me and held out a tomato for me to *smell the sunshine on.* We then got into a lengthy discussion about how much mozzarella I had, how many tomatoes I would need, how to slice into the mozzarella balls, and which olive oil Veronique had left me. Nunzio then snapped off some fresh basil leaves, threw them in the bag and sent me off to enjoy one of the simplest yet most flavorful meals I've ever had. But that's Naples.

Moral of the story? Go to Paestum. Buy fresh bufala mozzarella. Smell the sunshine. Fall in love with Naples.

23.
What to Eat in Naples

In Naples the sun shines brighter and the food tastes better.

~ George Byron

Street Food

Port towns like Palermo, Genoa and Naples have an amazing street food culture. In most of Italy, food is consumed at a table, not walking down the street. In port towns, street foods were born from necessity when sailors from all over the merchant trade world needed food on the run. Influenced by the cuisines of the various nationalities pulling into port and the interesting ingredients they brought with them, port city street foods are sensational.

You'll notice quite a few fried foods on the list here. These were perfect for hungry sailors and workers who needed small, portable foods. Hustling from ports, market stalls and worksites, these high fat, protein dense, carbo-loaded morsels not only gave them tons of energy, but they were inexpensive too.

So let's check out some Neapolitan street food!

1. Pizze Fritte

Piping hot, crispy on the outside, stuffed with fluffy ricotta, mozzarella and *ciccioli* (crunchy pork bits) and served to you on paper, you absolutely **must** *not miss* this classic Neapolitan street food.

Different theories abound as to when Napoli's fried pizzas were created. Cookbooks from as far back as the 1500s talk about recipes with fried dough. The prevailing theory today is that fried pizza became essential after World War II. The allies bombed the living daylights out of Naples, destroying the traditional wood burning pizza ovens and impoverishing the people. So as a matter of need, a new form of pizza evolved. This time pizza dough was pulled thin, filled with ricotta, mozzarella, ciccioli (fried pork bits a little like bacon) and maybe some tomato, folded over like a calzone, and flash fried.

This is not like deep frying a Domino's pizza – it's nothing of the sort. Instead, pizza fritta is puffed up, light, crisp on the outside and fluffy on the inside. It's not greasy either.

In post-war Naples this was known as 'the pizza of the people'. Street vendors fed impoverished customers with a system called *a ogge a otto* (eat it today and you have up to eight days to pay). You can even see this in the 1954 Sophia Loren movie *L'Oro di Napoli* (The Gold of Naples). In the chapter *Pizza a Credito* (Pizza on Credit), she is a pizza fritta maker who cheats on her husband.

Pizza Fritta is inexpensive and comes in small, medium and large sizes. Beware, large is *huge*. You can also choose from a variety of flavors, but I recommend starting with the original.

Although places like Sorbillo are *pizze-fritte*-Instagram-famous, you can enjoy this stupendous street food at any of hundreds of hole-in-the-wall joints scattered all over the city. Just look for a bunch of Neapolitans outside, leaning against the walls and hightop tables, chowing down on *pizze fritte* and you know you've found a winner. Other places like **Isabella de Cham** in the Sanità neighborhood have elevated the simple street delicacy into a chic new food. This super cool eatery is entirely female staffed in a male dominated industry, so is extra fun to visit and support. Check the website at Sanita.Isabelladecham.com

2. Taralli

Southern Italy offers us a variety of little dough rings known as *taralli*. You may already be familiar with the Pugliesi variation: small, crunchy snack foods that pair perfectly with an aperitivo. Napoli has its own version, and be warned, they are addictive!

The Neapolitan *tarallo* is larger, more rustic and, where the Pugliesi one is crunchy, this one is delectably flaky. They come in many flavors, both sweet and savory, but your *first* one should be the original. This is made with *'nzogna* (lard) pepper and toasted almonds. Before you turn your nose up at it, just know the secret ingredient is the lard – this is what creates the perfect texture. Lard has fewer bad fats than butter, so don't feel guilty – just enjoy.

The original tarallo flavor combo makes it spicy (the pepper) yet sweet (the almonds). These were created a few centuries ago when leftover bits of bread dough called *sfriddo* were mixed with lard and pepper, bent into circles and then baked. Somewhere along the line almonds were added. They were no doubt a lifesaver for the poorer classes: cheap carbohydrates with animal fat and protein, and goodness from the almonds from Sicily. They were also the ideal street food for sailors and workmen: you could eat them easily while making your way through the bustling streets of Naples as you headed back to your ship or worksite, and they are still a popular street food today.

It's fun to wander along the lungomare between Castel dell' Ovo and Mergellina, grab a hot tarallo and a beer and enjoy them sitting on the rocks watching a spectacular Neapolitan sunset. I don't drink beer myself, but all summer long you'll spot Neapolitans out here in the evening, a tarallo in one hand and a Peroni in the other.

Most bakeries sell taralli and you can buy bags of them to take home with you. I like to go to the temple of taralli, **Tarallaficio Leopoldo**, outside the Botanical Gardens on Via Foria, but I also buy them all over town. (And in a divine twist of fate, there is a Neapolitan food stand at my local Saturday market near my home in Tuscany. They always have fresh taralli and even throw in a couple of extras for me because they know how much I adore their hometown.)

3. Frittatina

This traditional Neapolitan dish is found both as a street food and on menus around town, as a starter or a lunch food. Most frequently seen as a ball or disc shape, *frittatine* are deep fried pasta balls. The traditional recipe calls for peas, ham, *besciamella* (bèchamel) and bucatini pasta, battered and breadcrumbed, then deep fried and served to you on paper.

I put these into the *don't try to reason, just bite* category. They sound heavy and fatty, but are in fact crunchy on the outside, soft on the inside and incredibly good. You **must** try frittatina at least once while you're in Naples.

4. Spaghetti Frittata

What's an enterprising Neapolitan mamma to do with leftover pasta? Like many of the best foods in Italy, this is *cucina povera* – poor people's food. During times of poverty, when every last morsel had to be used and no ingredient could be wasted, leftover spaghetti was mixed with eggs and cheese, rolled into balls, flattened to inch-thick discs and fried. The crunchy exterior and soft interior are surprisingly delicious. These cake-like frittatas are sliced in half and packed for lunches and picnics, or served to you in paper from a stall or shop to be eaten as you wander around. You can find them with a variety of other ingredients, and they even show up on gourmet menus. Yes, they're dense and filling, but this is Naples – you'll walk them off in no time!

5. Il Cuoppa

Think of this as the king of street food in Naples. Keep your eyes open and you'll spot people walking along with a brown paper cone in hand, a stick or two poking out the top and an assortment of deep-fried delicacies inside. You can order **terra** (foods of the land): a mixture of deep fried mini *frittatine*, vegetables, potato croquettes, *sciurilli* (battered zucchini flowers) salted *zeppoline* (fried dough balls) and fried polenta scraps. Or try my favorite, the **mare/pesche**, which is as assortment of small seafoods. Don't expect a *cuoppa* to weigh you down or be greasy or heavy – everything is lightly fried, so is crisp and delicious. This is another perfect food to enjoy on the run, as you make your way around the amazing sights of Naples.

The Pastas of Naples

Naples is known for several pasta dishes. Obviously, being a city on the Mediterranean, you'll find lots of seafood options.

Spaghetti alle Vongole (Spaghetti with Clams)

If you're going to eat Spaghetti alle Vongole anywhere in Italy, be sure to eat it in Naples. The blend of olive oil, garlic, parsley and clams is just perfect here, every time.

Frutti di Mare (Seafood Medley)

I love any of the Frutti di Mare (fruit of the sea/shellfish) pasta options here in Campania. Normally they are a combination of mussels, clams and shrimp, often with octopus too, all tossed in olive oil, garlic and parsley. Sometimes tomatoes are added as well. You'll normally see these served with spaghettis and linguinis. Another pasta you'll find everywhere here is *scialatielli*, a fresh, handmade square noodle that has been perfect in every seafood pasta I've eaten along the coast.

Pasta Puttanesca (Whore's Pasta)

The famous Pasta Puttanesca also hails from Naples. Although there is some dispute over how it was named, my favorite story involves the hookers of days gone by – prostitutes lured clients with the smell, smelled like the pungent pasta themselves, or regularly made it because the ingredients were cheap and accessible. Other translations suggest the *puttanesca* comes from cheap ingredients that are easily available and found in every pantry. However it came to its name, this pasta is a Neapolitan classic. Filets of anchovies are melted into fresh extra virgin olive oil, infusing the sauce with a deep, umami flavor, to which garlic, red pepper flakes, capers, black olives, tomatoes, oregano and parsley are added. Served with spaghetti, this super flavorful dish is a **must**-try while in Naples.

Pasta e Fagioli con Cozze

You'll find that lots of dishes here are made with mussels – *cozze*. This one comes in a ceramic bowl and combines short pasta, white beans and steamed mussels. Creamy and briny Paste e Fagioli con Cozze is rustic and hearty. I love it in cooler weather.

Sugo alla Genovese

Although named for its cousins in Genoa, this is a traditionally Neapolitan sauce. A soffritto of celery carrots and onions is sautéed in olive oil, to which veal or beef is added, along with white wine and slow cooked for up to 10 hours. You'll find it either served alone or with rigatoni style pastas.

Pasta alla Caprese

This summery pasta hails from Capri. Fresh tomatoes, mozzarella, basil and olive oil are combined with freshly cooked pasta. The dish is light, fragrant and delicious.

Manfredi con la Ricotta

This hearty pasta dish has a long history. In 1295 it was prepared for King Manfred of Sicily when he came to Sannio, near Naples. Made with rippled *mafaldine* pasta and ragù Napoletano, it is topped with a dollop of the king's favorite cheese, ricotta, just before serving. Although eaten year-round, I prefer it in cooler weather.

Spaghetti al Soffritto

Another Neapolitan specialty, this is not to be confused with the regular *soffritto* of celery, onions and carrots. Here instead, we have a rich and hearty sauce made from offal, most commonly pork. The lungs, heart, spleen, liver and whatever other parts of the fifth quarter were available are slow cooked with tomatoes and chili peppers.

Lemon Pastas

Fresh, summery lemon pastas are served all along the coast as well as here in Naples. Garlic is sautéed in olive oil with lemon zest and freshly squeezed lemon juice, then tossed with fresh from the pot spaghetti. Pasta water is added a ladle at a time until the pasta becomes creamy. Sometimes served with mint or basil, sometimes with ricotta or grated pecorino, every version I've had of these Campanian lemon pastas has been to die for.

Pastries in Naples

Naples is a city known for its incredible pastries. You will spot pastry shops (*pasticcerie*) everywhere you go.

The 17th century nuns of Naples were famous for their baking skills and played a big part in the city's pastry history. Each convent had its own pastry or dessert specialty. Many of these Brides of Christ were cloistered, so you couldn't see their faces, but you could smell and taste their wares. Nuns sold their divine desserts through barred windows or a rotating wheel, ensuring the pastry purchasers would never catch a glimpse of their faces. (With nunneries and churches standing cheek by jowl with the elaborate palazzi of Naples' elite, you have to wonder if the nuns lay awake at night listening to all the partying happening on the other side of the stone walls!) I'm sure the aromas from their baking wafted up over the other smells of this vibrant city.

At this time, Naples was under Bourbon rule. The Bourbon kings brought French pastry chefs to Naples. The two most sophisticated cities in Europe at that time were Paris and Naples, so it made sense that both cities, along with their artists, philosophers and socialites, would take great pleasure in indulging in the most luxurious sweet treats, some of which are still around today.

Sfogliatella

Legend says the most iconic Neapolitan pastry of them all was created by a nun. Supposedly, she soaked leftover semolina flour in milk, added ricotta, candied fruit and orange essence, wrapped it between lard-softened flaky pastry and formed it into the shape of a monk's hood.

A century later the shape changed to a shell made up of layers of flaky pastry. This is the *sfogliatella riccia*, my favorite of the two types.

Ideally try one fresh out of the oven, but either way, engage all five senses as it makes its way to your mouth. Sfogliatelle smell delicious and look intriguing with their crispy layers of pastry. Your ears are engaged with the crunch as you bite into one, your taste buds will swoon at the orange and ricotta flavor, and your sense of touch comes in as flakes of pastry drop everywhere.

The second type has the same ricotta and candied orange inside but, instead of a shell-shaped flaky pastry, the *sfogliatella frolla* is a dome-shaped short crust, baked golden brown.

Sfogliatelle are everywhere in Napoli but if you can, swing by **Pintauro** (Via Toledo, 275). They've been in business since 1793 and might be the most famous place to buy one. They also have a huge list of other delicacies in their glass cases.

Fiocchi di Neve (Snowflakes)

You see these all over Naples now, but this is a relatively new pastry. The snowflake is the brainchild of Ciro **Poppella**, a third-generation baker from the Sanità neighborhood. His real name Ciro Scognamiglio (Poppella was an amalgamation of his baker-grandparents' names).

In the early 2000s, Ciro wanted to create something new, a cake that was simple and light, but tasted incredibly good. After experimenting for a while he came up with one of the best things you've ever tasted (that's me talking) – a light, soft brioche type bread filled with a delicate cream made from sheep's ricotta and cow's milk. He called his airy creation *fiocco di neve* (a snowflake) and it really is as light as a feather.

With little foot traffic near his pasticceria in the Sanità, it took a while before the city even knew about the snowflake pastry. In fact, it wasn't until he donated a huge batch to a charity fundraiser that the snowflake became known – and *coveted*. People came not only from all over Naples, but from all over Campania to buy them. So much so that Ciro had to expand his business to keep up with demand for thousands of snowflakes per day.

The crazy thing is there's nothing much to them. They're not bitingly sweet, nor overly sugary. They are just perfect. Especially when you have one with a cup of Neapolitan espresso – the best coffee in the world. Even after you've overeaten next door at Isabella di Cham, somehow this is the perfect end to the meal.

Other pasticcerie have tried to copy him, but in my opinion, Ciro's are the best. Why go for a replica when you can have the original? Chances are you'll see Ciro sitting outside his place chatting with the neighbors. He is super friendly and happy to take photos with *fiocco di neve* lovers.

I should add here that Poppella make an enormous range of pastries. The glass case is both huge and enticing. If you are blessed enough to be in Naples during the Christmas season, the *panettone* from Poppella is also incredible and well worth taking home on the plane with you.

But don't leave Napoli without trying a fiocco di neve – let it snow!

Poppella

Address: Via Arena della Sanità, 29 (There are other branches, but come here to the original if you can.)

https://www.pasticceriapoppella.com

Babà

The next iconic Neapolitan pastry has to be the rum-soaked babà. These mushroom shaped spongey cakes come in two sizes – small and large – and stay moist due to the infusion of the sticky, rum-based syrup. Babà also has an interesting history.

While living in France, exiled Polish king Stanislav Lesczynski grew bored with *kugelhupf*, the dry Polish dessert made from flour, sugar, butter, eggs and sultanas. Supposedly he threw one across the table where it collided with an open bottle of rum, infusing the room with a heady pirate-like scent. He decided to try a bite of the rum-soaked cake and loved it, naming the new dessert *Ali Baba* after the hero of his favorite book *One Thousand and One Nights*.

This became a favorite at the court of Nancy where it was served with a Madeira sauce. A French pastry chef working at the court modified the recipe using sweet brioche formed in the shape of a hat and renamed it *babà*. It then made its way to Naples via the *monsu* (the French chefs working for the Neapolitan nobles). You will see babà everywhere in Naples and should at least try a small one!

Zeppola di San Giuseppe

Named for St Joseph and traditionally eaten on his saint's day, March 19, nonetheless you will find this delicacy year-round. This is a fluffy choux, typically fried in the shape of a ring, topped with a swirl of cream and macerated Amarena cherries.

Zeppola's origins are a bit murky, but the first documented mention was in 1837. Neapolitan baker Pasquale Pintauro made them super popular with the masses, selling them from a street cart. Most pastries at the time were associated with a specific saint, so Pintauro cleverly linked these to St Joseph's Day, and the story of Joseph feeding his family fried pancakes on their escape to Egypt.

You can also buy baked zeppole, but calories don't count in Italy, so go for the tastier fried one.

STRUFFOLI

This is a Christmas pastry you'll see literally everywhere from November through Epiphany. Originally from Greece, these delicious marble shaped balls of dough are deep fried, then dipped in honey. Around Christmas they're decorated with nonpareil sprinkles and bits of chopped orange rind. From pastry shops to coffee bars to supermarket racks, you'll see them everywhere, sold in sticky little bunches of goodness.

GRAFFA NAPOLETANA

This one is mostly associated with Carnevale season (pre-Lent), but you can find it year-round. The graffa Napoletana is an Italian donut, made with flour, boiled potatoes, eggs, yeast and butter. You'll find them in either a traditional ring or shaped like a hook, rolled in sugar. They're airy and light and when fresh out of the oven just melt in your mouth.

Apparently *graffe* arrived in Naples during the Austrian rule and are a contraction of the Austrian *krapfen*. The new name is definitely more appetizing. However they got here, these sugary delicacies are now considered Neapolitan, and you'll spot them everywhere.

Torta Caprese

Hailing from just across the bay on the island of Capri, this one came to fame when a baker forgot to add flour to his cake. (Or maybe he just ran out?) Regardless, this gluten-free chocolate cake combines dark chocolate, eggs, butter, sugar and ground almonds. Once cooked, the torte is dusted with powdered sugar or cocoa and served in thin wedges.

Open Thighs Lemonade

Italians, and particularly Neapolitans, take digestion seriously. They have rules about when and what order foods are eaten. There are rules about when milk is consumed (like cappuccino being a breakfast drink and not normally ordered after 11:00 am – although they will make you cappuccino any time of day). I recently had a waitress lock eyes with me in abject *horror* when one of my Glam Italia tour travelers ordered a cappuccino with her pasta.

In Italy it is normal to end a meal with a digestivo, like a limoncello, and then take a walk. In Naples you'll see something a little more drastic, the naughtily named *limonata a cosce aperte* or 'open thighs lemonade'. I've also seen it called 'open legs lemonade'.

This super refreshing, non-alcoholic digestivo uses locally grown Sorrento lemons, known worldwide for their distinctive aroma and flavor. The lemons are squeezed to order on a specially designed contraption that imparts the oils from the skin along with the juice. The vendor then pours in *aqua frizzante* (sparkling water) and at the last moment adds a dash of baking soda. This makes the lemonade erupt like Vesuvius in a tower of foam. The customer then grabs the drink and knocks it back in one go.

The only way to drink it without soaking your legs and shoes is to have your legs wide apart, bend at the hip, and hold the drink as far away from your body as possible. Hence the *open-thigh* part of the name.

It is both hilarious to watch and fun to do. Also, it really works. If you've overindulged in Naples' pizza, pastas or fried foods, an open-thighs lemonade will set you right. And it tastes so good! The magic is in the Sorrento lemons which have a flavor profile all of their own. Like its neighborhood friend limoncello, it's not the same and doesn't taste right when made with regular lemons.

Apparently at one time there were as many as 1700 of these *limonata a cosce aperte* stands scattered around Naples but now there are only a few. The most famous is **Acquafrescaio** in Piazza Triste e Trento. This stand has been in business since 1836 and has been run by the same family for 50+ years. You'll be in the neighborhood anyway, so why not try one? Even if you don't need help with your digestion, this is still a refreshing drink on a hot day.

Acquafrescaio
Address: Piazza Trieste e Trento, 4
What's nearby: This is right next to Piazza Plebiscito, Gran caffe Gambrinus, Palazzo Reale, Teatro San Carlo and Galleria Umberto.

24.
Naples – The Home of Pizza

To understand Naples, first you must taste its pizza and feel its passion.

~ Sophia Loren

Of course, you already know pizza comes from Naples. And so, of course, you have to eat pizza while you're here.

History books say pizza originated in the early 1700s, but archaeologists recently discovered a fresco in Pompeii that depicts what looks like a pizza. Instead of tomatoes (which didn't arrive in Italy until the 1500s), this painted pizza appears to have pomegranate seeds on top. Ancient Roman bread ovens in Pompeii are very similar to modern pizza ovens, so maybe pizza and Naples have been the perfect pair for more than two millennia?

Neapolitan pizza could not be more different from pizza at home. There's no sugar added to the dough and no sugar added to the tomato sauce. Pizza here doesn't have much cheese, has few if any toppings and isn't swimming in grease. This is not a chemical laden, manufactured food product designed to be cooked at home in an electric oven. Instead, this is real food, designed to be eaten within moments of coming out of the igloo-shaped wood-burning oven. Until you've eaten pizza in Naples, you've not eaten pizza.

In America, pizza tends to be made by high school kids and college students working a part-time job. In Italy, the work of a *pizzaioulo* is a specialty vocation, a career, and involves much more than sliding a franchised pizza into a commercial oven. There are around 15,000 *pizzaiouli* in Naples, all of whom work to rigorous and stringent standards. Consequently, it is hard to find a less than fantastic pizza here. In fact, their craft is so specialized and exacting that Neapolitan pizza is considered the best in the world. So much so that the art form has been placed on UNESCO's Cultural Heritage list – not a single pizza emporium, but the collective brilliance and tradition of the *entire city*.

BASE

Let's start with the base. The only ingredients in the dough are wheat flour, water, salt and yeast. The flour comes from untampered-with wheat. Remove the GMOs and chemicals found in American flour, and you have a product as different as apples and oranges. Apart from our crappy, highly allergenic flour (known to cause bloating and distressed tummies), at home in the US other chemical agents are added to most pizza bases, along with sugar to turbocharge the speed at which it rises. In Naples, it's just pure, real food.

Here, the base is stretched out thin – don't expect to find anything even remotely like a bready, Chicago deep-dish pizza. Instead, expect a soft, chewy base covered in scorch marks (leoparding) with a *cornicione* or edge that is pillowy and airy. Your pizza arrives thinner than the plate it's served on.

SAUCE

The base gets a swirl of tomatoes, grown in local volcanic soil, and is topped with chunks of local Campanian mozzarella. Thus prepped, the *pizzaioulo* slides your pizza into his oven where it is blast cooked for 90 seconds at about 900 degrees.

If you can, try to watch a *pizzaioulo* at work. With an intricate knowledge of the quirks of his particular oven, he'll be quickly moving the multiple pizzas around inside the blistering heat with a long handled wooden paddle, hitting the appropriate hotspots to create evenly cooked, perfect pizzas every time. (He'll be Neapolitan, so chances are he's going to be very easy on the eyes too.)

Toppings*

There are two versions of the traditional Neapolitan pizza, the **margherita** and the **marinara**. The margherita, named for Queen Margherita of Savoy shortly after the unification of Italy, comes in the red, white and green of the then new Italian flag (red tomato, white mozzarella, green basil). Meanwhile the cheese-less marinara has tomato, garlic, oregano and oil.

There are many variations available on pizza menus, but I recommend starting with a margherita, which is about as authentic as it gets. Once while in Rome, I posted a photo of a margherita pizza with arugula on social media. Mr. Mode immediately jumped on and commented *"What the hell is that???"* He was horrified that I would tamper with a margherita. (The only thing that could have made it worse was if I had added pineapple.)

The key is to keep it simple. The fewer ingredients, the better. Let the pizza work its magic.

* Be aware that in Italy *pepperoni* means large bell peppers.

Pineapple?

Outside of Italy, pineapple shows up frequently on pizzas. In Italy, pineapple pizza is considered a crime (although I did read that pizza legend Sorbillo is adding it to his menu, but that could be to appease tourists? Who knows.) My hilarious driver and great friend Pasquale often tells me that were he to find out I had pineapple on a pizza, our friendship would be over. (He also tells me if I support Juventus, I will be dead to him. I periodically send him stock photos of Juventus jerseys just to check he's still alive.)

Where to Eat

Along with **Sorbillo,** there are many famous pizzerias in Naples.

In business since 1738, the fantastic **Antica Pizzeria Port' Alba** is the oldest pizzeria in the world. (See the **Interesting & Unusual Things** Chapter.) If in season and on the menu, try the margherita with yellow and red tomatoes — it is incredibly good.

L'Antica Pizzeria da Michele in the Forcella neighborhood is super famous, as is **Da Attilio** in Pignasecca market and the Instagram-beloved **Pizzeria Concettina Ai Tre Santi** in Sanità. There are loads of high profile *pizzerie* in Naples.

Personally, rather than get in line at one of the famous joints, I prefer to wander into any loud pizzeria filled with happy Italians. Because it is intended to be eaten immediately, pizza is more than just a meal in Naples, it is a social event. Maybe it's a throwback to the boisterous nights we spent eating pizza with Mr. Mode and his friends, but I equate pizza in Naples with lots of laughter, noise and excitement. If you're going to indulge in something as iconic as eating pizza in Naples, why not go in for the whole experience?

Typically consumed with beer, not wine, you'll not only find cold Peronis served with pizza, but also many places now offer (what I am told are) excellent local craft beers. Not a beer drinker myself (even though I'm a Kiwi — go figure), I tend to be the philistine in the corner, happy as a clam, sipping house wine with my margherita.

Pizza here in Italy is ordered one per person, a pizza being slightly smaller than a dinner plate. Unlike in the US, it isn't a heavy food so, while you might balk at the idea of an entire pizza to yourself, here it won't weigh you down. Most of the time your pizza arrives unsliced and is frequently eaten with a knife and fork. A good rule of thumb is to observe the other patrons before manhandling your pizza. If they're using a knife and fork you may look like a barbarian eating with your hands. If *Italians* around you are folding slices in their hands, you are fine to follow suit.

At the time of writing this book, a margherita pizza in Naples costs around €6.

25.
Which Wines to Drink in Naples

In Vino Veritas. (In wine there is truth.)

-Pliny the Elder

I recently read a well-respected wine magazine telling readers to pair Spaghetti Puttanesca with a good Chianti. It took me a moment to pick myself back up off the floor. Had this person ever been to Naples or had so much as a single bite of puttanesca? Campania makes some fantastic wines including four DOCGs. So why would anyone advocate pairing this intensely Neapolitan food with a Tuscan wine?

In Italy, cuisine and wine are entirely regional. What you eat in Naples should be different to what you eat in Tuscany, and the same goes for the wines. Just as you should, in most cases, drink Tuscan wines with Tuscan foods, surely you should drink the wines of Campania while you're here.

I stick to this rule most of the time. Wherever I am in Italy I ask the waiter to help me choose a local wine to go with what I'm ordering. Almost always they select something from their *terre*. For example, in Rome I'll often get wine from Orvieto, which grows around the Umbria/Lazio border, so isn't entirely foreign. Or a waiter might insist on a crisp Ligurian or Sardinian Vermentino to go with the fish we're having. I can honestly say that in all the years of traveling to Campania and in the hundreds of times I must have eaten in restaurants in Naples and along the coast, I have never, ever had a waiter or anyone else recommend a Tuscan wine to pair with anything I'm eating. Not even once.

So, let me tell you about the wines of Campania.

The Wines of Campania

The Campania wine region is famous for its viticultural history and its indigenous grape varieties. Aristotle tells us of vines being planted here in the 5th century BC, so we know wine grapes have been grown on the slopes of Mount Vesuvius and the surrounding area for *more than 2500 years*. Vesuvius wine was renowned in every corner of the Roman Empire. Safe to say, they know a thing or two about wine.

Wines from this area are very distinctive. The combination of Mount Vesuvius' fertile volcanic soil, rich in volcanic ash and minerals, the gorgeous, sunny mediterranean climate and the cooling sea breezes, produces full bodied, robust and sometimes feisty reds and crisp fresh whites.

AGLIANICO

One of the local grape varieties is **Aglianico**. Aglianico-based reds tend to be complex, full bodied, high in tannin and, to my uneducated palate, quite minerally. One thing I learned from years of visiting Vesuvian wineries with my Glam Italia Tours is that Aglianico grapes vary depending on where they grow on the slope of the mountain. The vines closer to the top of the mountain produce a more delicate wine, while those lower down the slope make a more luscious, robust wine. Personally, I often find them quite peppery, and love curling up at night with a good book, a feisty Aglianico and a couple of squares of extra-dark chocolate.

Aglianico is considered the Barolo of the South. One of the four DOCGs from the region is the Aglianico-based **Taurasi**, the most celebrated red in Campania. A mineral forward, intensely flavored, velvety red often likened to Barberas and Brunellos, Taurasi ages well and is considered one of the best reds in all of Italy. (The other red DOCG is **Aglianico del Taburno**.)

I have been to the family owned and run Sorrentino Vesuvio winery multiple times per year with my tour groups. When the weather is oppressively hot down in Naples, it is markedly cooler and breezy just a short way up the hill at the winery. Maria Paola always tells us the **Don Paolo Aglianico** is complex and full bodied like her dad, which still makes me laugh even after all these years. I should warn you – if her dad Paolo pulls up a chair and sits at your table, cancel your plans. You are in for an afternoon of absolute hilarity, drenched in Vesuvian wines. My tour groups who have been graced with Don Paolo's presence at their wine lunch *still* talk about it, years later. Like Mr Mode, Paolo is another fantastic Neapolitan character who imprints so much fun and laughter on your visit, but this time with the addition of some wonderful wines.

LACRIMA CHRISTI (OR LACRYMA CHRISTI)

When residue discovered in 2000-year-old wine vessels was analyzed by bio-archaeologists, they discovered that **Lacryma Christi** is the closest equivalent to the wine drunk by the ancient Romans.

Lacryma Christi means *Christ's tears*, even though this wine is from long before Jesus. The Greeks were here planting vines centuries prior, and when the Romans came along and called the area *Campania Felix* (happy countryside), legend said Bacchus, the god of wine and debauchery, cried tears of joy, which in turn made the vines flourish. Once Christianity was in full swing the story was amended. It became Christ crying tears over either Lucifer falling from Heaven or dropping a stolen piece of paradise on Vesuvius. Now it's his tears that are attributed to the success of the vines. Although he did have that whole turning-water-into-wine trick, the vines had already been flourishing here for at least 500 years. So, who knows?

Produced with grapes native to Mount Vesuvius, this DOC wine comes in both red and white varieties. The reds are made from Piedirosso and Scianscinoso grapes, while the whites use Coda di Volpe and Caprettone. Funnily enough *caprettone* roughly translates to large goat, due to the grape bunches resembling a goat's beard. This grape is indigenous to the Naples province.

Whether opting for the red or the white, these wines pair beautifully with anything you eat in or near Naples. The reds can be fruity, full and bold while the whites are more citrusy and fresher. This past winter (2023) I was in Naples for an extended period. One rainy night, the waiter in the Vomero restaurant told me it was a night for a hearty pasta, which he chose for me. (Always let them – they make the best choices.) He then brought me a swoon-worthy glass of red Lacryma Christi. I'm not a fan of dense, heavy reds, but he pointed out that a lightweight red would be lost in the rich flavors of the pasta. He was so happy that I was so thrilled with his choices that he also brought me slivers of local cheeses he thought paired perfectly with the wine. And yet again I spent the evening trying to figure out how I could move to Napoli.

The Land of Crisp White Wines

As you eat your way up and down the coast, you'll become aware of two major factors:

1. The Vesuvian coast is sunny and warm/hot for much of the year.

2. The cuisine mostly revolves around fresh seafoods and fresh produce.

Both of these factors lend themselves to crisp, fresh white wines. If you are here on vacation chances are you've come during the warmer, sunnier months and you're not craving a heavy red wine. Or for that matter, a fat, buttery chardonnay. The volcanic soils of Campania lend themselves beautifully to mineral, acidic (think crisp) white wines, three of which I particularly love.

FIANO

This is a textured white wine with notes of florals and tropical fruits. **Fiano d' Avellino** is one of Campania's DOCG wines. Avellino wines differ from others up and down the region thanks to the Apennine Mountains around the town. There is more rainfall and as the vines are mostly grown at a higher altitude they live in interesting microclimates with warm days and cold nights, warm summers and cold winters. Having grown there for thousands of years, the grape has adapted beautifully to the conditions, making this a tremendous wine. As far as whites go Fiano is on the mineral side, but the altitude it grows at makes it a little less acidic.

I first had Fiano a lifetime ago on a hot summer night when one of my favorite waiters in Sorrento (he still works in the same restaurant) chose it as the ideal pairing with the seafood I ordered. I have loved it so much over the years that it took me a while and some persuading to venture into any of the other great whites from around here. If in doubt and you want a white wine, try this one first.

GRECO DI TUFO

Another of Campania's DOCG wines, **Greco di Tufo** might also be the region's most prestigious white. Thought to be named for the Greeks (*Greco*) who brought the grape (or a version of it) to Campania, and *Tufo* for the type of rock the grape grows on, an ash-based *tufa*.

The vines grow at an altitude of around 450–500 meters (1300–1600 ft, give or take), which means the grapes thrive in the Campania sunshine while the coolness of the altitude stops them overheating or becoming too sweet. Instead, they retain a nice acidity, making them crisp and refreshing. They have a mineral finish (crisp) and aromatic notes of pears and lemons.

This is another perfect wine for all the lemony foods and seafoods you'll find all over Campania. And again, this is an ideal wine for hot summer days along the coast.

FALANGHINA

There are two sub-varieties of **Falanghina**, the better known of the two being **Falanghina Flegrea**, a DOC wine grown in the Campi Flegrei area. The other is **Falanghina Beneventana**, an IGT from the Benevento area. Another grape brought to Campania by the ancient Greeks, Falanghina thrives in the volcanic soil and mediterranean climate and is another of Campania's fabulous signature whites.

This one is light, fresh and fragrant with a crisp minerality. Falanghina Flegrei is thought to be the grape used to make **Falerian**, the best-known wine of the ancient Romans era.

In my non-oenophile opinion (based not in science but in endless summers spent in Campania loving these three white wines), I think of Falanghina as being the lightest and crispest of the three. But all of them are just wonderful.

If in doubt...

If you're unsure, just ask the waiter to choose for you – they never seem to get it wrong. If you're standing in front of shelves of white wine and not sure which of the three to choose, maybe pick the prettiest bottle? You can pay a lot or ridiculously little, but you are bound to love whatever you choose. In all these years, I have never had a bad one. Summer nights in Campania were made for these three wines.

And as for the pairing with puttanesca? I double checked with a sommelier friend of mine. He too was gobsmacked at the Chianti recommendation. He recommended choosing a light local red or rosé, or a nice local white. Puttanesca is too intensely flavored to send into battle with a heavy red. He suggested avoiding anything too tannic and intense like an Aglianico or the Chianti talked about in the wine magazine. His recommendations were a Lacrima Cristi or a Falanghina. Whichever you choose, just make sure it's from Campania!

26.
The Best Coffee in the World

Quite simply, the very best coffee in the world is in Naples.

~ Corinna Cooke

Everyone knows that Italy makes the best coffee in the world, but until they've been here few realize that Naples makes the best coffee in all of Italy. (This is my personal opinion but ask any Italian who's been to Naples, and they'll likely tell you the same thing.)

Historically speaking

I go into depth about the story of coffee arriving in Italy and from there to the western world in my book *Glam Italia! 101 Fabulous Things To Do In Venice*. In a nutshell, the first western documentation of this magical drink was in 1591 when Prospero Alpini, a doctor working for the Venetian Consul in Cairo, wrote of the medicinal benefits of African coffee beans. Like a magic potion, this wonder drink revived the lethargic and those lacking energy. Before long, it became a cure-all for everything from headaches to gout.

Ethiopian coffee beans had already made their way to the Ottoman Empire. The business potential of this rich, energizing drink led the Ottomans to expand coffee bean farming to Yemen. At that time Venice was the merchant capital of the world. All goods coming from the east to the west passed through Venice. All goods passing from west to east did the same. So naturally the Ottomans routed coffee through Venice.

In Naples

Neapolitan coffee history needed a little prodding from one of the more intriguing women in European history, Princess Maria Carolina. (We meet Marie Antoinette's vastly more interesting sister in the **Caserta** chapter, and learn about some of her political prowess, however this beautiful Austrian princess also changed Naples' coffee culture forever.) Maria Carolina loved drinking coffee in the Hapsburg's Austrian court, so when she married King Ferdinand of Bourbon and moved to Naples, she introduced the custom here too. If you were invited into the court of Maria Carolina, chances were you'd be drinking coffee.

In around 1800 the first street coffee stands began to appear around Naples and this glorious drink became the drink of the people. As the coffee trade got going, beans were shipped to two main ports: Venice received the more delicate, sweeter, aromatic Arabica beans hailing from South America, Naples got the more intense, rich, dark, robusta beans from sub-Saharan Africa. At that time, these cheaper to farm African beans were more prone to diseases and bugs, sometimes arriving in questionable condition. If roasted in the normal manner, these defects would impact the taste of the coffee, so to disguise any imperfections, coffee in Naples was given a deep, dark roast.

What Makes Neapolitan Coffee So Special?

In a country known for its coffee culture, how has Neapolitan coffee been able to completely bewitch the taste buds of millions of (very) discerning coffee lovers? I am warning you, my friend, once you've experienced the magic of coffee in Naples, there is no turning back!

It starts with the intensely deep, rich aroma and the full-bodied taste, which are unique to the Neapolitan coffee blend and preparation. The combination of traditional Arabica beans with the aforementioned *robusta* beans lowers the sweetness while increasing the caffeine. The beans are roasted for longer and at a higher temperature, giving them additional depth and intensity.

In my opinion, the Neapolitan *baristas* are key to the process. Sit back and watch and you'll see them constantly adjusting the grind and the water temperature. They adjust and readjust in response to the humidity and the weather conditions throughout the day, so every cup is perfect. Remember that rather than a part-time job for college students, a barista is a fully fledged career in Italy, so the level of expertise cannot be compared.

Some will tell you it's about the machines they use, but I beg to differ. A coffee bar in Milan can use the exact same Ferrari-of-coffee-machines as its counterpart in Naples but, even if they use Neapolitan coffee, it won't taste the same. Others say it's the water, which admittedly comes from the Serino Springs in the Irpina mountains and is considered one of the purest waters in the world. I've often wondered if Vesuvius casts some kind of magic spell on the local water because frankly, everything tastes better in Naples.

The Old-Fashioned Method

If you spot a bar that uses the old school lever machine, hightail your way in there and order a cup. These machines have all kinds of interesting attributes and work in a similar manner to an internal combustion engine. (Not to imply I understand anything about either.) These machines not only look cool but also require a different barista skill set. Supposedly they make a better cup of coffee, but I can't tell the difference. To me it's all Neapolitan coffee perfection, regardless of the machine being used.

Prep Work

There are a couple of things to pay attention to with the preparation.

The cups are kept either in a bath of boiling water, or on top of the machine, making them almost too hot to handle. The coffee is short but maintains its optimal heat throughout your sipping experience.

Some baristas will automatically put sugar in the bottom of the cup before expressing the coffee. I don't question it – if they think the blend needs it, I trust them. I do keep an eye on it though, as tapping the sugar packet and pouring it into my coffee are part of my Italian coffee ritual. (Funnily enough, I never add sugar to coffee in America.) In the early years before I knew that coffee sometimes arrives pre-sugared, a barista once called out to me and put his hand up in a STOP motion to prevent me adding extra sugar.

Another thing to pay attention to is the rich layer of *crema* on top of your Neapolitan coffee. This is to do with the amount of *robusta* in the blend. Before you go whizzing a teaspoon around your cup, watch the locals. They either swirl the cup or do a different motion with the spoon. (I asked a barista to show me once, but that was mostly because he was not only a flirty Neapolitan but was also incredibly handsome.) Still, on occasion, I remember to do the spoon thing too.

Be aware that Neapolitan coffee tends to be stronger than its counterparts around the country. Because it tastes so amazing, when you knock back that first cup you'll instantly want more, but I recommend pacing yourself. Let some time lapse before you hit another one – at least enough time for that mega jolt of caffeine to kick in. (See the **Introduction** for my story about my first morning cruising Naples with Mr. Mode.)

One more thing to note: if all the pasta, pizza and bread you've been consuming have your personal plumbing backed up, make sure you're somewhere close to home base and try having a third espresso. Your hair might be standing on end for the rest of the day, but your pipes will be cleared for sure.

Caffé Sospeso

In a city renowned for the very best coffee in the world, it is unthinkable that someone should be denied this incredible pleasure just because they're poor. Everyone should be able to enjoy a piping hot espresso, no matter how down on their luck or impoverished they are. At least as far back as WWII, when Neapolitans suffered intense hardship, the custom of leaving *un caffé sospeso* ('suspending' a coffee for someone less fortunate) has become an integral part of Neapolitan culture.

Essentially, when you buy a cup (which costs around €1.20) you can pay for a second cup to be suspended. You'll notice some bars (you get coffee in a bar in Italy, hence the person who makes it is called a *barista*) may have a board with the words *caffé sospeso* and a number of check marks indicating how many coffees have been suspended. Or you may see a row of receipts taped to the bar window, or just hear someone ask the barista if there is a *caffé sospeso* available. Some bars have a bucket on the table where you can drop a euro, others you need to tell the barista you want to leave a coffee for someone else. Regardless, the concept is that someone who can't afford a coffee can still have one. It's a symbol of kindness, human decency and social solidarity, and I just love it.

One thing I always notice in Naples is the sense of community and civic pride shared amongst Neapolitans. They are very inclusive group and hold their culture close. You'll see opera house tickets suspended too (I talk about this in the **Teatro San Carlo** chapter), so whoever you are, from whichever walk of life, you too can enjoy your city's cultural heritage. Walking along the Via Tribunali I always notice receipts taped to street food vendors' windows providing a hot meal (be it a *pizza fritta*, a *cuoppa* or some other local street delicacy) to a Neapolitan who can't afford to eat. My friend and local guide Pina told me you even see it in some pharmacies where people will suspend commonly used over the counter products.

Next time you buy a coffee or a cappuccino in Naples, maybe think about suspending another for someone less fortunate than yourself. Rather than an act of charity, think of it as sharing a moment of pleasure.

Watch the Waiters

I can't even tell you how much I *love* this detail! Not all eateries have coffee machines, so when you order a coffee after your meal it sometimes comes from a bar up the street. Your waiter texts, calls or runs across the street with your coffee order. A few minutes later, a barista or waiter from said bar (frequently resplendent in black pants, white shirt and black tie, perhaps with a half-apron tied at his waist) races your way. With *Cirque du Soleil* levels of balance, he'll cut through the crowds and the traffic, flat-palming a tray over his head with your coffee on top.

It would be cool enough to watch this were he anywhere else in the world, but he's not. He is in the middle of crazy, chaotic Naples with Vespas weaving around him and cars whizzing past. Furthermore, he is *completely unfazed*. All the players in this madcap drama know their roles. He doesn't have to wait for a break in the traffic and they know the importance of a killer cup of Neapolitan coffee, so aren't about to hit him or make him drop his tray. He darts and sidesteps his way across the street not skipping a beat, this eccentric ballet playing out to the soundtrack of mayhem – horns honking, vendors shouting, Vespas, cars, traffic noises and church bells all at full volume. And, because he's Neapolitan and learned to flirt in utero, your coffee arrives with flourish, a wink and a smile.

Even on rainy days the same theatrical feat plays out, except then the coffee tray will be covered by a see-through plastic dome. Honestly, I could do this all day long.

The Cuccuma – The Neapolitan Coffee Pot

The *Morize* pot, the *Cuccumela*, the *Macchinetta* – this slice of Neapolitan coffee history has multiple names. Its original translation meant *little copper pot,* although they are now made of aluminum. Not to be confused with its more famous cousin, the moka pot, found in every home in Italy, the *Cuccuma* is unique to Naples. It even made its way into Neapolitan film culture in the 1967 movie *Questi Fantasmi,* when Sophia Loren spends a full two minutes on her rooftop terrace explaining to Vittorio Gassman how to make the perfect coffee. You can find the 2-minute sequence on YouTube if you don't want to watch the entire marvelous movie.

At first glance the cuccuma looks oddly incorrect – when not in use, its top portion has an upside-down spout. It is basically two pots with two handles, that screw into each other with a coffee filter in the middle. Like the moka pot, it is comprised of three parts. You fill the base chamber with water to just below the little hole in its side. (Look for the hole first.) This hole becomes a steam vent when the water gets boiling. You then insert the inner chamber, with its perforated screw top holding the coffee inside. The upside-down pot screws on top, and then you put the cuccuma on the stove.

Once the water boils and steam blows out the side hole like the vent in a volcano, the cuccuma is removed from the heat and turned upside down. Now the spout is facing the right way up. The boiling water moves through the coffee filter and into what was previously the top section. You then put a little paper cone over the spout to keep the aroma inside. Sophia Loren advocates putting this *cuppetiello* over the upside-down spout while the water is heating up. My Neapolitan friends say you put it on once you've flipped the pot. Either way it takes a few minutes, but you end up with an authentic cup of Neapolitan coffee.

Walking around the historic center of Naples you'll see these contraptions in shop windows. They make fantastic gifts and souvenirs – way better than a T-shirt made in China!

The big thing to remember here is that Neapolitans drink a lot of coffee. Most seem to drink 5–7 cups per day. More than just refueling, Neapolitan coffee is a ritual designed to be enjoyed with good company, at any time of day. If someone offers you a coffee, always say yes. It's part of the social structure and saying no would seem churlish. So what if you're wide awake until 4:00 am?

27.
Island Hopping: Procida, Ischia & Capri

Put a compass to paper and trace a circle. Then tell me which other country has a concentration of places like Amalfi, Naples, Ischia, Procida, Sorrento, Positano, Pompeii and Capri.

~ Diego della Valle

Yet another reason to devote multiple days to Naples is the access the city provides to the islands across the bay. The Gulf of Naples is home to an archipelago of five diverse islands. Unique, beautiful and glamorous, each has something special to offer. **Ischia** is the largest, **Capri** the most famous, **Procida** the most colorful. **Vivara** is a nature reserve. Crescent-shaped **Nisida** is the tiniest of them all.

Procida

Procida is one of the ten most colorful places on Earth and one of the most picturesque places on the planet. Just 40 minutes from Naples by boat, this jewel is well off the tourist radar, making it even more delicious.

No amount of googling images and videos prepares your brain for the explosion of color as you sail into **Marina Grande**, the island's main port. Traditional fishermen's houses painted in bright pastel shades of pink, yellow, blue, orange and red line the waterfront, offset by the intense blues of the Mediterranean and the Naples sky.

At less than two square miles, Procida is easily explored on foot in less than a day. On arrival you really must walk the waterfront, if only to take in all the color. It is so ridiculously *pretty*. From there, take time to wander the narrow streets and alleyways, listening out for Vespas whizzing past.

Terra Murata is the oldest village and the highest part of the island. The views from here are stunning. Dominated by the 16th century **Palazzo d'Avalos**, a monumental complex, it was home to the island's governors from 1563 until 1744 when the Bourbons turned it into a royal palace. By 1818, it became a military school, then a prison from 1830 until 1988. To visit Palazzo D'Avalos you can book a ticket in advance, but in the past I've been able to just wander in. Check ahead before coming to the island just in case.

After visiting Terra Murata wander down to Procida's most famous village, **Corricella**. This is a great spot to stop for lunch at one of the eateries along the seafront. I love sitting outdoors under the umbrellas, soaking up the atmosphere and views peppered with colorful old boats, and fishing nets drying in the sun. It's gorgeous. You'll feel like you're starring in your own Italian movie. In fact, this is where much of *Il Postino* was filmed, along the **Cala del Pozzo Vecchio** beach. You may also recognize parts of Procida from *The Talented Mr Ripley*.

Criss-crossing to the southern tip of the island you'll find the **Chiaiolella Marina** with its luxury boats. Along with a picture-postcard-pretty marina, this is where you'll find most of the hotels and many restaurants. From here you can access both the **Chiaiolello** and **Ciraccio** beaches, with both offering free public beach access as well as beach clubs. This is the most popular stretch of beach on the island, its shallow waters are ideal for swimming and its geography gives you sunshine all day long. If you are lucky enough to be on Procida later in the day, you can catch a dreamy sunset overlooking the islands of Vivara and Ischia from this point. This is also where you'll find the bridge to Vivara, from the promontory of **Santa Margherita**.

Foodie Paradise

Procida is a foodie paradise. Plenty of people pop over here purely for the pleasure of eating the local cuisine. If you're staying in Naples, you should come here for lunch at least once. I've never had an average meal on Procida – it has always been outstanding. Some dishes to keep an eye out for:

Spaghetti alla Pescatora Povere – A poor man's seafood spaghetti made with just anchovies and tomatoes.

Spaghetti ai Ricci di Mare – Sea urchin sautéed with olive oil, garlic, parsley and a touch of lemon.

Luveri al Sale – The local *pagello* sea bream, known here as *luvero*, is normally served in a salt crust.

Calamari Ripeni – Stuffed calamari.

Lemons – Procida is known for its large, sweet lemons. You'll find them in both sweet and savory dishes, in pastries – try the *Lingue di Procida* (tongues of Procida) – and also in the local *Insalata di Simone*, a refreshing lemon salad made with mint, garlic, olive oil and chili pepper. Before boarding the ferry back to Naples be sure to enjoy a next-level-fabulous lemon gelato in Marina Grande.

Coniglio alla Procidana – It's not all seafood here. Just like on neighboring Ischia, rabbit is popular on Procida too. Here it is prepared with cherry tomatoes, rosemary, garlic, white wine and olive oil.

Baldassare Cossa, the Pirate Pope

Procida was the home of my favorite bad pope. We met him earlier in this book, and I'm not kidding you – he and his two brothers were pirates! Born to a once noble but then impoverished family on Procida, the boys kept the family funded through piracy. I go into his story in depth in my book *Glam Italia! 101 Fabulous Things To Do In Florence*, but here's the abbreviated version – he earned doctorates in civil and canon law, became a cardinal then bought the papacy. He raided nunneries, stole all manner of treasures, and was eventually deemed Antipope John XXIII.

Getting there: Ferries and hydrofoils run throughout the day from Naples to Procida, Ischia and Capri.

Vivara

Connected to Procida by a 100-meter bridge, only crossable on foot, this small, crescent-shaped island is a protected nature reserve. Along with rare plants, migratory birds and rabbits, Vivara is also home to some incredibly important Mycenaean archaeological finds. It turns out the island was an important mediterranean trading center during the Bronze Age (16th and 15th centuries *BC*).

Vivara was a thriving community 4000 years ago, specializing in manufacturing ceramics as evidenced by vases discovered here. This was one of the most expansive and flourishing times in Greek history. They built a network of commercial hubs between the Aegean and Mediterranean Seas, with a series of important well-equipped ports along the way. This guaranteed the safe passage of goods to and from the east and west. Vivara was one of the main centers for processing metallic raw materials mined in Tuscany, Liguria and Sardegna. On the west side of the island at **Punta d' Alaca**, archaeologists have found metal objects, tools for sharpening blades, metal and copper droplets and waste from the smelting process.

Vivara has 3 km of coastline and is traversed by thousands of little paths cutting through the lush vegetation. The island is uninhabited and is under the protection of the State Nature Reserve. The only building on the island is a house built for Duke de Guevara in 1681. It later became a Bourbon hunting lodge.

You can come here as part of a (small) guided tour. Tours only run three days per week, between 10:00 am and 3:00 pm and require an online booking.

Website: https://www.vivarariservanaturalestatale.it
Email for reservations: prenotazionivivara@comune.procida.na.it

Ischia

At 46 square km, Ischia is the largest island in the archipelago. Famous for picturesque villages, thermal spas, hot springs and abundant nature, this is an ideal island to spend a multi-day getaway. There is plenty going on here to keep you busy, without a fraction of the crowds in nearby Capri. Ischia neither caters to the shopping whims of the superyacht crowd's luxe designer boutiques nor the cruise ship crowds' tacky souvenir stands. Any shopping here is mid-range, quality goods for regular Italians, who make up most of the visitors to the island. The restaurants and dining options are fantastic, and most are sensibly priced, again unlike Capri.

Ischia is also a great island for campers and there are several organized campsites close to the beaches. Scooters are a fun way to get around the island (if you know how to drive one) but be advised many rental places require your international driving permit to specify that you have a motorcycle license.

You could come here and just relax at the beach or a day spa, but there really is so much to do on Ischia. Along with spending a few lazy days doing nothing much at all, I recommend the following:

TAKE A BOAT TRIP AROUND THE ISLAND

This is always my favorite thing to do. Boat days are the best days! A local charter will take you to perfect swimming spots, while also pointing out interesting places as you circumvent the island. If you enjoy jumping off boats and swimming in the Med, this needs to be at the top of your list.

Charters often provide lunch, Prosecco and limoncello, but check first in case you need to pick up something at the marina before departing.

You can also rent boats and just meander out for an afternoon, but I prefer to have a local captain in charge.

VISIT THE ARAGONESE CASTLE

This most famous historical site on the island is not to be missed. Built on a huge rock (**insula minor**) connected to Ischia by a stone bridge, the original castle was built in the 5th century BC. At that time, it was known as Castrum Gironis, named for Girone/Hiero of Syracusa.

It had a fascinating history over the next two thousand years. In 1423 Alfonso of Aragon conquered the castle and it was renovated to its current splendor. The Avalos family governed the castle for the next two centuries, after which it changed hands several times, according to who was ruling Naples.

In 1911 the abandoned fortress was in ruins. A lawyer, Nicola Ernesto Mattera bought it from the state property office for the small sum of 25,000 lire. By 1913 he had purchased the surrounding land and moved in. Nicola spent the rest of his life restoring the property and the castle has stayed in his family, except for the fortified tower (**Il Maschio**) which was sold to a Neapolitan company by one of his sons. The remaining family members have returned the castle to its former glory.

It opened to the public in the late 90s. Along with the castle museum, there are eateries with gorgeous views. It is a tremendous place to visit. You can come alone or book a guided tour.

Hours: Open 365 days per year, 9:00 am until sunset.

Spend a Day at the Thermal Spa

For most visitors one of the main attractions on the island is a day spent at one of the thermal spas. And they are fantastic. Part of the larger Phlegraean Fields, the hot springs are a byproduct of all the geothermal action. Known for their curative properties, you can enjoy the natural mineral waters year-round, not just in summer.

Ischia offers an array of full-service day spas and free thermal baths. The most famous spas are **Negombo** and **Poseidon**, but there are plenty of natural springs scattered all over the island. Personally, I love anywhere with sun loungers, spritz-serving snack bars, bathrooms with hot running water and showers, and am happy to pay an entrance fee for this. Throw in the opportunity to have massages and facials? Count me in.

Visit the Archaeological Museum of Pithecusae

In 1952 publisher Angelo Rizzoli bought the 18th century **Villa Arbusto** in the little town of **Lacco Ameno.** Today it is a museum, housing artifacts from the oldest Greek settlement in the western Mediterranean. The most important piece here is the *Coppa di Nestore* (Nestor's Cup), a vase engraved with one of the most ancient examples of Greek writing. It dates back to the time of Homer, around the 8th century BC. At that time Ischia was called Pithecusae.

Excavations began here in 1950 and changed everything we knew about Greek colonization of southern Italy. The museum is small but fascinating to anyone with an interest in archaeology.

Hours: Open Tuesday to Sunday 9:30 am – 1:30 pm, then 3:00 pm – 6:30 pm October to May, and 4:00 pm – 7:30 pm June to September. Closed Mondays.
Tickets: €5

Forio

Forio, on the western coast of the island, is the largest of the six main towns on Ischia. It has a direct ferry connection to Naples and is beloved for its beautiful beaches and lovely historic center. Considered the cultural heart of Ischia, the town is full of artisan boutiques, art shops, art workshops as well as a summer cultural events calendar. There are plenty of historic churches and noble palazzi and it has a pretty marina full of colorful boats tied up to buoys. There are even a series of Saracen watch towers along the coastline. Be sure to watch the sunset over the Mediterranean from the terrace in front of the **Chiesa del Soccorso**.

One of the big local attractions is the **la Mortella Gardens**, a garden museum with over 3000 species of plants, that opened to the public in 1990. Concerts are held here over the summer.

The famous **Giardini Poseidon** is one of the island's most popular thermal parks. Spend the day here lying on the **Citara beach** and relaxing in the thermal pools. There are more hot springs bubbling up from below the seafloor in the nearby **Bay of Sorgeto**. Here you can enjoy the unique experience of hot spring water and cool sea water for free.

Forio is a great place to stay if you want a (slightly) busier town with more things to do. Think of it more as a fun trip destination than a lovers' retreat.

Sant' Angelo

Meanwhile, on the southern coast, Sant'Angelo is the most well-known village on the island and possibly the most picturesque. This is a great place for a lovers' getaway. Sant' Angelo is a suburb of

Serrara Fontana and is famous for the views of its tufa rock mini-island known as *La Torre*.

This fishing town is a bit more isolated and has a relaxed atmosphere with its pedestrian streets and chilled out vibe. It has some lovely hotels, and the town center is completely closed to traffic, which is worth considering if you plan on bringing excess luggage.

While beautiful and remote, it is a tad trickier to get to as it's not close to any of the ports. Your closest access is a 30-minute cab ride which costs around €40 (at the time of writing this). The public bus will get you here from the port in 45 minutes.

HIKE MOUNT EPOMEO

For those who enjoy hiking, climbing to the peak of Mount Epomeo (800 meters above sea level) is spectacular. This is the ancient volcano in the heart of Ischia. It takes about an hour (or longer if I'm with you). Along the way you'll see ruins of ancient cliff buildings including the **Eremo di San Nicola**, an old church carved out of the volcanic tufa stone. On a clear day from the peak, you can see all the way out to the islands of Ponza and Ventotene. You can also just enjoy the lush foliage taking a long walk on its slopes. You enter the walk from the village of **Fontana**, near Sant'Angelo.

WHAT TO EAT ON ISCHIA

Obviously, this is a seafood paradise. Everything you order was caught fresh last night and came in off the boats this morning. Everywhere you go here the food is outstanding. But what if you don't want fish?

The other super famous dish on Ischia is **Coniglio all'Ischitana**, or Ischian rabbit. I'm not a rabbit-eater but have zero problem with a fish staring up at me from my plate, so no judgement here. Your bunny is simmered in a mixture of tomatoes, basil, garlic, olive oil and white wine until tender and served as a stew of sorts.

Zingara is the most loved street food on the island. Two slices of rustic local bread, stuffed with fillings of your choice and grilled. The most popular is a bufala mozzarella, tomato and prosciutto combo. You can't go wrong.

Getting there: Ischia has three ports, and the island is quite large, so you need to find out which port is closest to your accommodation. There are cars on the island, and you can technically bring one, but be aware there's not a lot of parking and some towns don't allow cars. Do a little research first.

Capri

Capri is the island that gets most overcrowded with tourists. The reason for this is simple: Capri is staggeringly beautiful. Mind-bendingly stunning.

This is the island I've spent the most time on – along with my own adventures, for the past ten years I've brought almost all my Glam Italia tours here. (My tours have a maximum of six women, so before you think we're part of the overcrowding problem, be reassured that we're not.)

This is an island with loads of cool things to see and do. You'll fall in love with Capri. The smell of lemons and jasmine will haunt you, and the views will become screensavers on the inside of your eyelids forever more. For the past 10+ years my phone screensaver has been a photo overlooking the rocks and sea taken from the park beside **Villa Jovis**. Capri is in my thoughts every time I pick up my phone.

The Elephant in the Piazzetta

We can't move forward without addressing the elephant in the room (which in this case is the piazzetta). Yes, the crowds on Capri can be insane, especially when the cruise ships are in. Capri has a year-round population of 14,000, but during the high season as many as 24,000 tourists arrive *per day*. The annual tourist load is somewhere around 2.2 million people, most of whom spend their time loitering in the main piazza in Capri town. Or doing things in groups of 50. This means we must approach our time on Capri with a strategy. Since the bulk of the tourists clog up the city center, hanging out at the overly expensive cafes in the piazzetta and in the luxury designer stores, it's really easy to get away from them.

Although you can come here easily for a day trip, I recommend you plan to stay a couple of nights on the island. The final ferries depart quite early – normally around 6:30 – 7:30 pm. And then Capri – even the piazzetta – has transformed into the chic, gorgeous island of your dreams. The crowds are gone, leaving you with the real Capri and views out to forever, in some of the most beautiful light anywhere in the world.

Whether you are into history and archaeology, nature and hiking, beaches and wine tasting, or you're a foodie traveler who enjoys a little fashion flare, Capri has something wickedly fabulous for you.

Historical Capri

While clearing land to build new imperial buildings some 2000 years ago, the ancient Romans unearthed some very ancient history. Along with traces of Stone Age settlements they found remains of animals that had become extinct tens of thousands of years prior. Suetonius wrote that Emperor Augustus was so fascinated with the remains he created the first ever museum of paleontology in the garden of his villa.

In the 8th century BC, the Greeks had already settled on Ischia and at Cumae. At some point they also moved to Capri. In his book *Geographica*, Greek historian and philosopher Strabo (63 BC – 24 BC) wrote of two towns in Capri, later reduced to one. No doubt the 'one' was Capri town, where remains of Greek fortification walls and buildings date to around the 5th century BC. The other town is probably **Anacapri**, based on the **Phoenician Steps**, an ancient Greek staircase connecting Marina Grande and Anacapri. (More on the steps below.) It was only recently discovered that this famous staircase was in fact chiseled out of the rock face by the Greeks around 7th–6th century BC.

For ten years Tiberius, the second emperor, ruled the Roman Empire from Capri. He built twelve villas here, my favorite of which is **Villa Jovis** (below). After the fall of the Roman Empire, Capri was mostly under the rule of Naples. During the Middle Ages it suffered brutal pirate raids and multiple watch towers were built to help defend the island.

The first tourist to Capri may have been Jean Jacques Bouchard, a 17th century Frenchie, whose diary (discovered in 1850) is an important source of information about the island. By the second half of the 19th century, Capri had become a popular destination for writers, artists and celebrities. And now, today, there's you and me.

STRATEGY

So, let's talk about our strategy. A trip to Capri requires a little planning so you don't squander your precious time amid the fanny-packers. This is super easy if you're staying on the island, as during their peak hours you'll be chilling out on your terrace, soaking up the views. Or you'll be working on your tan at one of the wickedly chic beach clubs. (Even the not-chic ones are still ridiculously fabulous.) But whether you're staying or just coming for the day, you need a plan, a list of things to see and do, and an idea of where you'll eat. (Not the piazzetta!)

The first part of my strategy involves getting from the marina up to Capri town. When I get off the ferry, I deposit my group at a coffee place close to the funicular (the cable railway that runs you up and down the hill) and have them order my breakfast/cappuccino for me while I zip over to the ticket office to buy funicular tickets. The ticket office is diagonally opposite the funicular, where the bus and ferry tickets are sold.

Once done breakfasting/having coffee, I keep an eye on the line for the funicular. We either line up when there's a break in the action, or I time it using the neon people counter, so we are at the front of the *next* batch of humans heading up the hill. I want to be at the front A) so we get great seats with the best views and B) so we're not at the back of the bunch when we exit.

As you exit the funicular station, turn right and walk to the terrace for the first of your many fabulous photo-stops. This spot is wonderful but gets filled up fast. Remember, most of the people crowding you here won't adventure out much further, so you'll have oodles more opportunities for incredible photos of you and Capri.

From here you have to step into the piazzetta – it's in front of you. The plan is to soak it up later in the day when the crowds are thinning (or gone if you're overnighting), so don't panic when you see all the people squishing in there – we are literally 30 seconds from escaping them and things are about to get fabulous.

It gets hot on the island, and chances are you'll be coming here in the warmer months, so the first things we want to do are anything that involves exertion or walking. So let's go…

Villa Jovis

One of the things I love most about coming up here is that within 30 seconds of stepping away from the swarming masses in the piazzetta you enter a whole new world. You're immediately away from the crowds, and you have some of the most sensational views on the island largely to yourself. The first 15 minutes you'll encounter random travelers staying in accommodations along this stretch, but from then on it's just locals. It's glorious! Steep in places, but totally magnificent. There are multiple places to stop, each with progressively more astounding views. Shortly before reaching the top there's a restaurant/bar to your left. I always stop here either on the way up or the way down (or both) for a coffee/spritz/lemon soda and take in the spellbinding view from the terrace.

The Back Story

This one ties in with my favorite murderess in history (although my private guides in Rome say I'm not allowed to call her that). In 38 BC Livia divorced her husband Tiberius Claudius Nero (not *that* Nero) and married Julius Caesar's adopted heir, Octavian. She brought with her two sons from her previous marriage, Drusus and

Tiberius. In 27 BC, Octavian became Augustus, the first emperor of Rome and our friend Livia became the first empress. They were married for 52 years, until his death. She was ambitious, clever, a powerful political player, and it would seem, a great wife.

From the beginning Livia wanted her eldest son, Tiberius, to succeed Augustus. And funnily enough, *every single person* who came in line between Augustus and Tiberius mysteriously died. Including Augustus' grandsons. Ancient writers Tacitus and Suetonius both support my theory that Livia murdered them all. Augustus supposedly died of natural causes on August 19, 14 AD, but some speculate that Livia helped the process along. On one hand, he was 75 at the time. On the other hand, she was Livia. We'll never know the real story, but I think it's more interesting to think of her as a mastermind killer.

Tiberius becomes emperor. Twelve years into his reign he leaves Rome forever, moving to his island getaway in Capri. He lives out the rest of his life here, ruling the empire from the island. It makes sense in a way – at a time when everyone was getting assassinated, the island offered him incredible security and, away from Rome's prying eyes, it also gave him the privacy to live a life of absolute debauchery without consequence. Tiberius built 12 palaces here on Capri, the most celebrated of which is our next destination: the spectacular **Villa Jovis**.

High up on Mount Tiberio, the second highest mountain on the island, Tiberius' palace of Jupiter (Villa Jovis) has views stretching across the Bay of Sorrento to Naples in one direction, and the length of the Amalfi Coast in the other. The views up here are just *spectacular*.

Villa Jovis was around 7000 square feet of marble clad magnificence. With multiple levels and multiple terraces, the front face of the palace is thought to have been 40 meters tall. The white marble facade will have gleamed across the bay in the Caprese sunshine.

You can still visit Villa Jovis and walk through corridors and the remaining rooms of the palace across multiple levels. Plaques tell you about the various rooms, and you get a sense of the genius behind both the design and construction. You also get to enjoy the views of Tiberius – the wow factor is off the charts.

Along with swimming from a chartered boat all afternoon, this is my absolute favorite thing to do on Capri. I do it pretty much every time I come here, which can be five or six times per year.

The Tiberius Jump

Tiberius was a depraved fellow. One of his sources of entertainment was his celebrated Tiberius Jump. The convicted had a choice: go to jail or try your luck jumping to freedom from the cliff. From up here it looked like a back breaking 330-meter drop to the sea. In reality, bodies crashed into the spiked rocks a short way down, destroyed on impact. Tiberius also had those who simply fell out of favor with him hurled over the edge.

The Walk Up

Potential attackers would have been spotted making their way across the bay. But should they succeed in getting to Capri, they would then have to make their way up the steep path to the palace. Wide enough for a litter to carry the emperor up and down the hill, it was way too narrow to mount much of an attack, particularly the last stretch of the path.

As you walk up here, look to the homes that line the pathway. Some still have columns lining the entry to what would have been the homes of senators 2000 years ago.

THE NOSE KNOWS

There are all kinds of fabulous island summer smells to enjoy on the way up. For the rest of your life every time you smell the combination of jasmine and lemons, you'll be jolted back to Capri to re-live the intense colors and mad beauty of the island. But there's another smell to be aware of as you enter the final stretch up to the villa – wild mountain goats. Capra means goat, and Capri is the island of wild mountain goats. But good lord, the stench! They really are ripe. And inquisitive. And endearing. You'll smell them before you see them and will have plenty of time to get your camera ready.

When I've encountered them, they've been on goat paths slightly above me, faces bent and twisted from falling down cliff faces, and stinky as all get out. But also, incredibly cool. Depending on their moods, they may ignore you, tip their heads from side to side looking at you, or bare their teeth and shout at you in Caprese goat dialect. They are fantastic!

The walk up to Villa Jovis takes around 45 minutes, is quite steep, and requires decent shoes/sandals, not flip flops. As you turn left onto via Tiberio there's normally a group of old men hanging out chatting. They'll tell you if Villa Jovis is closed, and are 100% more reliable than the website, which I'm not sure is ever updated. I still go up anyway because the views are so insane. There is a little park on your right just before the palace. Be sure to walk out here for an entirely different set of views. You never know, your photos from here could well end up being your screensavers too.

I suggest googling images of Villa Jovis before coming to Capri. Once you see how amazing it is you'll invariably find a way to work it into your itinerary. Also, there is hardly anyone up here. In my experience it's mostly random, well-informed Brits and bilingual Germans, all of whom have vast banks of knowledge about what they're visiting and are happy to point things out to you.

ONE LAST THING...

On the way back down, instead of turning right onto Via Sopramonte, turn left. Follow this road (Via Matermania) until it becomes Via Arco Naturale. You are now in a gorgeous nature preserve with views of the other side of the island. There is a wonderful hidden restaurant here called **Le Grottelle**. The food is fabulous, and you'll feel like you're on your own paradise island.

Anacapri

There are two principal towns on the island, Capri and Anacapri. You definitely need to experience both.

THE PHOENICIAN STEPS

Along Via Palazzo a Mare, 400 meters from the port in Marina Grande, a majolica sign announces the beginning of the staircase. For thousands of years this was how everything was transported from the port, up Monte Solano to Anacapri. Of course, most of the hard work was done by women carrying heavy vases on their heads. In the late 18th century when travelers started coming to Anacapri, the women were replaced by donkeys. The road between Capri and Anacapri wasn't built until 1874.

The staircase is steep and arduous but rewards you with some of the most gorgeous views on the island. Look for crosses carved into the steps; these were to ask for protection from the rocks raining down on islanders using the stairs. (Steel netting now keeps loose rocks from falling on you.) Along the way you'll see the tiny white church of **Sant' Antonio**.

You can expect the climb to take around an hour. The steps were restored in 1998 and are quite safe, but very steep. To protect your knees, you are better to climb up rather than descend the staircase. Also pay attention to the heat – you may want to rethink this on a really hot day. Personally, I take one of the islands iconic convertible taxis from the port or Capri town to Anacapri. Hilariously, the slang for convertible is *decapitata* (decapitated). Taxis, like everything else on the island, are super expensive, but if there's a group of you it's great fun. There is also a specially designed bus that runs back and forth. The road is non-stop hairpin turns and steep, but the taxis and buses whip up and down like it ain't no thing. This is probably why (as far as I know) there are no rental cars on Capri. The very last thing you would want is to meet a tourist driver on this road.

At the top of the hill in Anacapri, be sure to visit the iconic **Villa San Michele**. Built 20 years after the completion of the road, most of the building materials were nonetheless transported up the stairs by men and donkeys. Anacapri has an entirely different vibe. It is much more chill, is very residential and has some lovely little shops. It also has some really cool old ruins to check out.

Villa Damecuta

Damecuta is another of Tiberius' fabulous palaces, this time in Anacapri, above the **Blue Grotto**. Based on the marble floors, art, decorations and stucco discovered during excavations, Damecuta was possibly the most luxurious of his palaces on the island. Volcanic dust found on the walls of the loggia indicate the palace was damaged by the eruption of Mount Vesuvius in 79 AD. Sadly, archaeologists have established Palazzo A Mare and Villa Damecuta suffered deliberate damage during Bourbon and English occupation, when they built their military fortifications.

To visit Villa Damecuta you stroll along a pathway with breathtaking scenery, then through a shaded pine grove. You can walk all through the ruins, taking in the same views Tiberius did, 2000 years ago.

Damecuta Tower

West of the villa you'll see the 12th century Damecuta tower, built to provide warning and protection from pirate raids. (There are multiple watchtowers around the island.) Some interesting artifacts were discovered here, including an Egyptian *cipollino* marble column with its capital and base, remains of floors, green marble columns and some Greek inscriptions.

The Blue Grotto

The Blue Grotto is a sea cave below Anacapri, filled with a surreal blue light. With only a very low opening from above the level of the sea, most of the sunlight is blocked from the entrance. The magic happens due to light passing through a *secondary* hole in the rocks somewhere below the surface. The secondary hole becomes the main source of light into the sea cave. As sunlight passes through the water, the red tones get filtered out, causing only blue light to bounce up through the hole and into the cave. Or something like that. However it happens, the effect is pure magic.

The domed cave is around 60 meters long and 25 meters wide, and apparently is 150 meters from the top of the cave to the sandy sea bottom below. The entrance is only 2 meters wide and around 1 meter high, when the tide is low.

History
This was Tiberius' private swimming cave and a marine temple of sorts. At that time the grotto was decorated with statues, three of which were recovered from the sea floor in 1964. Pliny the Elder wrote about the grotto, describing a statue of Triton playing on a shell. From this, it is believed the 1964 statues were in fact Tiberius' from the 1st century AD. In 2009, seven bases from statues were found, so there are possibly four more statues down there, somewhere.

There are three passageways at the back of the cave leading to the *Sala dei Nomi* (Room of Names) and two more passages leading from there to the stairs to Tiberius' palace.

Access
You access the grotto in a shallow rowboat, oared by one of the licensed Blue Grotto boatmen, of which there are very few. The boatman tells you to lie down as the boat slips through the narrow opening, and within seconds you enter the realm of the sirens, and one of the most beautiful sights you'll ever see.

Only the official Blue Grotto boatmen are allowed inside, and only in their special boats. Your charter boat captain cannot take you inside. Instead, you float around the bay waiting for a Blue Grotto boatman to approach you. On a good day this can be quite quick, however sometimes the bay is swarmed with tourist boats, particularly when the cruise ships are in, and you can wait well over an hour. If you come down the stairs from Capri you possibly have a shorter wait, but fewer boatmen service that dock.

In my opinion this needs to be on your **must-see** list, but with a caveat. If you come by private chartered boat your captain should advise you how long the wait will be. All the local boatmen know each other and communicate back and forth. If you have to wait longer than 30 minutes, just move on. Most of us only have a short time on the island, none of which should be wasted in long lines. Depending on how long you have your boat booked, you may be able to come back later in the day.

The grotto closes when the tide is high and when the waves get too choppy. Definitely put it on your itinerary but assume there's only a 50% chance you'll get in.

Swimming is forbidden in the grotto and can earn you a €10,000 fine.

Monte Solaro Chairlift

From the main piazza in Anacapri you can take a 10-minute chairlift ride to the summit of Monte Solaro. Of course, the views from up here are ridiculous. From the dramatic cliffs and rocks to the length of the Sorrento peninsula and the Amalfi Coast, from up here you can see it all. Before walking back down, stop at the **Hermitage of Santa Maria di Cetrella**. Facing Capri town and Marina Piccola, the Franciscan hermitage was built in the 1400s. It contains a Madonna revered by pilgrims. Capriote citizens prayed to her to protect their fishermen.

HAVE A FOODIE EXPERIENCE

Another super cool thing to do here in Anacapri is to have a foodie experience. The **Michel'angelo Cooking School** has taught more than 1500 cooking classes to visitors since 2015. Some of you will remember the former Michel'angelo restaurant in Capri, others will have read about it in Kevin Kwan's best-selling book *Sex & Vanity* (the follow up to his massively successful *Crazy Rich Asians*). Along with catering private dinner parties and events at villas, retreats, and on boats, the Anacapri-based Michel'angelo offers some incredible foodie experiences. From divine cooking classes to degustation menus, limoncello workshops to gelato workshops, tastings of local extra virgin olive oils, wines and cheeses, there are multiple options here to have a truly authentic Caprese experience, far from the crowds in the piazzetta. And all of them are super fun. There are loads of different cooking classes to choose from too – see the website below.

Another offering I just die over is Michel'angelo's gourmet picnics. Book a picnic ahead of time and either pick it up or have it delivered to your boat or location. Brunch, lunch or sunset, they even give you ideas for tourist-free spots to enjoy your banquet. (There are multiple food options too.) Capri is the chicest island in the Mediterranean and in my opinion, this is one of the most chic things you can do. Even the woven hessian bags your picnic arrives in (which you get to keep) are fashion forward fabulous, while the food packaging is biodegradable. On top of that, this is all done at the hands of one of the island's most celebrated chefs using locally grown, zero-km produce. Don't just take my word for it, they've been written up in Harper's Bazaar, Travel & Leisure, New York Times, and The New Yorker, along with TV shows and Italian publications.

The Most Romantic Thing You'll Ever Hear

You *must* listen to the **Untold Italy Podcast episode #42** before coming to Capri. Co-owner Holly Star tells the story of traveling to Capri on a whim, meeting and falling in love with Gianluca, the owner and chef at the Michel'angelo restaurant, marrying him and moving to Capri. Holly's story is about the most romantic thing you will ever hear.

Check out their website: www.giardinodicapri.com and follow them (Holly) on Instagram @michelangelo_capri

CHARTER A BOAT

My favorite thing to do on Capri, whether paired with a picnic or just a panino, is chartering a private boat for the afternoon. I prefer the traditional gozzo boats, although there's pretty much every kind of island boat you can imagine. The traditional boats are just more fun.

Your boat captain will circumnavigate the island, stopping at a variety of cool spots for you to swim. Over the years I've visited secret coves to dive into the sea from Roman ruins, and others where you swim through a hole in the rock into a private sea pool. We've floated on our backs in the beautiful Mediterranean Sea, gazing up at the crazy views, wondering how on earth this can possibly be our lives? We've swum through grottos and dived from the boat in front of the famous faraglioni rocks. If you like boats and swimming, you just cannot beat this experience. My captain's mother always puts a bottle of limoncello on the boat for us, made from the lemons in her garden. While we tool around the island, he points out every cool detail and tells stories you couldn't otherwise access. It's the greatest thing ever.

Enjoy a Beach Club

If you're not in the mood for ancient history or nature walks and don't feel like chartering a boat, spend an afternoon at a beach club in Capri. There are multiple beach clubs around the island to choose from, but you will probably need a reservation ahead of time. Rent sun loungers and an umbrella, order a spritz and love your life.

Getting here: Ferries run all day from Naples and Sorrento and a little less frequently from Positano and Salerno. You arrive in Marina Grande, then take a funicular up the hill to Capri town. If you have luggage you'll want to grab a taxi, but be aware there are plenty of areas they can't drive through. If you're staying overnight, check with your accommodation first.

Make sure you know the time of the last ferry crossing back home and buy tickets ahead of time. Normally the last ferries depart around 6:30 pm.

Nisida

This crescent-shaped island is the smallest in the archipelago. Connected to Posillipo by a bridge, this is home to Naples' juvenile detention center. Public access is normally forbidden here. Occasionally cultural events and guided tours are held here, but in general this island is out of bounds.

Fun fact: the island is thought to be the place in the Odyssey from where the sirens tried to lure Ulysses during his journey.

28.
The Reading List: Ten Wonderful Books Set in Naples

1. *THE GUARDIAN OF MERCY: HOW AN EXTRAORDINARY PAINTING BY CARAVAGGIO CHANGED AN ORDINARY LIFE TODAY* – TERENCE WARD

This is a fabulous odyssey into the life and work of Caravaggio and the creation of *The Seven Acts of Mercy*. The modern story unfolds as Ward moves to Florence and makes frequent trips to Naples. He and his girlfriend meet Angelo, a Neapolitan museum worker whose job is watching over the Caravaggio masterpiece. The ensuing story of art, eccentricity and Naples will have you desperate to visit both the painting and the city.

2. *THE POISON KEEPER* – DEBORAH SWIFT

This is the compelling story of Giulia Tofana, a 17th century professional poisoner of violent husbands. When the authorities arrest and then execute her mother, the original poisoner, Giulia flees to Naples. Here she sets up a secret shop and sells Aqua Tofana, an arsenic rich potion, to women being beaten by their husbands. Based on a true story this book takes you inside Naples under Spanish rule in the 1600s. It's part of a series that ends in Rome.

3. *FALLING PALACE: A ROMANCE OF NAPLES* – DAN HOFSTADTER

This is a gorgeous autobiography about the complexities of a boy from New York moving to Naples and falling for a local girl. His stories of Naples, the friends he makes and the crazy life he leads there are so beautifully written, you'll both fall in love with Naples and feel profoundly lost when it's over.

4. *LOST IN THE SPANISH QUARTER* – HEDDI GOODRICH

A poignant autobiographical tale of life and passionate first love in the crumbling Spanish Quarter of Naples. Arriving in Naples as a 16-year-old foreign exchange student, Heddi falls for the city and can't bring herself to leave. While earning a degree in linguistics, she tumbles into a life changing romance with fellow student Pietro. Goodrich leads us through her fierce love for a man and a city, languages and cultures, introducing us to the colorful characters who enriched her life along the way. This book is beautiful.

5. *THE NIGHT VILLA* – CAROL GOODMAN

This spellbinding novel of romance, treachery and intrigue takes place between Capri and Naples. Told through the stories of two women 2000 years apart – a slave girl in 79 AD and a modern-day Classics professor – I found it hard to put this book down.

6. *THE COLLABORATOR* – GERALD SEYMOUR

This thriller takes place between London and Naples. Immacolata Borelli is in London ostensibly as an accounting student, but really, she's there to watch over her gangster brother who is wanted for multiple murders in Naples. The Borelli family are deeply enmeshed in the Camorra, the Neapolitan crime network known to be more deadly and more ruthless than the Sicilian Mafia. When Immacolata's childhood friend dies, she reaches out to a senior Carabinieri Camorra investigator to help bring her crime family down, setting in motion a terrifying series of events. Thriller readers will love this one.

7. *I WILL HAVE VENGEANCE* – MAURIZIO DE GIOVANNI

This is the first book in the Commissario Ricciardi series. When one of the world's greatest tenors, Maestro Vezzi is found brutally murdered in his dressing room backstage at the Teatro San Carlo, Commissario Ricciadi is called in to investigate. Riccardi is cursed with a secret – he can see the ghosts of the victims he investigates and can hear their final thoughts. This book and series set in Naples are great for anyone who enjoys Donna Leon or Agatha Christie.

8. *THE WOLF DEN* – ELODIE HARPER

When Amara's loving father, a doctor in Greece, dies, her now impoverished mother sells her into slavery. Her new owner also owns the Wolf Den, Pompeii's most notorious brothel. The companionship and friendship of her fellow brothel workers stops her spirit from being broken and fuels her determination to fight for her freedom. This is book one in a trilogy set in Pompeii. Fabulous for lovers of historical fiction.

9. *THE TEMPTATION TO BE HAPPY* – LORENZO MARONE

This is the story of Cesare, a cantankerous 77-year-old widower who spends his days avoiding his children and his old cat lady neighbor. However, when the mysterious Emma and her sinister husband move in next door, he is suspicious that there's more here than meets the eye. Before long he enlists the other neighbors to help him investigate, giving him a whole new purpose in life and making him an unlikely hero. Charming and funny, this book will make you both laugh and cry. Truly wonderful.

10. *THE LADY QUEEN: THE NOTORIOUS REIGN OF JOANNA I* – NANCY GOLDSTONE

The enthralling story of a beautiful queen, a shocking murder, a papal trial and one of the most fascinating women in history. On March 15, 1348, 22-year-old Joanna I Queen of Naples stood trial before the Pope for the brutal murder of her cousin and husband, Prince Andrew of Hungary. She defended herself, in Latin no less, and eventually against enormous odds, was acquitted. Joanna went on to rule one of Europe's most glamorous courts for 30 years and was the only female European monarch at the time to rule in her own name. A brilliant leader, she successfully navigated Naples through the turmoil of wars and plagues, built hospitals and churches, and truly cared for her subjects. Her life was embroiled with intrigue and treachery, ultimately ending in murder. This book gives you fascinating insight both into her life and into the complexities of ruling during the turbulence of the Middle Ages. It also reads like Game of Thrones without the dragons – the subterfuge, deceit, intrigue going on inside the castle walls is astounding. The fact that this young girl could not only navigate her way through all of this but also keep her kingdom intact is testament to what a remarkable woman she truly was.

If you're not sure about reading this one, listen to the Noble Blood podcast below. You too will become fascinated with Joanna.

Podcasts

The following podcasts are tremendous and both are worth listening to if you're planning a trip to Naples.

NOBLE BLOOD PODCAST

Dana Schwartz' fabulous podcast introduces us to fascinating blue bloods throughout history. I particularly love that although some episodes are about well-known historical figures like Napoleon, she devotes most episodes to lesser-known characters. Her episode on Queen Joanna of Naples is wonderful.

Episode #114 The Trials of Joanna of Naples

THE REST IS HISTORY

Some history podcasts are a bit boring, but this one is narrated by two fun Brits. Tom Holland and Dominic Sandbrook manage to take weighty historical fact and make it super interesting and enjoyable to listen to.

Episode #224 Grand Villas on the Bay of Naples

29.

Arrivederci

Naples is a city where passion burns bright.

- Anonymous

When you find your stride in Naples, the city turns into an addiction, a siren song constantly calling you back.

I can't decide if it's the exhilarating madness of the place, the never-ending historical treasures lying in wait for me to discover like a cultural game of hide and seek, the fascinating characters living here, or the staggering beauty of the place. Then of course, there's a volcano as well. Naples is just everything, everywhere, all at once.

Don't expect to understand Naples, or for it to even make sense. Naples is like nowhere else on Earth. They speak in a secret code and live in yet another. As outsiders we'll never crack the code and we'll never be part of it, and that's fine – I will happily, giddily be a tourist here for the rest of my life.

Along with *Napoletano* – the second most spoken language in all of Italy – Napolitani also speak another language: the language of passion. Red hot, fiery, unbridled passion. They are fervently passionate in love and judging by the arguments you hear on the street, equally impassioned in war. Family rows, lovers' tiffs and neighbors' skirmishes happen at full volume, with intensity. Mind you, so do discussions about ham sandwiches, soccer and the weather report. Then the storm blows over and for a while at least, the seas are once again calm.

Don't confuse the never-ending honking of horns and shaking of fists with road rage – it's communication. One time, years ago, a taxi driver was blasting his horn and shouting and waving his fists and I was sure the cars would stop and the drivers would come to blows. He laughed and told me it was just his cousin, who is also his best friend and who he loves most in the world after his mamma. The horn honking and shouting are part of the crazy fun here. So long as I'm not driving, I'm here for it.

Whether you're a guest or a native, Mount Vesuvius takes part in every day spent in Naples. This big old composite stratovolcano is constantly watching, playing multiple roles in every story. Sometimes the protagonist – Vesuvius' fertile lands drew the Greeks and Romans here instead of somewhere else along the coast. Without Vesuvius there would be no Pompeii, no snapshot of life 2000 years ago.

Ever the backdrop, some find the volcano sinister and intimidating, while others like me find it equal parts enthralling and alluring. Every photo resonates when Vesuvius makes an appearance in the background. And yet the mountain is also the antagonist, the brooding arch villain in the story, glowering threateningly in the background. He scoops up all the attention while the real villain, the biggest threat of them all, is the all-powerful super-volcano lurking underwater in the Campi Flegrei. Should it blow, scientists believe the Earth will plunge into a global winter lasting several years. There will be 100-foot tsunamis, crop devastation and mass extinctions.

Will the super volcano blow during our lifetime? Who knows. Maybe? Or maybe centuries will pass before it erupts again. The big issue is if either of them start showing off again everything that is Naples will be gone forever. Perhaps that's why I feel such urgency to spend as much time as possible in Naples, to see all the things, eat all the food, drink all the wine, here and now while I still can. Or maybe it's just because Naples is so cool, and I feel so alive when I'm there.

When I moved into my home in Tuscany one of the first things I did was figure out which trains could get me to Naples the quickest, and if I could get there in time for breakfast. It wasn't merely *desire* to have easy access to Napoli, it was an overwhelming need. I've no idea how many times I've been to Naples at this point, but somewhere along the way I caught my rhythm here. I found my favorite coffee spots and my favorite *taralli* kiosk on the waterfront. I know where I like to wander to take in the views and from where I like to watch sunset. And along the way I've been finding my people too. Some are deep friendships that will last forever, others are the casual acquaintances you meet during the course of life.

Recently I buzzed down to Naples for the day from my Tuscan home. I arrived at 9:15 and by 9:35 was strolling down the street in the Vomero to my favorite breakfast place, the one on a quiet sloping street with a view of Capri across the water. It had been five months since my last adventure in the city, so I didn't expect anyone to recognize me. When I was still 100 meters away from the café the waiter spotted me, raised his hands in a wide V above his head and called out "I knew you'd be back!". He met me partway down the slope, gave me the customary cheek kisses, and guided me to my favorite table. I didn't need to give him my order, it's always the same

– cappuccino and cornetto (croissant). He told me to get comfortable and he'd bring my breakfast out. During the short time I was there, he managed to ask me a hundred questions about where I'd been, how long was I here this time, what were my plans, what was I doing today. I was so taken with his genuine interest, even though he knew it could be months before I returned, if I ever did. To me, he is a prime example of the people you meet in Naples. Gregarious, fun and caring. Just like Mr. Mode.

As I am writing this last paragraph, I have been messaging back and forth with my dear friend Pina. We normally coordinate my day trips to Naples with her private tour guiding schedule and plan an event or a spritz around the two. We just calendared a diving trip to Baiae to swim through the undersea ruins, for 3 weeks from today. I'll have time to roll into Vomero for breakfast beforehand and our train schedules allow us oodles of time to sip Aperol spritzes with a view of the sea in Pozzuoli after.

Veronique still messages me with random nights her apartment is available, coordinated with the calendar for the Teatro San Carlo. I'm determined to pair my overnights in Naples with performances at the theater – the San Carlo has me hooked. I can't wait to be back there again, hanging out in the courtyard with her and the artist whose front door opens to the sea, talking about tomatoes, volcanoes and Greek ruins, breathing in the lemons, soaking up the view.

Open yourself up to this crazy city, its mayhem and its quirks, the views, the history and above all the wonderful people, and you too will discover – Naples is magic.

30. What Next?

Thank you for reading *Glam Italia! 101 Fabulous Things To Do In Naples!*

Now that you've made it to the end of the book, can I ask you a favor? Please leave a review on Amazon. Reviews and 5-star ratings are crucial to the survival of indie books like mine and stop them from being swallowed up by the big corporate travel books.

More importantly, your review will help other travelers just like you who are trying to find helpful, interesting books to help them plan their trip and add value to their time in Naples.

THE GLAM ITALIA NEWSLETTER

Subscribe to my monthly newsletter at CorinnaCooke.com. Every month I'll update you on travel news and tell you about cool, off the radar towns and villages you probably have never heard of before and may want to add to a future Italy itinerary. I also talk about new sites and events opening in the bigger, more touristed towns and cities, giving you more great options to escape the crowds while enjoying your ultimate Italian experience.

Let's Get Social

My website CorinnaCooke.com has links to all my socials, but you can also find them here:

Instagram: @CorinnaTravels
Facebook: Corinna Cooke Author
Pinterest: @Corinnamakeup
TikTok: CorinnaTravels1

Download The Guides PDF

GlamItaliaBooks.com/Naples–Private–Guides

Download my list of private guides for Naples and the surrounding area. These are good people who I know and work with in real life.

The guides on this list are all **fully licensed, local** guides. The list not only helps you find a guide, it also meets my personal sustainable travel goals. By booking a guide directly rather than through a travel corporation, your travel dollars stay right here in Naples, paying real people's rent, food and electricity bills. The guide gets 100% of the fee. They don't pay to be on the list, and I take no kickbacks.

Become A *Glam Italia!* Traveler

Check out the other books in the series. The first book, *Glam Italia! How To Travel Italy* helps you with all the logistics of planning a trip to Italy, from figuring out where to stay and for how long, to how to use the trains, how to plan your money, what to eat in each region of Italy and what to do if something goes wrong. It is extremely helpful.

WHAT NEXT?

The other books take you inside Rome, Florence and Venice to show you things the mass tourism crowds *don't* see. Each of these cities is filled to bursting with incredible sites, wonderful foods and wines, and sensational experiences that most travelers have no idea exist.

All four books are bestsellers and are available worldwide, exclusively on Amazon.

Glam Italia! How To Travel Italy: Secrets To Glamorous Travel(On A Not So Glamorous Budget)

Glam Italia! 101 Fabulous Things To Do In Rome

Glam Italia! 101 Fabulous Things To Do in Florence

Glam Italia! 101 Fabulous Things To Do in Venice

Ciao!

So, my friend, I hope you have enjoyed this book and feel inspired to devote some time to exploring Naples. I also hope that while you're here you'll enjoy the local cuisine, sip local Campania wines and discover just how fantastic Neapolitan coffee is!

Chances are, if you see a red ponytail swinging its way across the piazza, it will be me. If you see me here in Naples (or anywhere else) please come over and say hi! I have met so many of my readers on the streets of Italy over the past few years, and in airports and train stations, ferries and taxi lines. It is always fun to meet you and hear how your trip is going.

Finally, I would like to send you best wishes for your trip to Italy.

Have a fantastic time, eat everything, do things you wouldn't normally do, and make it the trip of a lifetime!

See you in the piazza,

Corinna

xo

Acknowledgements

Growing up my mother Jennifer was always the most interesting person I ever met. Exciting and glamorous, she had traveled the world and lived in Europe, while no one else's mothers had done anything so incredibly cool.

I always loved looking at photos of her living her best life in London and in Paris and dreamed of a similar fabulous life for myself. It's fair to say my wanderlust and life of travel all began with her, and I am eternally grateful for the excitement and the passion she infused into my life. She taught me that there was a huge, exciting world out there waiting to be explored, and that I only got one shot at life, so I needed to make it count. So really, all of this, the books and the tours, all come back to her. She gets the biggest thank you of them all.

For more than a decade my dear friend Pina Paesano has been my wingman in Naples. I am endlessly grateful for all the laughter and stories told over Aperol spritzes, for leading my tour groups through the magic of Pompeii, and for being such a fabulous friend. Thank you Pina and I can't wait for our next aperitivo hour overlooking the sea, our plans to dive in Baiae, and whatever other craziness we come up with!

Thank you to Pasquale Aversa for years and years of hilarity, for all the fun I've had riding shotgun with you, and for letting me practice my Napoletano on you, even if I only get one word right :) (To be fair, it really is the best word anyway)

To Mr. Mode, thank you for making Napoli so much fun. Who else would take a day off work to show a stranger around Naples? Giovanni – you are the best!

Thank you also to Marta Halama, my fabulous illustrator. As always, it was a joy working with you. You are so brilliant and talented. I wish the world for you.

Thank you Katy Clarke for being such a great friend. I love recording Untold Italy podcast episodes with you and love that when we get together in real life it's in Rome! Hopefully we can get together in Naples soon when our next Italy adventures coincide.

As always, thank you to Tommy for being you, for following your dreams and creating an exciting life for yourself, and for being my proudest moment in every day.

Corinna Cooke

Corinna Cooke is a professional makeup artist and bestselling author.

A fascination with archaeology and history, paired with a love of languages, lured her into a lifetime of non-stop travel to Italy. Her blog posts about exploring Italy and discovering off-the-beaten-path places led to Corinna establishing a private boutique tour business, the Glam Italia Tours. Every summer Corinna brings small groups of women on glamor-filled, a la carte, boutique tours of Italy.

Her understanding of the stress points and concerns of people planning trips to Italy inspired her to write the *Glam Italia!* series. Her books are designed to help people just like you to build your dream trip to Italy, at whichever price point you need.

Originally from New Zealand, Corinna has lived around the world and now splits her time between her homes in Tuscany and Arizona.

Made in the USA
Middletown, DE
26 November 2024